ı|ııı|ıı
CISCO™

Course Booklet

Scaling Networks

Cisco | Networking Academy
Mind Wide Open

ciscopress.com

Scaling Networks Course Booklet

Published by:
Cisco Press
800 East 96th Street
Indianapolis, IN 46240 USA

Printed in the United States of America

First Printing   December 2013

Library of Congress data is on file.

ISBN-13: 978-1-58713-324-4

ISBN-10: 1-58713-324-5

Warning and Disclaimer

This book is designed to provide information about Cisco Networking Academy Scaling Networks course. Every effort has been made to make this book as complete and as accurate as possible, but no warranty or fitness is implied.

The information is provided on an "as is" basis. The authors, Cisco Press, and Cisco Systems, Inc. shall have neither liability nor responsibility to any person or entity with respect to any loss or damages arising from the information contained in this book or from the use of the discs or programs that may accompany it.

The opinions expressed in this book belong to the author and are not necessarily those of Cisco Systems, Inc.

Publisher
Paul Boger

Associate Publisher
Dave Dusthimer

Business Operations Manager, Cisco Press
Jan Cornelssen

Executive Editor
Mary Beth Ray

Managing Editor
Sandra Schroeder

Project Editor
Seth Kerney

Editorial Assistant
Vanessa Evans

Cover Designer
Louisa Adair

Interior Designer
Mark Shirar

Composition
Bronkella Publishing, LLC

Trademark Acknowledgments

All terms mentioned in this book that are known to be trademarks or service marks have been appropriately capitalized. Cisco Press or Cisco Systems, Inc., cannot attest to the accuracy of this information. Use of a term in this book should not be regarded as affecting the validity of any trademark or service mark.

Feedback Information

At Cisco Press, our goal is to create in-depth technical books of the highest quality and value. Each book is crafted with care and precision, undergoing rigorous development that involves the unique expertise of members from the professional technical community.

Readers' feedback is a natural continuation of this process. If you have any comments regarding how we could improve the quality of this book, or otherwise alter it to better suit your needs, you can contact us through email at feedback@ciscopress.com. Please make sure to include the book title and ISBN in your message.

We greatly appreciate your assistance.

Americas Headquarters	Asia Pacific Headquarters	Europe Headquarters
Cisco Systems, Inc.	Cisco Systems (USA) Pte. Ltd.	Cisco Systems International BV
San Jose, CA	Singapore	Amsterdam, The Netherlands

Cisco has more than 200 offices worldwide. Addresses, phone numbers, and fax numbers are listed on the Cisco Website at www.cisco.com/go/offices.

CCDE, CCENT, Cisco Eos, Cisco HealthPresence, the Cisco logo, Cisco Lumin, Cisco Nexus, Cisco StadiumVision, Cisco TelePresence, Cisco WebEx, DCE, and Welcome to the Human Network are trademarks; Changing the Way We Work, Live, Play, and Learn and Cisco Store are service marks; and Access Registrar, Aironet, AsyncOS, Bringing the Meeting To You, Catalyst, CCDA, CCDP, CCIE, CCIP, CCNA, CCNP, CCSP, CCVP, Cisco, the Cisco Certified Internetwork Expert logo, Cisco IOS, Cisco Press, Cisco Systems, Cisco Systems Capital, the Cisco Systems logo, Cisco Unity, Collaboration Without Limitation, EtherFast, EtherSwitch, Event Center, Fast Step, Follow Me Browsing, FormShare, GigaDrive, HomeLink, Internet Quotient, IOS, iPhone, iQuick Study, IronPort, the IronPort logo, LightStream, Linksys, MediaTone, MeetingPlace, MeetingPlace Chime Sound, MGX, Networkers, Networking Academy, Network Registrar, PCNow, PIX, PowerPanels, ProConnect, ScriptShare, SenderBase, SMARTnet, Spectrum Expert, StackWise, The Fastest Way to Increase Your Internet Quotient, TransPath, WebEx, and the WebEx logo are registered trademarks of Cisco Systems, Inc. and/or its affiliates in the United States and certain other countries.

All other trademarks mentioned in this document or website are the property of their respective owners. The use of the word partner does not imply a partnership relationship between Cisco and any other company. (0812R)

Contents at a Glance

Contents

Command Syntax Conventions

The conventions used to present command syntax in this book are the same conventions used in the IOS Command Reference. The Command Reference describes these conventions as follows:

- **Boldface** indicates commands and keywords that are entered literally as shown. In actual configuration examples and output (not general command syntax), boldface indicates commands that are manually input by the user (such as a **show** command).

- *Italic* indicates arguments for which you supply actual values.

- Vertical bars (|) separate alternative, mutually exclusive elements.

- Square brackets ([ ]) indicate an optional element.

- Braces ({ }) indicate a required choice.

- Braces within brackets ([{ }]) indicate a required choice within an optional element.

About This Course Booklet

Your Cisco Networking Academy Course Booklet is designed as a study resource you can easily read, highlight, and review on the go, wherever the Internet is not available or practical:

- The text is extracted directly, word-for-word, from the online course so you can highlight important points and take notes in the "Your Chapter Notes" section.

- Headings with the exact page correlations provide a quick reference to the online course for your classroom discussions and exam preparation.

- An icon system directs you to the online curriculum to take full advantage of the images imbedded within the Networking Academy online course interface and reminds you to perform the labs, Class activities, Interactive activities, Packet Tracer activities, and chapter quizzes and exams.

| Refer to **Online Course** for Illustration | Refer to **Lab Activity** for this chapter | Go to the online course to take the quiz and exam. | Refer to **Interactive Graphic** in online course. | Refer to **Packet Tracer Activity** for this chapter |

The *Course Booklet* is a basic, economical paper-based resource to help you succeed with the Cisco Networking Academy online course.

Companion Guide

Looking for more than the online curriculum? The Companion Guide is fully aligned to Networking Academy's online course chapters and offers additional book-based pedagogy to reinforce key concepts, enhance student comprehension, and promote retention. Using this full-fledged textbook, students can focus scarce study time, organize review for quizzes and exams, and get the day-to-day reference answers they're looking for.

The Companion Guide also offers instructors additional opportunities to assign take-home reading or vocabulary homework, helping students prepare more for in-class lab work and discussions.

Available in print and all major eBook formats (Book: 9781587133282   eBook: 9780133476408)

Course Introduction

0.0 Scaling Networks

0.0.1 Message to the Student

0.0.1.1 Welcome

Welcome to the CCNA R&S Scaling Networks course. The goal of this course is to introduce you to fundamental networking concepts and technologies. These online course materials will assist you in developing the skills necessary to plan and implement small networks across a range of applications. The specific skills covered in each chapter are described at the start of each chapter.

You can use your smart phone, tablet, laptop, or desktop to access your course, participate in discussions with your instructor, view your grades, read or review text, and practice using interactive media. However, some media are complex and must be viewed on a PC, as well as Packet Tracer activities, quizzes, and exams.

Refer to
Online Course
for Illustration

0.0.1.2 A Global Community

When you participate in the Networking Academy, you are joining a global community linked by common goals and technologies. Schools, colleges, universities, and other entities in over 160 countries participate in the program. A visualization of the global Networking Academy community is available at http://www.academynetspace.com.

Look for the Cisco Networking Academy official site on Facebook© and LinkedIn©. The Facebook site is where you can meet and engage with other Networking Academy students from around the world. The Cisco Networking Academy LinkedIn site connects you with job postings, and you can see how others are effectively communicating their skills.

Refer to
Online Course
for Illustration

0.0.1.3 More Than Just Information

The NetSpace learning environment is an important part of the overall course experience for students and instructors in the Networking Academy. These online course materials include course text and related interactive media, Packet Tracer simulation activities, real equipment labs, remote access labs, and many different types of quizzes. All of these materials provide important feedback to help you assess your progress throughout the course.

The material in this course encompasses a broad range of technologies that facilitate how people work, live, play, and learn by communicating with voice, video, and other data. Networking and the internet affect people differently in different parts of the world. Although we have worked with instructors from around the world to create these materials, it is important that you work with your instructor and fellow students to make the material in this course applicable to your local situation.

Refer to
Online Course
for Illustration

0.0.1.4 How We Teach

E-doing is a design philosophy that applies the principle that people learn best by doing. The curriculum includes embedded, highly interactive e-doing activities to help stimulate learning, increase knowledge retention, and make the whole learning experience much richer – and that makes understanding the content much easier.

Refer to
Online Course
for Illustration

0.0.1.5 Practice Leads to Mastery

In a typical lesson, after learning about a topic for the first time, you will check your understanding with some interactive media items. If there are new commands to learn, you will practice them with the Syntax Checker before using the commands to configure or troubleshoot a network in Packet Tracer, the Networking Academy network simulation tool. Next, you will do practice activities on real equipment in your classroom or accessed remotely over the internet.

Packet Tracer can also provide additional practice any time by creating your own activities or you may want to competitively test your skills with classmates in multi-user games. Packet Tracer skills assessments and skills integration labs give you rich feedback on the skills you are able to demonstrate and are great practice for chapter, checkpoint, and final exams.

Refer to
Online Course
for Illustration

0.0.1.6 Mind Wide Open

An important goal in education is to enrich you, the student, by expanding what you know and can do. It is important to realize, however, that the instructional materials and the instructor can only facilitate the process. You must make the commitment yourself to learn new skills. The following pages share a few suggestions to help you learn and prepare for transitioning your new skills to the workplace.

Refer to
Online Course
for Illustration

0.0.1.7 Engineering Journals

Professionals in the networking field often keep Engineering Journals in which they write down the things they observe and learn such as how to use protocols and commands. Keeping an Engineering Journal creates a reference you can use at work in your ICT job. Writing is one way to reinforce your learning – along with Reading, Seeing, and Practicing.

A sample entry for implementing a technology could include the necessary software commands, the purpose of the commands, command variables, and a topology diagram indicating the context for using the commands to configure the technology.

Refer to
Online Course
for Illustration

0.0.1.8 Explore the World of Networking

Packet Tracer is a networking learning tool that supports a wide range of physical and logical simulations. It also provides visualization tools to help you understand the internal workings of a network.

The pre-made Packet Tracer activities consist of network simulations, games, activities, and challenges that provide a broad range of learning experiences. These tools will help you develop an understanding of how data flows in a network.

Refer to
Online Course
for Illustration

0.0.1.9   Create Your Own Worlds

You can also use Packet Tracer to create your own experiments and networking scenarios. We hope that, over time, you consider using Packet Tracer - not only for experiencing the pre-built activities, but also to become an author, explorer, and experimenter.

The online course materials have embedded Packet Tracer activities that will launch on computers running Windows® operating systems, if Packet Tracer is installed. This integration may also work on other operating systems using Windows emulation.

Refer to **Packet Tracer Activity** for this chapter

0.0.1.10   How Packet Tracer Helps Master Concepts

Educational Games

Packet Tracer Multi-User games enable you or a team to compete with other students to see who can accurately complete a series of networking tasks the fastest. It is an excellent way to practice the skills you are learning in Packet Tracer activities and hands-on labs.

Cisco Aspire is a single-player, standalone strategic simulation game. Players test their networking skills by completing contracts in a virtual city. The Networking Academy Edition is specifically designed to help you prepare for the CCENT certification exam. It also incorporates business and communication skills ICT employers seek in job candidates.

Performance-Based Assessments

The Networking Academy performance-based assessments have you do Packet Tracer activities like you have been doing all along, only now integrated with an online assessment engine that will automatically score your results and provide you with immediate feedback. This feedback helps you to more accurately identify the knowledge and skills you have mastered and where you need more practice. There are also questions on chapter quizzes and exams that use Packet Tracer activities to give you additional feedback on your progress.

Refer to
Online Course
for Illustration

0.0.1.11   Course Overview

The focus of this course is on the architecture, components, and operations of routers and switches in a larger and more complex network. You will learn how to configure routers and switches for advanced functionality. You will do the following:

- Configure and troubleshoot DHCP and DNS operations for IPv4 and IPv6
- Describe the operations and benefits of the Spanning Tree Protocol (STP)
- Configure and troubleshoot STP operations
- Describe the operations and benefits of link aggregation and Cisco VLAN Trunk Protocol (VTP)
- Configure and troubleshoot VTP, STP, and RSTP
- Configure and troubleshoot basic operations of routers in a complex routed network for IPv4 and IPv6
- Configure and troubleshoot advanced operations of routers and implement RIP, OSPF, and EIGRP routing protocols for IPv4 and IPv6
- Manage Cisco IOS® Software licensing and configuration files

By the end of this course, you will be able to configure and troubleshoot routers and switches and resolve common issues with OSPF, EIGRP, STP, and VTP in both IPv4 and IPv6 networks. You will also develop the knowledge and skills needed to implement DHCP and DNS operations in a network.

Refer to
Interactive Graphic
in online course.

0.1.1.1   Course GUI Tutorial

Go to the online course to take the quiz and exam.

Chapter 0 Quiz

This quiz is designed to provide an additional opportunity to practice the skills and knowledge presented in the chapter and to prepare for the chapter exam. You will be allowed multiple attempts and the grade does not appear in the gradebook.

Chapter 0 Exam

The chapter exam assesses your knowledge of the chapter content.

Your Chapter Notes

Introduction to Scaling Networks

1.0 Introduction to Scaling Networks

1.0.1.1 Introduction

As a business grows, so does its networking requirements. Businesses rely on the network infrastructure to provide mission-critical services. Network outages can result in lost revenue and lost customers. Network designers must design and build an enterprise network that is scalable and highly available.

This chapter introduces strategies that can be used to systematically design a highly functional network, such as the hierarchical network design model, the Cisco Enterprise Architecture, and appropriate device selections. The goals of network design are to limit the number of devices impacted by the failure of a single network device, provide a plan and path for growth, and create a reliable network.

Refer to
Lab Activity
for this chapter

1.0.1.2 Class Activity - Network by Design

Network by Design

Your employer is opening a new, branch office.

You have been reassigned to the site as the network administrator where your job will be to design and maintain the new branch network.

The network administrators at the other branches used the Cisco three-layer hierarchical model when designing their networks. You decide to use the same approach.

To get an idea of what using the hierarchical model can do to enhance the design process, you research the topic.

Refer to
Interactive Graphic
in online course.

1.1 Implementing a Network Design

1.1.1 Hierarchical Network Design

1.1.1.1 The Need to Scale the Network

Businesses increasingly rely on their network infrastructure to provide mission-critical services. As businesses grow and evolve, they hire more employees, open branch offices, and expand into global markets. These changes directly affect the requirements of a network. A large business environment with many users, locations, and systems is referred to as an enterprise. The network that is used to support the business enterprise is called an enterprise network.

Click the Play button in the figure to view an animation of a small network expanding into an enterprise network.

An enterprise network must support the exchange of various types of network traffic, including data files, email, IP telephony, and video applications for multiple business units. All enterprise networks must:

- Support critical applications
- Support converged network traffic
- Support diverse business needs
- Provide centralized administrative control

Refer to
Online Course
for Illustration

1.1.1.2   Enterprise Business Devices

Users expect enterprise networks, such as the example shown in the figure, to be up 99.999 percent of the time. Outages in the enterprise network prevent the business from performing normal activities, which can result in a loss of revenue, customers, data, and opportunities.

To obtain this level of reliability, high-end, enterprise class equipment is commonly installed in the enterprise network. Designed and manufactured to more stringent standards than lower-end devices, enterprise equipment moves large volumes of network traffic.

Enterprise class equipment is designed for reliability, with features such as redundant power supplies and failover capabilities. Failover capability refers to the ability of a device to switch from a non-functioning module, service or device, to a functioning one with little or no break in service.

Purchasing and installing enterprise class equipment does not eliminate the need for proper network design.

Refer to
Online Course
for Illustration

1.1.1.3   Hierarchical Network Design

To optimize bandwidth on an enterprise network, the network must be organized so that traffic stays local and is not propagated unnecessarily onto other portions of the network. Using the three-layer hierarchical design model helps organize the network.

This model divides the network functionality into three distinct layers, as shown in Figure 1:

- Access layer
- Distribution layer
- Core layer

Each layer is designed to meet specific functions.

The access layer provides connectivity for the users. The distribution layer is used to forward traffic from one local network to another. Finally, the core layer represents a high-speed backbone layer between dispersed networks. User traffic is initiated at the access layer and passes through the other layers if the functionality of those layers is required.

Even though the hierarchical model has three layers, some smaller enterprise networks may implement a two-tier hierarchical design. In a two-tier hierarchical design, the core and distribution layers are collapsed into one layer, reducing cost and complexity, as shown in Figure 2.

Refer to **Online Course** for Illustration

1.1.1.4   Cisco Enterprise Architecture

The Cisco Enterprise Architecture divides the network into functional components while still maintaining the core, distribution, and access layers. As the figure shows, the primary Cisco Enterprise Architecture modules include:

■ Enterprise Campus

■ Enterprise Edge

■ Service Provider Edge

■ Remote

Enterprise Campus

The Enterprise Campus consists of the entire campus infrastructure, to include the access, distribution, and core layers. The access layer module contains Layer 2 or Layer 3 switches to provide the required port density. Implementation of VLANs and trunk links to the building distribution layer occurs here. Redundancy to the building distribution switches is important. The distribution layer module aggregates building access using Layer 3 devices. Routing, access control, and QoS are performed at this distribution layer module. The core layer module provides high-speed interconnectivity between the distribution layer modules, data center server farms, and the enterprise edge. Redundancy, fast convergence, and fault tolerance are the focus of the design in this module.

In addition to these modules, the Enterprise Campus can include other submodules such as:

■ **Server Farm and Data Center Module**- This area provides high-speed connectivity and protection for servers. It is critical to provide security, redundancy, and fault tolerance. The network management systems monitor performance by monitoring device and network availability.

■ **Services Module**- This area provides access to all services, such as IP Telephony services, wireless controller services, and unified services.

Enterprise Edge

The Enterprise Edge consists of the Internet, VPN, and WAN modules connecting the enterprise with the service provider's network. This module extends the enterprise services to remote sites and enables the enterprise to use Internet and partner resources. It provides QoS, policy reinforcement, service levels, and security.

Service Provider Edge

The Service Provider Edge provides Internet, Public Switched Telephone Network (PSTN), and WAN services.

All data that enters or exits the Enterprise Composite Network Model (ECNM) passes through an edge device. This is the point that all packets can be examined and a decision made whether the packet should be allowed on the enterprise network. Intrusion detection systems (IDS) and intrusion prevention systems (IPS) can also be configured at the enterprise edge to protect against malicious activity.

Refer to
Online Course
for Illustration

1.1.1.5 Failure Domains

A well-designed network not only controls traffic, but also limits the size of failure domains. A failure domain is the area of a network that is impacted when a critical device or network service experiences problems.

The function of the device that initially fails determines the impact of a failure domain. For example, a malfunctioning switch on a network segment normally affects only the hosts on that segment. However, if the router that connects this segment to others fails, the impact is much greater.

The use of redundant links and reliable enterprise-class equipment minimize the chance of disruption in a network. Smaller failure domains reduce the impact of a failure on company productivity. They also simplify the troubleshooting process, thereby, shortening the downtime for all users.

In the figure, click each network device to view the associated failure domain.

Limiting the Size of Failure Domains

Because a failure at the core layer of a network can have a potentially large impact, the network designer often concentrates on efforts to prevent failures. These efforts can greatly increase the cost of implementing the network. In the hierarchical design model, it is easiest and usually least expensive to control the size of a failure domain in the distribution layer. In the distribution layer, network errors can be contained to a smaller area; thus, affecting fewer users. When using Layer 3 devices at the distribution layer, every router functions as a gateway for a limited number of access layer users.

Switch Block Deployment

Routers, or multilayer switches, are usually deployed in pairs, with access layer switches evenly divided between them. This configuration is referred to as a building, or departmental, switch block. Each switch block acts independently of the others. As a result, the failure of a single device does not cause the network to go down. Even the failure of an entire switch block does not affect a significant number of end users.

Refer to
Interactive Graphic
in online course.

1.1.1.6 Activity – Identify Cisco Enterprise Architecture Modules

1.1.2 Expanding the Network

Refer to
Online Course
for Illustration

1.1.2.1 Design for Scalability

To support an enterprise network, the network designer must develop a strategy to enable the network to be available and to scale effectively and easily. Included in a basic network design strategy are the following recommendations:

- Use expandable, modular equipment or clustered devices that can be easily upgraded to increase capabilities. Device modules can be added to the existing equipment to support new features and devices without requiring major equipment upgrades. Some devices can be integrated in a cluster to act as one device to simplify management and configuration.

- Design a hierarchical network to include modules that can be added, upgraded, and modified, as necessary, without affecting the design of the other functional areas of the network. For example, creating a separate access layer that can be expanded without affecting the distribution and core layers of the campus network.

- Create an IPv4 or IPv6 address strategy that is hierarchical. Careful IPv4 address planning eliminates the need to re-address the network to support additional users and services.

- Choose routers or multilayer switches to limit broadcasts and filter other undesirable traffic from the network. Use Layer 3 devices to filter and reduce traffic to the network core.

As shown in the figure, more advanced network design requirements include:

- Implementing redundant links in the network between critical devices and between access layer and core layer devices.

- Implementing multiple links between equipment, with either link aggregation (EtherChannel) or equal cost load balancing, to increase bandwidth. Combining multiple Ethernet links into a single, load-balanced EtherChannel configuration increases available bandwidth. EtherChannel implementations can be used when budget restrictions prohibit purchasing high-speed interfaces and fiber runs.

- Implementing wireless connectivity to allow for mobility and expansion.

- Using a scalable routing protocol and implementing features within that routing protocol to isolate routing updates and minimize the size of the routing table.

Refer to
Online Course
for Illustration

1.1.2.2   Planning for Redundancy

Implementing Redundancy

For many organizations, the availability of the network is essential to supporting business needs. Redundancy is an important part of network design for preventing disruption of network services by minimizing the possibility of a single point of failure. One method of implementing redundancy is by installing duplicate equipment and providing failover services for critical devices.

Another method of implementing redundancy is redundant paths, as shown in the figure. Redundant paths offer alternate physical paths for data to traverse the network. Redundant paths in a switched network support high availability. However, due to the operation of switches, redundant paths in a switched Ethernet network may cause logical Layer 2 loops. For this reason, Spanning Tree Protocol (STP) is required.

STP allows for the redundancy required for reliability, but eliminates the switching loops. It does this by providing a mechanism for disabling redundant paths in a switched network until the path is necessary, such as when failures occur. STP is an open standard protocol, used in a switched environment to create a loop-free logical topology.

More details about LAN redundancy and the operation of STP are covered in the chapter titled "LAN Redundancy".

Refer to
Online Course
for Illustration

1.1.2.3   Increasing Bandwidth

Implementing EtherChannel

In hierarchical network design, some links between access and distribution switches may need to process a greater amount of traffic than other links. As traffic from multiple links converges onto a single, outgoing link, it is possible for that link to become a bottleneck. Link aggregation allows an administrator to increase the amount of bandwidth between devices by creating one logical link made up of several physical links. EtherChannel is a form of link aggregation used in switched networks, as shown in the figure.

EtherChannel uses the existing switch ports; therefore, additional costs to upgrade the link to a faster and more expensive connection are not necessary. The EtherChannel is seen as one logical link using an EtherChannel interface. Most configuration tasks are done on the EtherChannel interface, instead of on each individual port, ensuring configuration consistency throughout the links. Finally, the EtherChannel configuration takes advantage of load balancing between links that are part of the same EtherChannel, and depending on the hardware platform, one or more load-balancing methods can be implemented.

EtherChannel operation and configuration will be covered in more detail in the chapter titled "Link Aggregation".

Refer to
Online Course
for Illustration

1.1.2.4   Expanding the Access Layer

Implementing Wireless Connectivity

The network must be designed to be able to expand network access to individuals and devices, as needed. An increasingly important aspect of extending access layer connectivity is through wireless connectivity. Providing wireless connectivity offers many advantages, such as increased flexibility, reduced costs, and the ability to grow and adapt to changing network and business requirements.

To communicate wirelessly, end devices require a wireless NIC that incorporates a radio transmitter/receiver and the required software driver to make it operational. Additionally, a wireless router or a wireless access point (AP) is required for users to connect, as shown in the figure.

There are many considerations when implementing a wireless network, such as the types of wireless devices to use, wireless coverage requirements, interference considerations, and security considerations.

Wireless operation and implementation will be covered in more detail in the chapter titled "Wireless LANs".

Refer to
Online Course
for Illustration

1.1.2.5   Fine-tuning Routing Protocols

Managing the Routed Network

Enterprise networks and ISPs often use more advanced protocols, such as link-state protocols, because of their hierarchical design and ability to scale for large networks.

Link-state routing protocols such as Open Shortest Path First (OSPF), as shown in Figure 1, works well for larger hierarchical networks where fast convergence is important. OSPF routers establish and maintain neighbor adjacency or adjacencies, with other connected OSPF routers. When routers initiate an adjacency with neighbors, an exchange of link-state updates begins. Routers reach a FULL state of adjacency when they have synchronized views on their link-state database. With OSPF, link state updates are sent when network changes occur.

OSPF is a popular link-state routing protocol that can be fine-tuned in many ways. The chapter titled "Adjust and Troubleshoot Single-Area OSPF" will cover some of the more advanced features of OSPF configuration and troubleshooting.

Additionally, OSPF supports a two-layer hierarchical design, or multiarea OSPF, as shown in Figure 2. All OSPF networks begin with Area 0, also called the backbone area. As the network is expanded, other, non-backbone areas can be created. All non-backbone areas must directly connect to area 0. The chapter titled "Multiarea OSPF" introduces the benefits, operation, and configuration of Multiarea OSPF.

Another popular routing protocol for larger networks is Enhanced Interior Gateway Routing Protocol (EIGRP). Cisco developed EIGRP as a proprietary distance vector routing protocol with enhanced capabilities. Although configuring EIGRP is relatively simple, the underlying features and options of EIGRP are extensive and robust. For example, EIGRP uses multiple tables to manage the routing process, as shown in Figure 3. EIGRP contains many features that are not found in any other routing protocols. It is an excellent choice for large, multi-protocol networks that employ primarily Cisco devices.

The chapter titled "EIGRP" introduces the operation and configuration of the EIGRP routing protocol, while the chapter titled "EIGRP Advanced Configurations and Troubleshooting" covers some of the more advanced configuration options of EIGRP.

> Refer to
> **Interactive Graphic**
> in online course.

1.1.2.6   Activity: Identify Scalability Terminology

> Refer to
> **Online Course**
> for Illustration

1.2   Selecting Network Devices

1.2.1   Switch Hardware

1.2.1.1   Switch Platforms

When designing a network, it is important to select the proper hardware to meet current network requirements, as well as allow for network growth. Within an enterprise network, both switches and routers play a critical role in network communication.

There are five categories of switches for enterprise networks, as shown in Figure 1:

- **Campus LAN Switches-** To scale network performance in an enterprise LAN, there arc core, distribution, access, and compact switches. These switch platforms vary from fanless switches with eight fixed ports to 13-blade switches supporting hundreds of ports. Campus LAN switch platforms include the Cisco 2960, 3560, 3750, 3850, 4500, 6500, and 6800 Series.

- **Cloud-Managed Switches-** The Cisco Meraki cloud-managed access switches enable virtual stacking of switches. They monitor and configure thousands of switch ports over the web, without the intervention of onsite IT staff.

- **Data Center Switches-** A data center should be built based on switches that promote infrastructure scalability, operational continuity, and transport flexibility. The data center switch platforms include the Cisco Nexus Series switches and the Cisco Catalyst 6500 Series switches.

- **Service Provider Switches**- Service provider switches fall under two categories: aggregation switches and Ethernet access switches. Aggregation switches are carrier-grade Ethernet switches that aggregate traffic at the edge of a network. Service provider Ethernet access switches feature application intelligence, unified services, virtualization, integrated security, and simplified management.

- **Virtual Networking**- Networks are becoming increasingly virtualized. Cisco Nexus virtual networking switch platforms provide secure multi-tenant services by adding virtualization intelligence technology to the data center network.

When selecting switches, network administrators must determine the switch form factors. This includes fixed configuration (Figure 2), modular configuration (Figure 3), stackable (Figure 4), or non-stackable. The thickness of the switch, which is expressed in the number of rack units, is also important for switches that are mounted in a rack. For example, the fixed configuration switches shown in Figure 2 are all one rack units (1U).

In addition to these considerations, Figure 5 highlights other common business considerations when selecting switch equipment.

Refer to
Online Course
for Illustration

1.2.1.2   Port Density

The port density of a switch refers to the number of ports available on a single switch. The figure shows the port density of three different switches.

Fixed configuration switches typically support up to 48 ports on a single device. They have options for up to four additional ports for small form-factor pluggable (SFP) devices. High-port densities allow for better use of limited space and power. If there are two switches that each contain 24 ports, they would be able to support up to 46 devices, because at least one port per switch is lost with the connection of each switch to the rest of the network. In addition, two power outlets are required. Alternatively, if there is a single 48-port switch, 47 devices can be supported, with only one port used to connect the switch to the rest of the network, and only one power outlet needed to accommodate the single switch.

Modular switches can support very high-port densities through the addition of multiple switch port line cards. For example, some Catalyst 6500 switches can support in excess of 1,000 switch ports.

Large enterprise networks that support many thousands of network devices require high density, modular switches to make the best use of space and power. Without using a high-density modular switch, the network would need many fixed configuration switches to accommodate the number of devices that need network access. This approach can consume many power outlets and a lot of closet space.

The network designer must also consider the issue of uplink bottlenecks: A series of fixed configuration switches may consume many additional ports for bandwidth aggregation between switches, for the purpose of achieving target performance. With a single modular switch, bandwidth aggregation is less of an issue, because the backplane of the chassis can provide the necessary bandwidth to accommodate the devices connected to the switch port line cards.

Refer to
Online Course
for Illustration

1.2.1.3   Forwarding Rates

Forwarding rates define the processing capabilities of a switch by rating how much data the switch can process per second. Switch product lines are classified by forwarding rates, as shown in the figure. Entry-level switches have lower forwarding rates than enterprise-level switches. Forwarding rates are important to consider when selecting a switch. If the switch forwarding rate is too low, it cannot accommodate full wire-speed communication across all of its switch ports. Wire speed is the data rate that each Ethernet port on the switch is capable of attaining. Data rates can be 100 Mb/s, 1 Gb/s, 10 Gb/s, or 100 Gb/s.

For example, a typical 48-port gigabit switch operating at full wire speed generates 48 Gb/s of traffic. If the switch only supports a forwarding rate of 32 Gb/s, it cannot run at full wire speed across all ports simultaneously. Fortunately, access layer switches typically do not need to operate at full wire speed, because they are physically limited by their uplinks to the distribution layer. This means that less expensive, lower performing switches can be used at the access layer, and more expensive, higher performing switches can be used at the distribution and core layers, where the forwarding rate has a greater impact on network performance.

Refer to
Online Course
for Illustration

1.2.1.4   Power over Ethernet

PoE allows the switch to deliver power to a device over the existing Ethernet cabling. This feature can be used by IP phones and some wireless access points. Click the highlighted icons in Figure 1 to view PoE ports on each device.

PoE allows more flexibility when installing wireless access points and IP phones, allowing them to be installed anywhere that there is an Ethernet cable. A network administrator should ensure that the PoE features are required, because switches that support PoE are expensive.

The relatively new Cisco Catalyst 2960-C and 3560-C Series compact switches support PoE pass-through. PoE pass-through allows a network administrator to power PoE devices connected to the switch, as well as the switch itself, by drawing power from certain upstream switches. Click the highlighted icon in Figure 2 to view a Cisco Catalyst 2960-C.

Refer to
Online Course
for Illustration

1.2.1.5   Multilayer Switching

Multilayer switches are typically deployed in the core and distribution layers of an organization's switched network. Multilayer switches are characterized by their ability to build a routing table, support a few routing protocols, and forward IP packets at a rate close to that of Layer 2 forwarding. Multilayer switches often support specialized hardware, such as application-specific integrated circuits (ASICs). ASICs along with dedicated software data structures can streamline the forwarding of IP packets independent of the CPU.

There is a trend in networking toward a pure Layer 3 switched environment. When switches were first used in networks, none of them supported routing; now, almost all switches support routing. It is likely that soon all switches will incorporate a route processor because the cost of doing so is decreasing relative to other constraints. Eventually the term multilayer switch will be redundant.

As shown in the figure, the Catalyst 2960 switches illustrate the migration to a pure Layer 3 environment. With IOS versions prior to 15.x, these switches supported only one active switched virtual interface (SVI). With IOS 15.x, these switches now support multiple active

SVIs. This means that the switch can be remotely accessed via multiple IP addresses on distinct networks.

Refer to **Interactive Graphic** in online course.

1.2.1.6   Activity - Selecting Switch Hardware

Refer to **Packet Tracer Activity** for this chapter

1.2.1.7   Packet Tracer - Comparing 2960 and 3560 Switches

Background/Scenario

In this activity, you will use various commands to examine three different switching topologies and compare the similarities and differences between the 2960 and 3560 switches. You will also compare the routing table of a 1941 router with a 3560 switch.

Refer to **Lab Activity** for this chapter

1.2.1.8   Lab - Selecting Switching Hardware

In this lab, you will complete the following objectives:

- Part 1: Explore Cisco Switch Products
- Part 2: Select an Access Layer Switch
- Part 3: Select a Distribution/Core Layer Switch

Refer to **Online Course** for Illustration

1.2.2   Router Hardware

1.2.2.1   Router Requirements

In the distribution layer of an enterprise network, routing is required. Without the routing process, packets cannot leave the local network.

Routers play a critical role in networking by interconnecting multiple sites within an enterprise network, providing redundant paths, and connecting ISPs on the Internet. Routers can also act as a translator between different media types and protocols. For example, a router can accept packets from an Ethernet network and re-encapsulate them for transport over a Serial network.

Routers use the network portion of the destination IP address to route packets to the proper destination. They select an alternate path if a link goes down or traffic is congested. All hosts on a local network specify the IP address of the local router interface in their IP configuration. This router interface is the default gateway.

Routers also serve other beneficial functions:

- Provide broadcast containment
- Connect remote locations
- Group users logically by application or department
- Provide enhanced security

Click each highlighted area in the figure for more information on the functions of routers.

With the enterprise and the ISP, the ability to route efficiently and recover from network link failures is critical to delivering packets to their destination.

Refer to
Online Course
for Illustration

1.2.2.2 Cisco Routers

As the network grows, it is important to select the proper routers to meet its requirements. As shown in the figure, there are three categories of routers:

- **Branch Routers**- Branch routers optimize branch services on a single platform while delivering an optimal application experience across branch and WAN infrastructures. Maximizing service availability at the branch requires networks designed for 24x7x365 uptime. Highly available branch networks must ensure fast recovery from typical faults, while minimizing or eliminating the impact on service, and provide simple network configuration and management.

- **Network Edge Routers**- Network edge routers enable the network edge to deliver high-performance, highly secure, and reliable services that unite campus, data center, and branch networks. Customers expect a high-quality media experience and more types of content than ever before. Customers want interactivity, personalization, mobility, and control for all content. Customers also want to access content anytime and anyplace they choose, over any device, whether at home, at work, or on the go. Network edge routers must deliver enhance quality of service and nonstop video and mobile capabilities.

- **Service Provider Routers**- Service provider routers differentiate the service portfolio and increase revenues by delivering end-to-end scalable solutions and subscriber-aware services. Operators must optimize operations, reduce expenses, and improve scalability and flexibility, to deliver next-generation Internet experiences across all devices and locations. These systems are designed to simplify and enhance the operation and deployment of service-delivery networks.

Refer to
Online Course
for Illustration

1.2.2.3 Router Hardware

Routers also come in many form factors, as shown in the figure. Network administrators in an enterprise environment should be able to support a variety of routers, from a small desktop router to a rack-mounted or blade model.

Routers can also be categorized as fixed configuration or modular. With the fixed configuration, the desired router interfaces are built-in. Modular routers come with multiple slots that allow a network administrator to change the interfaces on the router. As an example, a Cisco 1841 router comes with two Fast Ethernet RJ-45 interfaces built-in, and two slots that can accommodate many different network interface modules. Routers come with a variety of different interfaces, such as Fast Ethernet, Gigabit Ethernet, Serial, and Fiber-Optic.

Refer to
Interactive Graphic
in online course.

1.2.2.4 Activity – Identify the Router Category

Refer to
Online Course
for Illustration

1.2.3 Managing Devices

1.2.3.1 Managing IOS Files and Licensing

With such a wide selection of network devices to choose from in the Cisco product line, an organization can carefully determine the ideal combination to meet the needs of the employees and the customers.

When selecting or upgrading a Cisco IOS device, it is important to choose the proper IOS image with the correct feature set and version. IOS refers to the package of routing, switching, security, and other internetworking technologies integrated into a single multitasking operating system. When a new device is shipped, it comes preinstalled with the software image and the corresponding permanent licenses for the customer-specified packages and features.

For routers, beginning with Cisco IOS Software release 15.0, Cisco modified the process to enable new technologies within the IOS feature sets, as shown in the figure.

The chapter title "IOS Images and Licensing" covers more information on managing and maintaining the Cisco IOS licenses.

Refer to
Online Course
for Illustration

1.2.3.2 In-Band versus Out-of-Band Management

Regardless of the Cisco IOS network device being implemented, there are two methods for connecting a PC to that network device for configuration and monitoring tasks. These methods include out-of-band and in-band management, as shown in the figure.

Out-of-band management is used for initial configuration or when a network connection is unavailable. Configuration using out-of-band management requires:

- Direct connection to console or AUX port

- Terminal emulation client

In-band management is used to monitor and make configuration changes to a network device over a network connection. Configuration using in-band management requires:

- At least one network interface on the device to be connected and operational

- Telnet, SSH, or HTTP to access a Cisco device

Refer to
Online Course
for Illustration

1.2.3.3 Basic Router CLI Commands

A basic router configuration includes the hostname for identification, passwords for security, assignment of IP addresses to interfaces for connectivity, and basic routing. Figure 1 shows the commands entered to enable a router with OSPF. Verify and save configuration changes using the `copy running-config startup-config` command. Figure 2 shows the results of the configuration commands that were entered in Figure 1. To clear the router configuration, use the `erase startup-config` command and then the `reload` command.

On Figure 3, use the Syntax Checker to verify router configurations using these `show` commands.

Refer to
Online Course
for Illustration

1.2.3.4 Basic Router Show Commands

Here are some of the most commonly used IOS commands to display and verify the operational status of the router and related network functionality. These commands are divided into several categories.

Routing Related:

- `show ip protocols`- Displays information about the routing protocols configured. If OSPF is configured, this includes the OSPF process ID, the router ID, networks the router is advertising, the neighbors the router is receiving updates from, and the default administrative distance, which is 110 for OSPF. (Figure 1)

- `show ip route`- Displays routing table information, including: routing codes, known networks, administrative distance and metrics, how routes were learned, next hop, static routes, and default routes. (Figure 2)

- `show ip ospf neighbor`- Displays information about OSPF neighbors that have been learned, including the Router ID of the neighbor, priority, the state (Full = adjacency has been formed), the IP address, and the local interface that learned of the neighbor. (Figure 3)

Interface Related:

- `show interfaces`- Displays interfaces with line (protocol) status, bandwidth, delay, reliability, encapsulation, duplex, and I/O statistics. If specified without a specific interface designation, all interfaces will be displayed. If a specific interface is specified after the command, information about that interface only will be displayed. (Figure 4)

- `show ip interfaces`- Displays interface information, including: protocol status, the IP address, if a helper address is configured, and whether an ACL is enabled on the interface. If specified without a specific interface designation, all interfaces will be displayed. If a specific interface is specified after the command, information about that interface only will be displayed. (Figure 5)

- `show ip interface brief`- Displays all interfaces with IP addressing information and interface and line protocols status. (Figure 6)

- `show protocols`- Displays information about the routed protocol that is enabled, and the protocol status of interfaces. (Figure 7)

Other connectivity related commands include the `show cdp neighbors` command (Figure 8). This command displays information on directly connected devices including Device ID, the local interface the device is connected to, capability (R = router, S = switch), the platform, and Port ID of the remote device. The details option includes IP addressing information and the IOS version.

Use the Syntax Checker in Figure 9 to verify router configurations using these `show` commands.

1.2.3.5   Basic Switch CLI commands

Refer to
Online Course
for Illustration

Basic switch configuration includes the hostname for identification, passwords for security, and assignment of IP addresses for connectivity. In-band access requires the switch to have an IP address. Figure 1 shows the commands entered to enable a switch.

Figure 2 shows the results of the configuration commands that were entered in Figure 1. Verify and save the switch configuration using the `copy running-config startup-config` command. To clear the switch configuration, use the `erase startup-config` command and then the reload command. It may also be necessary to erase any VLAN information using the command `delete flash:vlan.dat`. When switch configurations are in place, view the configurations using the `show running-config` command.

Refer to
Online Course
for Illustration

1.2.3.6   Basic Switch Show Commands

Switches make use of common IOS commands for configuration, to check for connectivity and to display current switch status. Click buttons 1 to 4 for sample outputs of the commands and the important pieces of information that an administrator can gather from it.

Interface / Port Related:

- `show port-security`- Displays any ports with security activated. To examine a specific interface, include the interface ID. Information included in the output: the maximum addresses allowed, current count, security violation count, and action to be taken. (Figure 1)

- `show port-security address`- Displays all secure MAC addresses configured on all switch interfaces. (Figure 2)

- `show interfaces`- Displays one or all interfaces with line (protocol) status, bandwidth, delay, reliability, encapsulation, duplex, and I/O statistics. (Figure 3)

- `show mac-address-table`- Displays all MAC addresses that the switch has learned, how those addresses were learned (dynamic/static), the port number, and the VLAN assigned to the port. (Figure 4)

Like the router, the switch also supports the `show cdp neighbors` command.

The same in-band and out-of-band management techniques that apply to routers also applies to switch configuration.

Refer to
Online Course
for Illustration

1.3   Summary

Refer to
Lab Activity
for this chapter

1.3.1.1   Class Activity - Layered Network Design Simulation

Layered Network Design Simulation

As the network administrator for a very small network, you want to prepare a simulated-network presentation for your branch manager to explain how the network currently operates.

The small network includes the following equipment:

- One 2911 series router
- One 3560 switch
- One 2960 switch
- Four user workstations (PCs or laptops)
- One printer

Refer to
Online Course
for Illustration

1.3.1.2   Basic Switch Configurations

Refer to **Packet
Tracer Activity**
for this chapter

1.3.1.3   Packet Tracer - Skills Integration Challenge

Background/Scenario

As a recently hired LAN technician, your network manager has asked you to demonstrate your ability to configure a small LAN. Your tasks include configuring initial settings on two switches using the Cisco IOS and configuring IP address parameters on host devices to provide end-to-end connectivity. You are to use two switches and two hosts/PCs on a cabled and powered network.

Refer to
Online Course
for Illustration

1.3.1.4   Summary

The hierarchical network design model divides network functionality into the access layer, the distribution layer, and the core layer. The Cisco Enterprise Architecture further divides the network into functional components.

A well-designed network controls traffic and limits the size of failure domains. Routers and multilayer switches can be deployed in pairs so that the failure of a single device does not cause service disruptions.

A network design should include an IP addressing strategy, scalable, and fast-converging routing protocols, appropriate Layer 2 protocols, and modular or clustered devices that can be easily upgraded to increase capacity.

A mission-critical server should have a connection to two different access layer switches. It should have redundant modules when possible, and a power backup source. It may be appropriate to provide multiple connections to one or more ISPs.

Security monitoring systems and IP telephony systems must have high availability and often have special design considerations.

The network designer should specify a router from the appropriate category: branch router, network edge router, or service provider router. It is important to also deploy the appropriate type of switches for a given set of requirements, switch features and specifications, and expected traffic flow.

Go to the online course to take the quiz and exam.

Chapter 1 Quiz

This quiz is designed to provide an additional opportunity to practice the skills and knowledge presented in the chapter and to prepare for the chapter exam. You will be allowed multiple attempts and the grade does not appear in the gradebook.

Chapter 1 Exam

The chapter exam assesses your knowledge of the chapter content.

Your Chapter Notes

LAN Redundancy

2.0 LAN Redundancy

2.0.1.1 Introduction

Network redundancy is a key to maintaining network reliability. Multiple physical links between devices provide redundant paths. The network can then continue to operate when a single link or port has failed. Redundant links can also share the traffic load and increase capacity.

Multiple paths need to be managed so that Layer 2 loops are not created. The best paths are chosen, and an alternate path is immediately available should a primary path fail. The Spanning Tree Protocols are used to manage Layer 2 redundancy.

Redundant devices, such as multilayer switches or routers, provide the capability for a client to use an alternate default gateway should the primary default gateway fail. A client may now have multiple paths to more than one possible default gateway. First Hop Redundancy Protocols are used to manage how a client is assigned a default gateway, and to be able to use an alternate default gateway should the primary default gateway fail.

This chapter focuses on the protocols used to manage these forms of redundancy. It also covers some of the potential redundancy problems and their symptoms.

Refer to
Lab Activity
for this chapter

2.0.1.2 Class Activity - Stormy Traffic

Stormy Traffic

It is your first day on the job as a network administrator for a small- to medium-sized business. The previous network administrator left suddenly after a network upgrade took place for the business.

During the upgrade, a new switch was added. Since the upgrade, many employees complain that they are having trouble accessing the Internet and servers on your network. In fact, most of them cannot access the network at all. Your corporate manager asks you to immediately research what could be causing these connectivity problems and delays.

So you take a look at the equipment operating on your network at your main distribution facility in the building. You notice that the network topology seems to be visually correct and that cables have been connected correctly, routers and switches are powered on and operational, and switches are connected together to provide backup or redundancy.

However, one thing you do notice is that all of your switches' status lights are constantly blinking at a very fast pace to the point that they almost appear solid. You think you have found the problem with the connectivity issues your employees are experiencing.

Use the Internet to research STP. As you research, take notes and describe:

■ Broadcast storm

■ Switching loops

■ The purpose of STP

■ Variations of STP

Complete the reflection questions that accompany the PDF file for this activity. Save your work and be prepared to share your answers with the class.

Refer to **Interactive Graphic** in online course.

2.1   Spanning Tree Concepts

2.1.1   Purpose of Spanning Tree

2.1.1.1   Redundancy at OSI Layers 1 and 2

The three-tier hierarchical network design that uses core, distribution, and access layers with redundancy, attempts to eliminate a single point of failure on the network. Multiple cabled paths between switches provide physical redundancy in a switched network. This improves the reliability and availability of the network. Having alternate physical paths for data to traverse the network makes it possible for users to access network resources, despite path disruption.

Click the Play button in Figure 1 to view an animation on redundancy.

1. PC1 is communicating with PC4 over a redundant network topology.

2. When the network link between S1 and S2 is disrupted, the path between PC1 and PC4 is automatically adjusted to compensate for the disruption.

3. When the network connection between S1 and S2 is restored, the path is then readjusted to route traffic directly from S2 to S1 to get to PC4.

For many organizations, the availability of the network is essential to supporting business needs; therefore, the network infrastructure design is a critical business element. Path redundancy is a solution for providing the necessary availability of multiple network services by eliminating the possibility of a single point of failure.

Note   The OSI Layer 1 redundancy is illustrated using multiple links and devices, but more than just physical planning is required to complete the network setup. For the redundancy to work in a systematic way, the use of OSI Layer 2 protocols, such as STP is also required.

Redundancy is an important part of hierarchical design for preventing disruption of network services to users. Redundant networks require adding physical paths; but, logical redundancy must also be part of the design. However, redundant paths in a switched Ethernet network may cause both physical and logical Layer 2 loops.

Logical Layer 2 loops may occur due to the natural operation of switches, specifically, the learning and forwarding process. When multiple paths exist between two devices on a network, and there is no spanning tree implementation on the switches, a Layer 2 loop occurs. A Layer 2 loop can result in three primary issues, as listed in Figure 2.

Refer to **Online Course** for Illustration

2.1.1.2   Issues with Layer 1 Redundancy: MAC Database Instability

MAC Database Instability

Ethernet frames do not have a time to live (TTL) attribute, like IP packets. As a result, if there is no mechanism enabled to block continued propagation of these frames on a switched network, they continue to propagate between switches endlessly, or until a link is disrupted and breaks the loop. This continued propagation between switches can result in MAC database instability. This can occur due to broadcast frames forwarding.

Broadcast frames are forwarded out all switch ports, except the original ingress port. This ensures that all devices in a broadcast domain are able to receive the frame. If there is more than one path for the frame to be forwarded out, an endless loop can result. When a loop occurs, it is possible for the MAC address table on a switch to constantly change with the updates from the broadcast frames, resulting in MAC database instability.

Click the Play button in the figure to view the animation. When the animation pauses, read the text to the left of the topology. The animation will continue after the short pause.

In the animation:

1. PC1 sends out a broadcast frame to S2. S2 receives the broadcast frame on F0/11. When S2 receives the broadcast frame, it updates its MAC address table to record that PC1 is available on port F0/11.

2. Because it is a broadcast frame, S2 forwards the frame out all ports, including Trunk1 and Trunk2. When the broadcast frame arrives at S3 and S1, they update their MAC address tables to indicate that PC1 is available out port F0/1 on S1 and out port F0/2 on S3.

3. Because it is a broadcast frame, S3 and S1 forward the frame out all ports, except the ingress port. S3 sends the broadcast frame from PC1 to S1. S1 sends the broadcast frame from PC1 to S3. Each switch updates its MAC address table with the incorrect port for PC1.

4. Each switch again forwards the broadcast frame out all of its ports, except the ingress port, resulting in both switches forwarding the frame to S2.

5. When S2 receives the broadcast frames from S3 and S1, the MAC address table is updated again, this time with the last entry received from the other two switches.

This process repeats over and over again until the loop is broken by physically disconnecting the connections causing the loop or powering down one of the switches in the loop. This creates a high CPU load on all switches caught in the loop. Because the same frames are constantly being forwarded back and forth between all switches in the loop, the CPU of the switch must process a lot of data. This slows down performance on the switch when legitimate traffic arrives.

A host caught in a network loop is not accessible to other hosts on the network. Additionally, due to the constant changes in the MAC address table, the switch does not know out of which port to forward unicast frames. In the example above, the switches will have the incorrect ports listed for PC1. Any unicast frame destined for PC1 loops around the network, just as the broadcast frames do. More and more frames looping around the network eventually create a broadcast storm.

Refer to
Online Course
for Illustration

2.1.1.3   Issues with Layer 1 Redundancy: Broadcast Storms

Broadcast Storm

A broadcast storm occurs when there are so many broadcast frames caught in a Layer 2 loop that all available bandwidth is consumed. Consequently, no bandwidth is available for legitimate traffic and the network becomes unavailable for data communication. This is an effective denial of service.

A broadcast storm is inevitable on a looped network. As more devices send broadcasts over the network, more traffic is caught within the loop, consuming resources. This eventually creates a broadcast storm that causes the network to fail.

There are other consequences of broadcast storms. Because broadcast traffic is forwarded out every port on a switch, all connected devices have to process all broadcast traffic that is being flooded endlessly around the looped network. This can cause the end device to malfunction because of the high processing requirements for sustaining such a high traffic load on the NIC.

Click the Play button in the figure to view an animation of a broadcast storm. When the animation pauses, read the text to the right of the topology. The animation will continue after the short pause.

In the animation:

1. PC1 sends a broadcast frame out onto the looped network.

2. The broadcast frame loops between all the interconnected switches on the network.

3. PC4 also sends a broadcast frame out on to the looped network.

4. The PC4 broadcast frame also gets caught in the loop between all the interconnected switches, just like the PC1 broadcast frame.

5. As more devices send broadcasts over the network, more traffic is caught within the loop, consuming resources. This eventually creates a broadcast storm that causes the network to fail.

6. When the network is fully saturated with broadcast traffic that is looping between the switches, new traffic is discarded by the switch because it is unable to process it.

Because devices connected to a network are regularly sending out broadcast frames, such as ARP requests, a broadcast storm can develop in seconds. As a result, when a loop is created, the switched network is quickly brought down.

Refer to
Online Course
for Illustration

2.1.1.4   Issues with Layer 1 Redundancy: Duplicate Unicast Frames

Multiple Frame Transmissions

Broadcast frames are not the only type of frames that are affected by loops. Unicast frames sent onto a looped network can result in duplicate frames arriving at the destination device.

Click the Play button in the figure to view an animation of this issue. When the animation pauses, read the text to the right of the topology. The animation will continue after the short pause.

In the animation:

1. PC1 sends a unicast frame destined for PC4.

2. S2 does not have an entry for PC4 in its MAC table, so it floods the unicast frame out all switch ports in an attempt to find PC4.

3. The frame arrives at switches S1 and S3.

4. S1 does have a MAC address entry for PC4, so it forwards the frame out to PC4.

5. S3 also has an entry in its MAC address table for PC4, so it forwards the unicast frame out Trunk3 to S1.

6. S1 receives the duplicate frame and forwards the frame out to PC4.

7. PC4 has now received the same frame twice.

Most upper layer protocols are not designed to recognize, or cope with, duplicate transmissions. In general, protocols that make use of a sequence-numbering mechanism assume that the transmission has failed and that the sequence number has recycled for another communication session. Other protocols attempt to hand the duplicate transmission to the appropriate upper layer protocol to be processed and possibly discarded.

Layer 2 LAN protocols, such as Ethernet, lack a mechanism to recognize and eliminate endlessly looping frames. Some Layer 3 protocols implement a TTL mechanism that limits the number of times a Layer 3 networking device can retransmit a packet. Lacking such a mechanism, Layer 2 devices continue to retransmit looping traffic indefinitely. A Layer 2 loop-avoidance mechanism, STP, was developed to address these problems.

To prevent these issues from occurring in a redundant network, some type of spanning tree must be enabled on the switches. Spanning tree is enabled, by default, on Cisco switches to prevent Layer 2 loops from occurring.

Refer to **Packet Tracer Activity** for this chapter

2.1.1.5   Packet Tracer - Examining a Redundant Design

Background/Scenario

In this activity, you will observe how STP operates, by default, and how it reacts when faults occur. Switches have been added to the network "out of the box". Cisco switches can be connected to a network without any additional action required by the network administrator. For the purpose of this activity, the bridge priority was modified.

Refer to **Online Course** for Illustration

2.1.2   STP Operation

2.1.2.1   Spanning Tree Algorithm: Introduction

Redundancy increases the availability of the network topology by protecting the network from a single point of failure, such as a failed network cable or switch. When physical redundancy is introduced into a design, loops and duplicate frames occur. Loops and duplicate frames have severe consequences for a switched network. The Spanning Tree Protocol (STP) was developed to address these issues.

STP ensures that there is only one logical path between all destinations on the network by intentionally blocking redundant paths that could cause a loop. A port is considered blocked when user data is prevented from entering or leaving that port. This does not include bridge protocol data unit (BPDU) frames that are used by STP to prevent loops. Blocking the redundant paths is critical to preventing loops on the network. The physical paths still exist to provide redundancy, but these paths are disabled to prevent the loops from occurring. If the path is ever needed to compensate for a network cable or switch failure, STP recalculates the paths and unblocks the necessary ports to allow the redundant path to become active.

Click the Play button in Figure 1 to view STP in action.

In the example, all switches have STP enabled:

1. PC1 sends a broadcast out onto the network.

2. S2 is configured with STP and has set the port for Trunk2 to a blocking state. The blocking state prevents ports from being used to forward user data, thus preventing a loop from occurring. S2 forwards a broadcast frame out all switch ports, except the originating port from PC1 and the port for Trunk2.

3. S1 receives the broadcast frame and forwards it out all of its switch ports, where it reaches PC4 and S3. S3 forwards the frame out the port for Trunk2 and S2 drops the frame. The Layer 2 loop is prevented.

Click the Play in Figure 2 to view STP recalculation when a failure occurs.

In this example:

1. PC1 sends a broadcast out onto the network.

2. The broadcast is then forwarded around the network, just as in the previous animation.

3. The trunk link between S2 and S1 fails, resulting in the previous path being disrupted.

4. S2 unblocks the previously blocked port for Trunk2 and allows the broadcast traffic to traverse the alternate path around the network, permitting communication to continue. If this link comes back up, STP reconverges and the port on S2 is again blocked.

STP prevents loops from occurring by configuring a loop-free path through the network using strategically placed "blocking-state" ports. The switches running STP are able to compensate for failures by dynamically unblocking the previously blocked ports and permitting traffic to traverse the alternate paths.

Up to now, we have used the term Spanning Tree Protocol and the acronym STP. The usage of the Spanning Tree Protocol term and the STP acronym can be misleading. Many professionals generically use these to refer to various implementations of spanning tree, such as Rapid Spanning Tree Protocol (RSTP) and Multiple Spanning Tree Protocol (MSTP). In order to communicate spanning tree concepts correctly, it is important to refer to the particular implementation or standard in context. The latest IEEE documentation on spanning tree, IEEE-802-1D-2004, says "STP has now been superseded by the Rapid Spanning Tree Protocol (RSTP)"; so one sees that the IEEE uses "STP" to refer to the original implementation of spanning tree and "RSTP" to describe the version of spanning tree specified in IEEE-802.1D-2004. In this curriculum, when the original Spanning Tree Protocol is the context of a discussion, the phrase "original 802.1D spanning tree" is used to avoid confusion.

Note   STP is based on an algorithm invented by Radia Perlman while working for Digital Equipment Corporation, and published in the 1985 paper "An Algorithm for Distributed Computation of a Spanning Tree in an Extended LAN".

Refer to
Online Course
for Illustration

2.1.2.2   Spanning Tree Algorithm: Port Roles

IEEE 802.1D STP uses the Spanning Tree Algorithm (STA) to determine which switch ports on a network must be put in blocking state to prevent loops from occurring. The STA designates a single switch as the root bridge and uses it as the reference point for all path calculations. In the figure, the root bridge (switch S1) is chosen through an election process. All switches participating in STP exchange BPDU frames to determine which switch has the lowest bridge ID (BID) on the network. The switch with the lowest BID automatically becomes the root bridge for the STA calculations.

Note   For simplicity, assume until otherwise indicated that all ports on all switches are assigned to VLAN 1. Each switch has a unique MAC address associated with VLAN 1.

A BPDU is a messaging frame exchanged by switches for STP. Each BPDU contains a BID that identifies the switch that sent the BPDU. The BID contains a priority value, the MAC address of the sending switch, and an optional extended system ID. The lowest BID value is determined by the combination of these three fields.

After the root bridge has been determined, the STA calculates the shortest path to it. Each switch uses the STA to determine which ports to block. While the STA determines the best paths to the root bridge for all switch ports in the broadcast domain, traffic is prevented from being forwarded through the network. The STA considers both path and port costs when determining which ports to block. The path costs are calculated using port cost values associated with port speeds for each switch port along a given path. The sum of the port cost values determines the overall path cost to the root bridge. If there is more than one path to choose from, STA chooses the path with the lowest path cost.

When the STA has determined which paths are most desirable relative to each switch, it assigns port roles to the participating switch ports. The port roles describe their relation in the network to the root bridge and whether they are allowed to forward traffic:

- **Root ports**- Switch ports closest to the root bridge. In the figure, the root port on S2 is F0/1 configured for the trunk link between S2 and S1. The root port on S3 is F0/1, configured for the trunk link between S3 and S1. Root ports are selected on a per-switch basis.

- **Designated ports**- All non-root ports that are still permitted to forward traffic on the network. In the figure, switch ports (F0/1 and F0/2) on S1 are designated ports. S2 also has its port F0/2 configured as a designated port. Designated ports are selected on a per-trunk basis. If one end of a trunk is a root port, then the other end is a designated port. All ports on the root bridge are designated ports.

- **Alternate and backup ports**- Alternate ports and backup ports are configured to be in a blocking state to prevent loops. In the figure, the STA configured port F0/2 on S3 in the alternate role. Port F0/2 on S3 is in the blocking state. Alternate ports are selected only on trunk links where neither end is a root port. Notice in the figure that only one end of the trunk is blocked. This allows for faster transition to a forwarding state, when necessary. (Blocking ports only come into play when two ports on the same switch are connected to each other via a hub or single cable.)

■ **Disabled ports**- A disabled port is a switch port that is shut down.

Refer to
Online Course
for Illustration

2.1.2.3   Spanning Tree Algorithm: Root Bridge

As shown in Figure 1, every spanning tree instance (switched LAN or broadcast domain) has a switch designated as the root bridge. The root bridge serves as a reference point for all spanning tree calculations to determine which redundant paths to block.

An election process determines which switch becomes the root bridge.

Figure 2 shows the BID fields. The BID is made up of a priority value, an extended system ID, and the MAC address of the switch.

All switches in the broadcast domain participate in the election process. After a switch boots, it begins to send out BPDU frames every two seconds. These BPDUs contain the switch BID and the root ID.

As the switches forward their BPDU frames, adjacent switches in the broadcast domain read the root ID information from the BPDU frames. If the root ID from a BPDU received is lower than the root ID on the receiving switch, then the receiving switch updates its root ID, identifying the adjacent switch as the root bridge. Actually, it may not be an adjacent switch, but could be any other switch in the broadcast domain. The switch then forwards new BPDU frames with the lower root ID to the other adjacent switches. Eventually, the switch with the lowest BID ends up being identified as the root bridge for the spanning tree instance.

There is a root bridge elected for each spanning tree instance. It is possible to have multiple distinct root bridges. If all ports on all switches are members of VLAN 1, then there is only one spanning tree instance. The extended system ID plays a role in how spanning tree instances are determined.

Refer to
Online Course
for Illustration

2.1.2.4   Spanning Tree Algorithm: Path Cost

When the root bridge has been elected for the spanning tree instance, the STA starts the process of determining the best paths to the root bridge from all destinations in the broadcast domain. The path information is determined by summing up the individual port costs along the path from the destination to the root bridge. Each "destination" is actually a switch port.

The default port costs are defined by the speed at which the port operates. As shown in Figure 1, 10 Gb/s Ethernet ports have a port cost of 2, 1 Gb/s Ethernet ports have a port cost of 4, 100 Mb/s Fast Ethernet ports have a port cost of 19, and 10 Mb/s Ethernet ports have a port cost of 100.

Note   As newer, faster Ethernet technologies enter the marketplace, the path cost values may change to accommodate the different speeds available. The non-linear numbers in the table accommodate some improvements to the older Ethernet standard. The values have already been changed to accommodate the 10 Gb/s Ethernet standard. To illustrate the continued change associated with high-speed networking, Catalyst 4500 and 6500 switches support a longer path cost method; for example, 10 Gb/s has a 2000 path cost, 100 Gb/s has a 200 path cost, and 1 Tb/s has a 20 path cost.

Although switch ports have a default port cost associated with them, the port cost is configurable. The ability to configure individual port costs gives the administrator the flexibility to manually control the spanning tree paths to the root bridge.

To configure the port cost of an interface (Figure 2), enter the `spanning-tree cost` value command in interface configuration mode. The value can be between 1 and 200,000,000.

In the example, switch port F0/1 has been configured with a port cost of 25 using the `spanning-tree cost 25` interface configuration mode command on the F0/1 interface.

To restore the port cost back to the default value of 19, enter the `no spanning-tree cost` interface configuration mode command.

The path cost is equal to the sum of all the port costs along the path to the root bridge (Figure 3). Paths with the lowest cost become preferred, and all other redundant paths are blocked. In the example, the path cost from S2 to the root bridge S1, over path 1 is 19 (based on the IEEE-specified individual port cost), while the path cost over path 2 is 38. Because path 1 has a lower overall path cost to the root bridge, it is the preferred path. STP then configures the redundant path to be blocked, preventing a loop from occurring.

To verify the port and path cost to the root bridge, enter the `show spanning-tree` command (Figure 4). The Cost field near the top of the output is the total path cost to the root bridge. This value changes depending on how many switch ports must be traversed to get to the root bridge. In the output, each interface is also identified with an individual port cost of 19.

Refer to
Online Course
for Illustration

2.1.2.5   802.1D BPDU Frame Format

The spanning tree algorithm depends on the exchange of BPDUs to determine a root bridge. A BPDU frame contains 12 distinct fields that convey path and priority information used to determine the root bridge and paths to the root bridge.

Click the BPDU fields in Figure 1 to see more detail.

- The first four fields identify the protocol, version, message type, and status flags.

- The next four fields are used to identify the root bridge and the cost of the path to the root bridge.

- The last four fields are all timer fields that determine how frequently BPDU messages are sent and how long the information received through the BPDU process (next topic) is retained.

Figure 2 shows a BPDU frame that was captured using Wireshark. In the example, the BPDU frame contains more fields than previously described. The BPDU message is encapsulated in an Ethernet frame when it is transmitted across the network. The 802.3 header indicates the source and destination addresses of the BPDU frame. This frame has a destination MAC address of 01:80:C2:00:00:00, which is a multicast address for the spanning tree group. When a frame is addressed with this MAC address, each switch that is configured for spanning tree accepts and reads the information from the frame; all other devices on the network disregard the frame.

In the example, the root ID and the BID are the same in the captured BPDU frame. This indicates that the frame was captured from a root bridge. The timers are all set to the default values.

Refer to
Online Course
for Illustration

2.1.2.6   BPDU Propagation and Process

Each switch in the broadcast domain initially assumes that it is the root bridge for a spanning tree instance, so the BPDU frames sent contain the BID of the local switch as the root ID. By default, BPDU frames are sent every two seconds after a switch is booted; that is, the default value of the Hello timer specified in the BPDU frame is two seconds. Each switch maintains local information about its own BID, the root ID, and the path cost to the root.

When adjacent switches receive a BPDU frame, they compare the root ID from the BPDU frame with the local root ID. If the root ID in the BPDU is lower than the local root ID, the switch updates the local root ID and the ID in its BPDU messages. These messages indicate the new root bridge on the network. The distance to the root bridge is also indicated by the path cost update. For example, if the BPDU was received on a Fast Ethernet switch port, the path cost would increment by 19. If the local root ID is lower than the root ID received in the BPDU frame, the BPDU frame is discarded.

After a root ID has been updated to identify a new root bridge, all subsequent BPDU frames sent from that switch contain the new root ID and updated path cost. That way, all other adjacent switches are able to see the lowest root ID identified at all times. As the BPDU frames pass between other adjacent switches, the path cost is continually updated to indicate the total path cost to the root bridge. Each switch in the spanning tree uses its path costs to identify the best possible path to the root bridge.

The following summarizes the BPDU process:

Note   Priority is the initial deciding factor when electing a root bridge. If the priorities of all the switches are the same, the device with the lowest MAC address becomes the root bridge.

1. Initially, each switch identifies itself as the root bridge. S2 forwards BPDU frames out all switch ports. (Figure 1)

2. When S3 receives a BPDU from switch S2, S3 compares its root ID with the BPDU frame it received. The priorities are equal, so the switch is forced to examine the MAC address portion to determine which MAC address has a lower value. Because S2 has a lower MAC address value, S3 updates its root ID with the S2 root ID. At that point, S3 considers S2 as the root bridge. (Figure 2)

3. When S1 compares its root ID with the one in the received BPDU frame, it identifies its local root ID as the lower value and discards the BPDU from S2. (Figure 3)

4. When S3 sends out its BPDU frames, the root ID contained in the BPDU frame is that of S2. (Figure 4)

5. When S2 receives the BPDU frame, it discards it after verifying that the root ID in the BPDU matched its local root ID. (Figure 5)

6. Because S1 has a lower priority value in its root ID, it discards the BPDU frame received from S3. (Figure 6)

7. S1 sends out its BPDU frames. (Figure 7)

8. S3 identifies the root ID in the BPDU frame as having a lower value and, therefore, updates its root ID values to indicate that S1 is now the root bridge. (Figure 8)

9. S2 identifies the root ID in the BPDU frame as having a lower value and, therefore, updates its root ID values to indicate that S1 is now the root bridge. (Figure 9)

Refer to
Online Course
for Illustration

2.1.2.7   Extended System ID

The bridge ID (BID) is used to determine the root bridge on a network. The BID field of a BPDU frame contains three separate fields:

- Bridge priority

- Extended system ID

- MAC address

Each field is used during the root bridge election.

Bridge Priority

The bridge priority is a customizable value that can be used to influence which switch becomes the root bridge. The switch with the lowest priority, which implies the lowest BID, becomes the root bridge because a lower priority value takes precedence. For example, to ensure that a specific switch is always the root bridge, set the priority to a lower value than the rest of the switches on the network. The default priority value for all Cisco switches is 32768. The range is 0 to 61440 in increments of 4096. Valid priority values are 0, 4096, 8192, 12288, 16384, 20480, 24576, 28672, 32768, 36864, 40960, 45056, 49152, 53248, 57344, and 61440. All other values are rejected. A bridge priority of 0 takes precedence over all other bridge priorities.

Extended System ID

Early implementations of IEEE 802.1D were designed for networks that did not use VLANs. There was a single common spanning tree across all switches. For this reason, in older Cisco switches, the extended system ID could be omitted in BPDU frames. As VLANs became common for network infrastructure segmentation, 802.1D was enhanced to include support for VLANs, requiring the VLAN ID to be included in the BPDU frame. VLAN information is included in the BPDU frame through the use of the extended system ID. All newer switches include the use of the extended system ID by default.

As shown in Figure 1, the bridge priority field is 2 bytes or 16-bits in length; 4-bits used for the bridge priority and 12-bits for the extended system ID, which identifies the VLAN participating in this particular STP process. Using these 12 bits for the extended system

ID reduces the bridge priority to 4 bits. This process reserves the rightmost 12 bits for the VLAN ID and the far left 4 bits for the bridge priority. This explains why the bridge priority value can only be configured in multiples of 4096, or 2^12. If the far left bits are 0001, then the bridge priority is 4096; if the far left bits are 1111, then the bridge priority is 61440 (= 15 x 4096). The Catalyst 2960 and 3560 Series switches do not allow the configuration of a bridge priority of 65536 (= 16 x 4096) because it assumes use of a 5th bit that is unavailable due to the use of the extended system ID.

The extended system ID value is added to the bridge priority value in the BID to identify the priority and VLAN of the BPDU frame.

When two switches are configured with the same priority and have the same extended system ID, the switch having the MAC address with the lowest hexadecimal value will have the lower BID. Initially, all switches are configured with the same default priority value. The MAC address is then the deciding factor on which switch is going to become the root bridge. To ensure that the root bridge decision best meets network requirements, it is recommended that the administrator configure the desired root bridge switch with a lower priority. This also ensures that the addition of new switches to the network does not trigger a new spanning tree election, which can disrupt network communication while a new root bridge is being selected.

In Figure 2, S1 has a lower priority than the other switches; therefore, it is preferred as the root bridge for that spanning tree instance.

When all switches are configured with the same priority, as is the case with all switches kept in the default configuration with a priority of 32768, the MAC address becomes the deciding factor for which switch becomes the root bridge (Figure 3).

Note   In the example, the priority of all the switches is 32769. The value is based on the 32768 default priority and the VLAN 1 assignment associated with each switch (32768+1).

The MAC address with the lowest hexadecimal value is considered to be the preferred root bridge. In the example, S2 has the lowest value for its MAC address and is, therefore, designated as the root bridge for that spanning tree instance.

Refer to
Interactive Graphic
in online course.

2.1.2.8   Activity - Identify 802.1D Port Roles

Refer to
Interactive Graphic
in online course.

2.1.2.9   Video Demonstration - Observing Spanning Tree Protocol Operation

Refer to
Lab Activity
for this chapter

2.1.2.10   Lab – Building a Switched Network with Redundant Links

In this lab, you will complete the following objectives:

- Part 1: Build the Network and Configure Basic Device Settings
- Part 2: Determine the Root Bridge
- Part 3: Observe STP Port Selection Based on Port Cost
- Part 4: Observe STP Port Selection Based on Port Priority

Refer to
Online Course
for Illustration

2.2   Varieties of Spanning Tree Protocols

2.2.1   Overview

2.2.1.1   List of Spanning Tree Protocols

Several varieties of spanning tree protocols have emerged since the original IEEE 802.1D.

The varieties of spanning tree protocols include:

- **STP**- This is the original IEEE 802.1D version (802.1D-1998 and earlier) that provides a loop-free topology in a network with redundant links. Common Spanning Tree (CST) assumes one spanning tree instance for the entire bridged network, regardless of the number of VLANs.

- **PVST+**- This is a Cisco enhancement of STP that provides a separate 802.1D spanning tree instance for each VLAN configured in the network. The separate instance supports PortFast, UplinkFast, BackboneFast, BPDU guard, BPDU filter, root guard, and loop guard.

- **802.1D-2004**- This is an updated version of the STP standard, incorporating IEEE 802.1w.

- **Rapid Spanning Tree Protocol (RSTP) or IEEE 802.1w**- This is an evolution of STP that provides faster convergence than STP.

- **Rapid PVST+**- This is a Cisco enhancement of RSTP that uses PVST+. Rapid PVST+ provides a separate instance of 802.1w per VLAN. The separate instance supports PortFast, BPDU guard, BPDU filter, root guard, and loop guard.

- **Multiple Spanning Tree Protocol (MSTP)**- This is an IEEE standard inspired by the earlier Cisco proprietary Multiple Instance STP (MISTP) implementation. MSTP maps multiple VLANs into the same spanning tree instance. The Cisco implementation of MSTP is MST, which provides up to 16 instances of RSTP and combines many VLANs with the same physical and logical topology into a common RSTP instance. Each instance supports PortFast, BPDU guard, BPDU filter, root guard, and loop guard.

A network professional, whose duties include switch administration, may be required to decide which type of spanning tree protocol to implement.

Note   The legacy Cisco-proprietary features UplinkFast and BackboneFast are not described in this course. These features are superseded by the implementation of Rapid PVST+, which incorporates these features as part of the implementation of the RSTP standard.

Refer to
Online Course
for Illustration

2.2.1.2   Characteristics of the Spanning Tree Protocols

These are characteristics of the various spanning tree protocols. The italicized words indicate whether the particular spanning tree protocol is Cisco-proprietary or an IEEE standard implementation:

- **STP**- Assumes one *IEEE 802.1D* spanning tree instance for the entire bridged network, regardless of the number of VLANs. Because there is only one instance, the CPU and memory requirements for this version are lower than for the other protocols. However, because there is only one instance, there is only one root bridge and one tree. Traffic for all VLANs flows over the same path, which can lead to suboptimal traffic flows. Because of the limitations of 802.1D, this version is slow to converge.

- **PVST+**- A Cisco enhancement of STP that provides a separate instance of the Cisco implementation of 802.1D for each VLAN that is configured in the network. The separate instance supports PortFast, UplinkFast, BackboneFast, BPDU guard, BPDU filter, root guard, and loop guard. Creating an instance for each VLAN increases the CPU and memory requirements, but allows for per-VLAN root bridges. This design allows the spanning tree to be optimized for the traffic of each VLAN. Convergence of this version is similar to the convergence of 802.1D. However, convergence is per-VLAN.

- **RSTP** (or *IEEE 802.1w*) - An evolution of spanning tree that provides faster convergence than the original 802.1D implementation. This version addresses many convergence issues, but because it still provides a single instance of STP, it does not address the suboptimal traffic flow issues. To support that faster convergence, the CPU usage and memory requirements of this version are slightly higher than those of CST, but less than those of RSTP+.

- **Rapid PVST+**- A Cisco enhancement of RSTP that uses PVST+. It provides a separate instance of 802.1w per VLAN. The separate instance supports PortFast, BPDU guard, BPDU filter, root guard, and loop guard. This version addresses both the convergence issues and the suboptimal traffic flow issues. However, this version has the largest CPU and memory requirements.

- **MSTP**- The *IEEE 802.1s* standard, inspired by the earlier Cisco proprietary MISTP implementation. To reduce the number of required STP instances, MSTP maps multiple VLANs that have the same traffic flow requirements into the same spanning tree instance.

- **MST**- The Cisco implementation of MSTP, which provides up to 16 instances of RSTP (802.1w) and combines many VLANs with the same physical and logical topology into a common RSTP instance. Each instance supports PortFast, BPDU guard, BPDU filter, root guard, and loop guard. The CPU and memory requirements of this version are less than those of Rapid PVST+, but more than those of RSTP.

The default spanning tree mode for Cisco Catalyst switches is PVST+, which is enabled on all ports. PVST+ has much slower convergence after a topology change than Rapid PVST+.

Note   It is important to distinguish between the legacy IEEE 802.1D-1998 (and earlier) standard and the IEEE 802.1D-2004 standard. IEEE 802.1D-2004 incorporates RSTP functionality, while IEEE 802.1D-1998 refers to the original implementation of the spanning tree algorithm. Newer Cisco switches running newer versions of the IOS, such as Catalyst 2960 switches with IOS 15.0, run PVST+ by default, but incorporate many of the specifications of IEEE 802.1D-1998 in this mode (such as alternate ports in place of the former non-designated ports); but to run rapid spanning tree on such a switch it still must be explicitly configured for rapid spanning tree mode.

Refer to
Interactive Graphic
in online course.

2.2.1.3   Activity - Identify Types of Spanning Tree Protocols

Refer to
Online Course
for Illustration

2.2.2   PVST+

2.2.2.1   Overview of PVST+

The original IEEE 802.1D standard defines a Common Spanning Tree (CST) that assumes only one spanning tree instance for the entire switched network, regardless of the number of VLAN. A network running CST has these characteristics:

- No load sharing is possible. One uplink must block for all VLANs.

- The CPU is spared. Only one instance of spanning tree must be computed.

Cisco developed PVST+ so that a network can run an independent instance of the Cisco implementation of IEEE 802.1D for each VLAN in the network. With PVST+, it is possible for one trunk port on a switch to be blocking for a VLAN while not blocking for other VLANs. PVST+ can be used to implement Layer 2 load balancing. Because each VLAN runs a separate instance of STP, the switches in a PVST+ environment require greater CPU process and BPDU bandwidth consumption than a traditional CST implementation of STP.

In a PVST+ environment, spanning tree parameters can be tuned so that half of the VLANs forward on each uplink trunk. In the figure, port F0/3 on S2 is the forwarding port for VLAN 20, and F0/2 on S2 is the forwarding port for VLAN 10. This is accomplished by configuring one switch to be elected the root bridge for half of the VLANs in the network, and a second switch to be elected the root bridge for the other half of the VLANs. In the figure, S3 is the root bridge for VLAN 20, and S1 is the root bridge for VLAN 10. Multiple STP root bridges per VLAN increases redundancy in the network.

Networks running PVST+ have these characteristics:

- Optimum load balancing can result.

- One spanning tree instance for each VLAN maintained can mean a considerable waste of CPU cycles for all the switches in the network (in addition to the bandwidth that is used for each instance to send its own BPDU). This would only be problematic if a large number of VLANs are configured.

Refer to
Online Course
for Illustration

2.2.2.2   Port States and PVST+ Operation

STP facilitates the logical loop-free path throughout the broadcast domain. The spanning tree is determined through the information learned by the exchange of the BPDU frames between the interconnected switches. To facilitate the learning of the logical spanning tree, each switch port transitions through five possible port states and three BPDU timers.

The spanning tree is determined immediately after a switch is finished booting up. If a switch port transitions directly from the blocking to the forwarding state without information about the full topology during the transition, the port can temporarily create a data loop. For this reason, STP introduces the five port states. The figure describes the following port states that ensure no loops are created during the creation of the logical spanning tree:

- **Blocking**- The port is an alternate port and does not participate in frame forwarding. The port receives BPDU frames to determine the location and root ID of the root bridge switch and what port roles each switch port should assume in the final active STP topology.

- **Listening**- Listens for the path to the root. STP has determined that the port can participate in frame forwarding according to the BPDU frames that the switch has received thus far. At this point, the switch port not only receives BPDU frames, it also transmits its own BPDU frames and inform adjacent switches that the switch port is preparing to participate in the active topology.

- **Learning**- Learns the MAC addresses. The port prepares to participate in frame forwarding and begins to populate the MAC address table.

- **Forwarding**- The port is considered part of the active topology. It forwards data frames and sends and receives BPDU frames.

- **Disabled**- The Layer 2 port does not participate in spanning tree and does not forward frames. The disabled state is set when the switch port is administratively disabled.

Note that the number of ports in each of the various states (blocking, listening, learning, or forwarding) can be displayed with the `show spanning-tree summary` command.

For each VLAN in a switched network, PVST+ performs four steps to provide a loop-free logical network topology:

1. **Elects one root bridge**- Only one switch can act as the root bridge (for a given VLAN). The root bridge is the switch with the lowest bridge ID. On the root bridge, all ports are designated ports (in particular, no root ports).

2. **Selects the root port on each non-root bridge**- STP establishes one root port on each non-root bridge. The root port is the lowest-cost path from the non-root bridge to the root bridge, indicating the direction of the best path to the root bridge. Root ports are normally in the forwarding state.

3. **Selects the designated port on each segment**- On each link, STP establishes one designated port. The designated port is selected on the switch that has the lowest-cost path to the root bridge. Designated ports are normally in the forwarding state, forwarding traffic for the segment.

4. **The remaining ports in the switched network are alternate ports**- Alternate ports normally remain in the blocking state, to logically break the loop topology. When a port is in the blocking state, it does not forward traffic, but can still process received BPDU messages.

Refer to **Online Course** for Illustration

2.2.2.3   Extended System ID and PVST+ Operation

In a PVST+ environment, the extended switch ID ensures each switch has a unique BID for each VLAN.

For example, the VLAN 2 default BID would be 32770 (priority 32768, plus the extended system ID of 2). If no priority has been configured, every switch has the same default priority and the election of the root for each VLAN is based on the MAC address. This method is a random means of selecting the root bridge.

There are situations where the administrator may want a specific switch selected as the root bridge. This may be for a variety of reasons, including the switch is more centrally located within the LAN design, the switch has higher processing power, or the switch is simply easier to access and manage remotely. To manipulate the root bridge election, simply assign a lower priority to the switch that should be selected as the root bridge.

Refer to **Interactive Graphic** in online course.

2.2.2.4 Activity - Identifying PVST+ Operation

Refer to **Online Course** for Illustration

2.2.3 Rapid PVST+

2.2.3.1 Overview of Rapid PVST+

RSTP (IEEE 802.1w) is an evolution of the original 802.1D standard and is incorporated into the IEEE 802.1D-2004 standard. The 802.1w STP terminology remains primarily the same as the original IEEE 802.1D STP terminology. Most parameters have been left unchanged, so users familiar with STP can easily configure the new protocol. Rapid PVST+ is simply the Cisco implementation of RSTP on a per-VLAN basis. With Rapid PVST+, an independent instance of RSTP runs for each VLAN.

The figure shows a network running RSTP. S1 is the root bridge with two designated ports in a forwarding state. RSTP supports a new port type: port F0/3 on S2 is an alternate port in discarding state. Notice that there are no blocking ports. RSTP does not have a blocking port state. RSTP defines port states as discarding, learning, or forwarding.

RSTP speeds the recalculation of the spanning tree when the Layer 2 network topology changes. RSTP can achieve much faster convergence in a properly configured network, sometimes in as little as a few hundred milliseconds. RSTP redefines the type of ports and their state. If a port is configured to be an alternate port or a backup port, it can immediately change to forwarding state without waiting for the network to converge. The following briefly describes RSTP characteristics:

- RSTP is the preferred protocol for preventing Layer 2 loops in a switched network environment. Many of the differences were established by Cisco-proprietary enhancements to the original 802.1D. These enhancements, such as BPDUs carrying and sending information about port roles only to neighboring switches, require no additional configuration and generally perform better than the earlier Cisco-proprietary versions. They are now transparent and integrated in the protocol's operation.

- Cisco-proprietary enhancements to the original 802.1D, such as UplinkFast and BackboneFast, are not compatible with RSTP.

- RSTP (802.1w) supersedes the original 802.1D while retaining backward compatibility. Much of the original 802.1D terminology remains and most parameters are unchanged. In addition, 802.1w is capable of reverting back to legacy 802.1D to interoperate with legacy switches on a per-port basis. For example, the RSTP spanning tree algorithm elects a root bridge in exactly the same way as the original 802.1D.

- RSTP keeps the same BPDU format as the original IEEE 802.1D, except that the version field is set to 2 to indicate RSTP, and the flags field uses all 8 bits.

■ RSTP is able to actively confirm that a port can safely transition to the forwarding state without having to rely on any timer configuration.

Refer to
Online Course
for Illustration

2.2.3.2   RSTP BPDU

RSTP uses type 2, version 2 BPDUs. The original 802.1D STP uses type 0, version 0 BPDUs. However, a switch running RSTP can communicate directly with a switch running the original 802.1D STP. RSTP sends BPDUs and populates the flag byte in a slightly different manner than in the original 802.1D:

■ Protocol information can be immediately aged on a port if Hello packets are not received for three consecutive Hello times, six seconds by default, or if the max age timer expires.

■ Because BPDUs are used as a keepalive mechanism, three consecutively missed BPDUs indicate lost connectivity between a bridge and its neighboring root or designated bridge. The fast aging of the information allows failures to be detected quickly.

Note   Like STP, an RSTP switch sends a BPDU with its current information every Hello time period (two seconds, by default), even if the RSTP bridge does not receive any BPDUs from the root bridge.

As shown in the figure, RSTP uses the flag byte of version 2 BPDU:

■ Bits 0 and 7 are used for topology change and acknowledgment as they are in the original 802.1D.

■ Bits 1 and 6 are used for the Proposal Agreement process (used for rapid convergence).

■ Bits from 2 to 5 encode the role and state of the port.

■ Bits 4 and 5 are used to encode the port role using a 2-bit code.

Refer to
Online Course
for Illustration

2.2.3.3   Edge Ports

An RSTP edge port is a switch port that is never intended to be connected to another switch device. It immediately transitions to the forwarding state when enabled.

The RSTP edge port concept corresponds to the PVST+ PortFast feature; an edge port is directly connected to an end station and assumes that no switch device is connected to it. RSTP edge ports should immediately transition to the forwarding state, thereby skipping the time-consuming original 802.1D listening and learning port states.

The Cisco RSTP implementation, Rapid PVST+, maintains the PortFast keyword, using the `spanning-tree portfast` command for edge port configuration. This makes the transition from STP to RSTP seamless.

Figure 1 shows examples of ports that can be configured as edge ports. Figure 2 shows examples of ports that are non-edge ports.

Note   Configuring an edge port to be attached to another switch is not recommended. This can have negative implications for RSTP because a temporary loop may result, possibly delaying the convergence of RSTP.

Refer to
Online Course
for Illustration

2.2.3.4   Link Types

The link type provides a categorization for each port participating in RSTP by using the duplex mode on the port. Depending on what is attached to each port, two different link types can be identified:

- **Point-to-Point**- A port operating in full-duplex mode typically connects a switch to a switch and is a candidate for rapid transition to forwarding state.

- **Shared**- A port operating in half-duplex mode connects a switch to a hub that attaches multiple devices.

In the figure, click each link to learn about the link types.

The link type can determine whether the port can immediately transition to forwarding state, assuming certain conditions are met. These conditions are different for edge ports and non-edge ports. Non-edge ports are categorized into two link types, point-to-point and shared. The link type is automatically determined, but can be overridden with an explicit port configuration using the `spanning-tree link-type` parameter command.

Edge port connections and point-to-point connections are candidates for rapid transition to forwarding state. However, before the link-type parameter is considered, RSTP must determine the port role. Characteristics of port roles with regard to link types include the following:

- Root ports do not use the link-type parameter. Root ports are able to make a rapid transition to the forwarding state as soon as the port is in sync.

- Alternate and backup ports do not use the link-type parameter in most cases.

- Designated ports make the most use of the link-type parameter. Rapid transition to the forwarding state for the designated port occurs only if the link-type parameter is set to point-to-point.

Refer to
Interactive Graphic
in online course.

2.2.3.5   Activity - Identify Port Roles in Rapid PVST+

Refer to
Interactive Graphic
in online course.

2.2.3.6   Activity - Compare PVST+ and Rapid PVST+

Refer to
Online Course
for Illustration

2.3   Spanning Tree Configuration

2.3.1   PVST+ Configuration

2.3.1.1   Catalyst 2960 Default Configuration

The table shows the default spanning tree configuration for a Cisco Catalyst 2960 series switch. Notice that the default spanning tree mode is PVST+.

Refer to
Online Course
for Illustration

2.3.1.2   Configuring and Verifying the Bridge ID

When an administrator wants a specific switch to become a root bridge, the bridge priority value must be adjusted to ensure it is lower than the bridge priority values of all the other switches on the network. There are two different methods to configure the bridge priority value on a Cisco Catalyst switch.

Method 1

To ensure that the switch has the lowest bridge priority value, use the `spanning-tree vlan` vlan-id `root primary` command in global configuration mode. The priority for the switch is set to the predefined value of 24,576 or to the highest multiple of 4,096, less than the lowest bridge priority detected on the network.

If an alternate root bridge is desired, use the `spanning-tree vlan` vlan-id `root secondary` global configuration mode command. This command sets the priority for the switch to the predefined value of 28,672. This ensures that the alternate switch becomes the root bridge if the primary root bridge fails. This assumes that the rest of the switches in the network have the default 32,768 priority value defined.

In Figure 1, S1 has been assigned as the primary root bridge using the `spanning-tree vlan 1 root primary` command, and S2 has been configured as the secondary root bridge using the `spanning-tree vlan 1 root secondary` command.

Method 2

Another method for configuring the bridge priority value is using the `spanning-tree vlan` vlan-id `priority` value global configuration mode command. This command gives more granular control over the bridge priority value. The priority value is configured in increments of 4,096 between 0 and 61,440.

In the example, S3 has been assigned a bridge priority value of 24,576 using the `spanning-tree vlan 1 priority 24576` command.

To verify the bridge priority of a switch, use the `show spanning-tree` command. In Figure 2, the priority of the switch has been set to 24,576. Also notice that the switch is designated as the root bridge for the spanning tree instance.

Use the Syntax Checker in Figure 3 to configure switches S1, S2, and S3. Using Method 2 described above, configure S3 manually, setting the priority to 24,576 for VLAN 1. Using Method 1, configure S2 as the secondary root VLAN 1 and configure S1 as the primary root for VLAN 1. Verify the configuration with the `show spanning-tree` command on S1.

Refer to
Online Course
for Illustration

2.3.1.3   PortFast and BPDU Guard

PortFast is a Cisco feature for PVST+ environments. When a switch port is configured with PortFast that port transitions from blocking to forwarding state immediately, bypassing the usual 802.1D STP transition states (the listening and learning states). You can use PortFast on access ports to allow these devices to connect to the network immediately, rather than waiting for IEEE 802.1D STP to converge on each VLAN. Access ports are ports which are connected to a single workstation or to a server.

In a valid PortFast configuration, BPDUs should never be received, because that would indicate that another bridge or switch is connected to the port, potentially causing a spanning tree loop. Cisco switches support a feature called BPDU guard. When it is enabled,

BPDU guard puts the port in an *error-disabled* state on receipt of a BPDU. This will effectively shut down the port. The BPDU guard feature provides a secure response to invalid configurations because you must manually put the interface back into service.

Cisco PortFast technology is useful for DHCP. Without PortFast, a PC can send a DHCP request before the port is in forwarding state, denying the host from getting a usable IP address and other information. Because PortFast immediately changes the state to forwarding, the PC always gets a usable IP address.

Note   Because the purpose of PortFast is to minimize the time that access ports must wait for spanning tree to converge, it should only be used on access ports. If you enable PortFast on a port connecting to another switch, you risk creating a spanning tree loop.

To configure PortFast on a switch port, enter the `spanning-tree portfast` interface configuration mode command on each interface that PortFast is to be enabled, as shown in Figure 2. The `spanning-tree portfast default` global configuration mode command enables PortFast on all nontrunking interfaces.

To configure BPDU guard on a Layer 2 access port, use the `spanning-tree bpduguard enable` interface configuration mode command. The `spanning-tree portfast bpduguard default` global configuration command enables BPDU guard on all PortFast-enabled ports.

To verify that PortFast and BPDU guard has been enabled for a switch port, use the `show running-config` command, as shown in Figure 3. PortFast and BPDU guard are disabled, by default, on all interfaces.

Use the Syntax Checker in Figure 4 to configure and verify switches S1 and S2 with PortFast and BPDU guard.

Refer to
Online Course
for Illustration

2.3.1.4   PVST+ Load Balancing

The topology in Figure 1 shows three switches with 802.1Q trunks connecting them. There are two VLANs, 10 and 20, that are being trunked across these links. The goal is to configure S3 as the root bridge for VLAN 20 and S1 as the root bridge for VLAN 10. Port F0/3 on S2 is the forwarding port for VLAN 20 and the blocking port for VLAN 10. Port F0/2 on S2 is the forwarding port for VLAN 10 and the blocking port for VLAN 20.

In addition to establishing a root bridge, it is also possible to establish a secondary root bridge. A secondary root bridge is a switch that may become the root bridge for a VLAN if the primary root bridge fails. Assuming the other bridges in the VLAN retain their default STP priority, this switch becomes the root bridge if the primary root bridge fails.

The steps to configure PVST+ on this example topology are:

Step 1.   Select the switches you want for the primary and secondary root bridges for each VLAN. For example, in Figure 1, S3 is the primary bridge for VLAN 20 and S1 is the secondary bridge for VLAN 20.

Step 2.   Configure the switch to be a primary bridge for the VLAN by using the `spanning-tree vlan` number `root primary` command, as shown in Figure 2.

Step 3.   Configure the switch to be a secondary bridge for the VLAN by using the `spanning-tree vlan` number `root secondary` command.

Another way to specify the root bridge is to set the spanning tree priority on each switch to the lowest value so that the switch is selected as the primary bridge for its associated VLAN.

Notice that in Figure 2, S3 is configured as the primary root bridge for VLAN 20, S1 is configured as the primary root bridge for VLAN 10. S2 retained its default STP priority.

The figure also shows that S3 is configured as the secondary root bridge for VLAN 10, and S1 is configured as the secondary root bridge for VLAN 20. This configuration enables spanning tree load balancing, with VLAN 10 traffic passing through S1 and VLAN 20 traffic passing through S3.

Another way to specify the root bridge is to set the spanning tree priority on each switch to the lowest value so that the switch is selected as the primary bridge for its associated VLAN, as shown in Figure 3. The switch priority can be set for any spanning tree instance. This setting affects the likelihood that a switch is selected as the root bridge. A lower value increases the probability that the switch is selected. The range is 0 to 61,440 in increments of 4,096; all other values are rejected. For example, a valid priority value is 4,096 x 2 = 8,192.

As shown in Figure 4, the `show spanning-tree active` command displays spanning tree configuration details for the active interfaces only. The output shown is for S1 configured with PVST+. There are a number of Cisco IOS command parameters associated with the `show spanning-tree` command.

In Figure 5, the output shows that the priority for VLAN 10 is 4,096, the lowest of the three respective VLAN priorities.

Use the Syntax Checker in Figure 6 to configure and verify spanning tree for S1 and S3.

Refer to **Packet Tracer Activity** for this chapter

2.3.1.5   Packet Tracer - Configuring PVST+

Background/Scenario

In this activity, you will configure VLANs and trunks, and examine and configure the Spanning Tree Protocol primary and secondary root bridges. You will also optimize the switched topology using PVST+, PortFast, and BPDU guard.

Refer to **Online Course** for Illustration

2.3.2   Rapid PVST+ Configuration

2.3.2.1   Spanning Tree Mode

Rapid PVST+ is the Cisco implementation of RSTP. It supports RSTP on a per-VLAN basis. The topology in Figure 1 has two VLANs: 10 and 20.

Note   The default spanning tree configuration on a Catalyst 2960 Series switch is PVST+. A Catalyst 2960 switch supports PVST+, Rapid PVST+, and MST, but only one version can be active for all VLANs at any time.

Rapid PVST+ commands control the configuration of VLAN spanning tree instances. A spanning tree instance is created when an interface is assigned to a VLAN and is removed when the last interface is moved to another VLAN. As well, you can configure STP switch and port parameters before a spanning tree instance is created. These parameters are applied when a spanning tree instance is created.

Figure 2 displays the Cisco IOS command syntax needed to configure Rapid PVST+ on a Cisco switch. The `spanning-tree mode rapid-pvst` global configuration mode command is the one required command for the Rapid PVST+ configuration. When specifying an interface to configure, valid interfaces include physical ports, VLANs, and port channels. The VLAN ID range is 1 to 4094 when the enhanced software image (EI) is installed and 1 to 1005 when the standard software image (SI) is installed. The port-channel range is 1 to 6.

Figure 3 shows Rapid PVST+ commands configured on S1.

In Figure 4, the `show spanning-tree vlan 10` command shows the spanning tree configuration for VLAN 10 on switch S1. Notice that the BID priority is set to 4,096. In the output, the statement "Spanning tree enabled protocol rstp" indicates that S1 is running Rapid PVST+. Because S1 is the root bridge for VLAN 10, all of its interfaces are designated ports.

In Figure 5, the `show running-config` command is used to verify the Rapid PVST+ configuration on S1.

Note   Generally, it is unnecessary to configure the point-to-point *link-type* parameter for Rapid PVST+, because it is unusual to have a shared *link-type*. In most cases, the only difference between configuring PVST+ and Rapid PVST+ is the `spanning-tree mode rapid-pvst` command.

Refer to **Packet Tracer Activity** for this chapter

2.3.2.2   Packet Tracer - Configuring Rapid PVST+

Background/Scenario

In this activity, you will configure VLANs and trunks, and examine and configure the Spanning Tree primary and secondary root bridges. You will also optimize it by using rapid PVST+, PortFast, and BPDU guard.

Refer to **Lab Activity** for this chapter

2.3.2.3   Lab - Configuring Rapid PVST+, PortFast and BPDU Guard

In this lab, you will complete the following objectives:

■ Part 1: Build the Network and Configure Basic Device Settings

■ Part 2: Configure VLANs, Native VLAN, and Trunks

■ Part 3: Configure the Root Bridge and Examine PVST+ Convergence

■ Part 4: Configure Rapid PVST+, PortFast, BPDU Guard, and Examine Convergence

Refer to
Online Course
for Illustration

2.3.3   STP Configuration Issues

2.3.3.1   Analyzing the STP Topology

To analyze the STP topology, follow these steps:

Step 1.   Discover the Layer 2 topology. Use network documentation if it exists or use the `show cdp neighbors` command to discover the Layer 2 topology.

Step 2.   After discovering the Layer 2 topology, use STP knowledge to determine the expected Layer 2 path. It is necessary to know which switch is the root bridge.

Step 3.   Use the `show spanning-tree vlan` command to determine which switch is the root bridge.

Step 4.   Use the `show spanning-tree vlan` command on all switches to find out which ports are in blocking or forwarding state and confirm your expected Layer 2 path.

Refer to
Online Course
for Illustration

2.3.3.2   Expected Topology versus Actual Topology

In many networks, the optimal STP topology is determined as part of the network design and then implemented through manipulation of STP priority and cost values. Situations may occur where STP was not considered in the network design and implementation, or where it was considered or implemented before the network underwent significant growth and change. In such situations, it is important to know how to analyze the actual STP topology in the operational network.

A big part of troubleshooting consists of comparing the actual state of the network against the expected state of the network and spotting the differences to gather clues about the troubleshooting problem. A network professional should be able to examine the switches and determine the actual topology, and be able to understand what the underling spanning tree topology should be.

Refer to
Online Course
for Illustration

2.3.3.3   Overview of Spanning Tree Status

Using the `show spanning-tree` command without specifying any additional options provides a quick overview of the status of STP for all VLANs that are defined on a switch. If interested only in a particular VLAN, limit the scope of this command by specifying that VLAN as an option.

Use the `show spanning-tree vlan` vlan_id command to get STP information for a particular VLAN. Use this command to get information about the role and status of each port on the switch. The example output on switch S1 shows all three ports in the forwarding (FWD) state and the role of the three ports as either designated ports or root ports. Any ports being blocked display the output status as "BLK".

The output also gives information about the BID of the local switch and the root ID, which is the BID of the root bridge.

Refer to
Online Course
for Illustration

2.3.3.4   Spanning Tree Failure Consequences

With many protocols, a malfunction means that you lose the functionality which the protocol was providing. For example, if OSPF malfunctions on a router, connectivity to networks that are reachable via that router might be lost. This would generally not affect the rest of the OSPF network. If connectivity to the router is still available, it is possible to troubleshoot to diagnose and fix the problem.

With STP, there are two types of failure. The first is similar to the OSPF problem; STP might erroneously block ports that should have gone into the forwarding state. Connectivity might be lost for traffic that would normally pass through this switch, but the rest of the network remains unaffected. The second type of failure is much more disruptive, as shown in Figure 1. It happens when STP erroneously moves one or more ports into the forwarding state.

Remember that an Ethernet frame header does not include a TTL field, which means that any frame that enters a bridging loop continues to be forwarded by the switches indefinitely. The only exceptions are frames that have their destination address recorded in the MAC address table of the switches. These frames are simply forwarded to the port that is associated with the MAC address and do not enter a loop. However, any frame that is flooded by a switch enters the loop (Figure 2). This may include broadcasts, multicasts, and unicasts with a globally unknown destination MAC address.

What are the consequences and corresponding symptoms of STP failure (Figure 3)?

The load on all links in the switched LAN quickly starts increasing as more and more frames enter the loop. This problem is not limited to the links that form the loop, but also affects any other links in the switched domain because the frames are flooded on all links. When the spanning tree failure is limited to a single VLAN only links in that VLAN are affected. Switches and trunks that do not carry that VLAN operate normally.

If the spanning tree failure has created a bridging loop, traffic increases exponentially. The switches will then flood the broadcasts out multiple ports. This creates copies of the frames every time the switches forward them.

When control plane traffic starts entering the loop (for example, OSPF Hellos or EIGRP Hellos), the devices that are running these protocols quickly start getting overloaded. Their CPUs approach 100 percent utilization while they are trying to process an ever-increasing load of control plane traffic. In many cases, the earliest indication of this broadcast storm in progress is that routers or Layer 3 switches are reporting control plane failures and that they are running at a high CPU load.

The switches experience frequent MAC address table changes. If a loop exists, a switch may see a frame with a certain source MAC address coming in on one port and then see the another frame with the same source MAC address coming in on a different port a fraction of a second later. This will cause the switch to update the MAC address table twice for the same MAC address.

Due to the combination of very high load on all links and the switch CPUs running at maximum load, these devices typically become unreachable. This makes it very difficult to diagnose the problem while it is happening.

Refer to
Online Course
for Illustration

2.3.3.5   Repairing a Spanning Tree Problem

One way to correct spanning tree failure is to manually remove redundant links in the switched network, either physically or through configuration, until all loops are eliminated from the topology. When the loops are broken, the traffic and CPU loads should quickly drop to normal levels, and connectivity to devices should be restored.

Although this intervention restores connectivity to the network, it is not the end of the troubleshooting process. All redundancy from the switched network has been removed, and now the redundant links must be restored.

If the underlying cause of the spanning tree failure has not been fixed, chances are that restoring the redundant links will trigger a new broadcast storm. Before restoring the redundant links, determine and correct the cause of the spanning tree failure. Carefully monitor the network to ensure that the problem is fixed.

Refer to
Interactive Graphic
in online course.

2.3.3.6   Activity - Troubleshoot STP Configuration Issues

Refer to
Online Course
for Illustration

2.4   First Hop Redundancy Protocols

2.4.1   Concept of First Hop Redundancy Protocols

2.4.1.1   Default Gateway Limitations

Spanning tree protocols enable physical redundancy in a switched network. However, a host at the access layer of a hierarchical network also benefits from alternate default gateways. If a router or router interface (that serves as a default gateway) fails, the hosts configured with that default gateway are isolated from outside networks. A mechanism is needed to provide alternate default gateways in switched networks where two or more routers are connected to the same VLANs.

Note   For the purposes of the discussion on router redundancy, there is no functional difference between a multilayer switch and a router at the distribution layer. In practice, it is common for a multilayer switch to act as the default gateway for each VLAN in a switched network. This discussion focuses on the functionality of *routing*, regardless of the physical device used.

In a switched network, each client receives only one default gateway. There is no way to configure a secondary gateway, even if a second path exists to carry packets off the local segment.

In the figure, R1 is responsible for routing packets from PC1. If R1 becomes unavailable, the routing protocols can dynamically converge. R2 now routes packets from outside networks that would have gone through R1. However, traffic from the inside network associated with R1, including traffic from workstations, servers, and printers configured with R1 as their default gateway, are still sent to R1 and dropped.

End devices are typically configured with a single IP address for a default gateway. This address does not change when the network topology changes. If that default gateway IP address cannot be reached, the local device is unable to send packets off the local network segment, effectively disconnecting it from the rest of the network. Even if a redundant router exists that could serve as a default gateway for that segment, there is no dynamic method by which these devices can determine the address of a new default gateway.

Refer to
Online Course
for Illustration

2.4.1.2   Router Redundancy

One way prevent a single point of failure at the default gateway, is to implement a virtual router. To implement this type of router redundancy, multiple routers are configured to work together to present the illusion of a single router to the hosts on the LAN, as shown in the figure. By sharing an IP address and a MAC address, two or more routers can act as a single virtual router.

The IP address of the virtual router is configured as the default gateway for the workstations on a specific IP segment. When frames are sent from host devices to the default gateway, the hosts use ARP to resolve the MAC address that is associated with the IP address of the default gateway. The ARP resolution returns the MAC address of the virtual router. Frames that are sent to the MAC address of the virtual router can then be physically processed by the currently active router within the virtual router group. A protocol is used to identify two or more routers as the devices that are responsible for processing frames that are sent to the MAC or IP address of a single virtual router. Host devices send traffic to the address of the virtual router. The physical router that forwards this traffic is transparent to the host devices.

A redundancy protocol provides the mechanism for determining which router should take the active role in forwarding traffic. It also determines when the forwarding role must be taken over by a standby router. The transition from one forwarding router to another is transparent to the end devices.

The ability of a network to dynamically recover from the failure of a device acting as a default gateway is known as first-hop redundancy.

Refer to
Online Course
for Illustration

2.4.1.3   Steps for Router Failover

When the active router fails, the redundancy protocol transitions the standby router to the new active router role. These are the steps that take place when the active router fails:

1. The standby router stops seeing Hello messages from the forwarding router.

2. The standby router assumes the role of the forwarding router.

3. Because the new forwarding router assumes both the IP and MAC addresses of the virtual router, the host devices see no disruption in service.

Refer to
Interactive Graphic
in online course.

2.4.1.4   Activity - Identify FHRP Terminology

Refer to
Online Course
for Illustration

2.4.2   Varieties of First Hop Redundancy Protocols

2.4.2.1   First Hop Redundancy Protocols

The following list defines the options available for First Hop Redundancy Protocols (FHRPs), as shown in the figure.

- **Hot Standby Router Protocol (HSRP)**- A Cisco-proprietary FHRP designed to allow for transparent failover of a first-hop IPv4 device. HSRP provides high network availability by providing first-hop routing redundancy for IPv4 hosts on networks configured with an IPv4 default gateway address. HSRP is used in a group of routers for selecting an active device and a standby device. In a group of device interfaces, the active device is the device that is used for routing packets; the standby device is the device that takes over when the active device fails, or when pre-set conditions are met. The function of the HSRP standby router is to monitor the operational status of the HSRP group and to quickly assume packet-forwarding responsibility if the active router fails.

- **HSRP for IPv6**- Cisco-proprietary FHRP providing the same functionality of HSRP, but in an IPv6 environment. An HSRP IPv6 group has a virtual MAC address derived from the HSRP group number and a virtual IPv6 link-local address derived from the HSRP virtual MAC address. Periodic router advertisements (RAs) are sent for the HSRP virtual IPv6 link-local address when the HSRP group is active. When the group becomes inactive these RAs stop after a final RA is sent.

- **Virtual Router Redundancy Protocol version 2 (VRRPv2)**- A non-proprietary election protocol that dynamically assigns responsibility for one or more virtual routers to the VRRP routers on an IPv4 LAN. This allows several routers on a multiaccess link to use the same virtual IPv4 address. A VRRP router is configured to run the VRRP protocol in conjunction with one or more other routers attached to a LAN. In a VRRP configuration, one router is elected as the virtual router master, with the other routers acting as backups, in case the virtual router master fails.

- **VRRPv3**- Provides the capability to support IPv4 and IPv6 addresses. VRRPv3 works in multi-vendor environments and is more scalable than VRRPv2.

- **Gateway Load Balancing Protocol (GLBP)**- Cisco-proprietary FHRP that protects data traffic from a failed router or circuit, like HSRP and VRRP, while also allowing load balancing (also called load sharing) between a group of redundant routers.

- **GLBP for IPv6**- Cisco-proprietary FHRP providing the same functionality of GLBP, but in an IPv6 environment. GLBP for IPv6 provides automatic router backup for IPv6 hosts configured with a single default gateway on a LAN. Multiple first-hop routers on the LAN combine to offer a single virtual first-hop IPv6 router while sharing the IPv6 packet forwarding load.

- **ICMP Router Discovery Protocol (IRDP)**- Specified in RFC 1256, is a legacy FHRP solution. IRDP allows IPv4 hosts to locate routers that provide IPv4 connectivity to other (nonlocal) IP networks.

Refer to
Interactive Graphic
in online course.

2.4.2.2   Activity - Identify the Type of FHRP

Refer to
Online Course
for Illustration

2.4.3   FHRP Verification

2.4.3.1   HSRP Verification

An HSRP active router has the following characteristics:

- Responds to default gateway's ARP requests with the virtual router's MAC.

- Assumes active forwarding of packets for the virtual router.

- Sends Hello messages.

- Knows the virtual router IP address.

An HSRP standby router has the following characteristics:

- Listens for periodic Hello messages.

- Assumes active forwarding of packets if it does not hear from the active router.

Use the **show standby** command to verify the HSRP state. In the figure, the output shows that the router is in the active state.

Refer to
Online Course
for Illustration

2.4.3.2   GLBP Verification

Although HSRP and VRRP provide gateway resiliency, for the standby members of the redundancy group, the upstream bandwidth is not used while the device is in standby mode.

Only the active router in HSRP and VRRP groups forwards traffic for the virtual MAC address. Resources that are associated with the standby router are not fully utilized. You can accomplish some load balancing with these protocols by creating multiple groups and assigning multiple default gateways, but this configuration creates an administrative burden.

GLBP is a Cisco proprietary solution to allow automatic selection and simultaneous use of multiple available gateways in addition to automatic failover between those gateways. Multiple routers share the load of frames that, from a client perspective, are sent to a single default gateway address, as shown in Figure 1.

With GLBP, you can fully utilize resources without the administrative burden of configuring multiple groups and managing multiple default gateway configurations. GLBP has the following characteristics:

- Allows full use of resources on all devices without the administrative burden of creating multiple groups.

- Provides a single virtual IP address and multiple virtual MAC addresses.

- Routes traffic to single gateway distributed across routers.

- Provides automatic rerouting in the event of any failure.

Use the **show glbp** command to verify the GLBP status. Figure 2 shows that GLBP group 1 is in the active state with virtual IP address 192.168.2.100.

Refer to
Online Course
for Illustration

2.4.3.3   Syntax Checker - HSRP and GLBP

Configuration of HSRP and GLBP are beyond the scope of this course. However, familiarity with the commands used to enable HSRP and GLBP aid in understanding the configuration output. For this reason, the syntax checker and subsequent lab are available as optional exercises.

Refer to
Lab Activity
for this chapter

2.4.3.4   Lab - Configuring HSRP and GLBP

In this lab, you will complete the following objectives:

- Part 1: Build the Network and Verify Connectivity

- Part 2: Configure First Hop Redundancy Using HSRP

- Part 3: Configure First Hop Redundancy Using GLBP

Refer to
Online Course
for Illustration

Refer to
Lab Activity
for this chapter

2.5   Summary

2.5.1.1   Class Activity - Documentation Tree

Documentation Tree

The employees in your building are having difficulty accessing a web server on the network. You look for the network documentation that the previous network engineer used before he transitioned to a new job; however, you cannot find any network documentation whatsoever.

Therefore, you decide to create your own network record-keeping system. You decide to start at the access layer of your network hierarchy. This is where redundant switches are located, as well as the company servers, printers, and local hosts.

You create a matrix to record your documentation and include access layer switches on the list. You also decide to document switch names, ports in use, cabling connections, root ports, designated ports, and alternate ports.

Refer to
Online Course
for Illustration

2.5.1.2   Summary

Problems that can result from a redundant Layer 2 network include broadcast storms, MAC database instability, and duplicate unicast frames. STP is a Layer 2 protocol that ensures that there is only one logical path between all destinations on the network by intentionally blocking redundant paths that could cause a loop.

STP sends BPDU frames for communication between switches. One switch is elected as the root bridge for each instance of spanning tree. An administrator can control this election by changing the bridge priority. Root bridges can be configured to enable spanning tree load balancing by VLAN or by a group of VLANs, depending on the spanning tree protocol used. STP then assigns a port role to each participating port using a path cost. The path cost is equal to the sum of all the port costs along the path to the root bridge. A port cost is automatically assigned to each port; however, it can also be manually configured. Paths with the lowest cost become preferred, and all other redundant paths are blocked.

PVST+ is the default configuration of IEEE 802.1D on Cisco switches. It runs one instance of STP for each VLAN. A newer, faster-converging spanning tree protocol, RSTP, can be implemented on Cisco switches on a per-VLAN basis in the form of Rapid PVST+. Multiple Spanning Tree (MST) is the Cisco implementation of Multiple Spanning Tree Protocol (MSTP), where one instance of spanning tree runs for a defined group of VLANs. Features such as PortFast and BPDU guard ensure that hosts in the switched environment are provided immediate access to the network without interfering with spanning tree operation.

First Hop Redundancy Protocols, such as HSRP, VRRP, and GLBP provide alternate default gateways for hosts in the redundant router or multilayer switched environment. Multiple routers share a virtual IP address and MAC address that is used as the default gateway on a client. This ensures that hosts maintain connectivity in the event of the failure of one device serving as a default gateway for a VLAN or set of VLANs. When using HSRP or VRRP, one router is active or forwarding for a particular group while others are in standby mode. GLBP allows the simultaneous use of multiple gateways in addition to providing automatic failover.

Go to the online course to take the quiz and exam.

Chapter 2 Quiz

This quiz is designed to provide an additional opportunity to practice the skills and knowledge presented in the chapter and to prepare for the chapter exam. You will be allowed multiple attempts and the grade does not appear in the gradebook.

Chapter 2 Exam

The chapter exam assesses your knowledge of the chapter content.

Your Chapter Notes

Link Aggregation

3.0   Introduction

3.0.1.1   Introduction

Link aggregation is the ability to create one logical link using multiple physical links between two devices. This allows load sharing among the physical links, rather than having STP block one or more of the links. EtherChannel is a form of link aggregation used in switched networks.

This chapter describes EtherChannel and the methods used to create an EtherChannel. An EtherChannel can be manually configured or can be negotiated by using the Cisco-proprietary protocol Port Aggregation Protocol (PAgP) or the IEEE 802.3ad-defined protocol Link Aggregation Control Protocol (LACP). The configuration, verification, and troubleshooting of EtherChannel are discussed.

Refer to
Lab Activity
for this chapter

3.0.1.2   Class Activity - Imagine This

Imagine This

It is the end of the work day. In your small- to medium-sized business, you are trying to explain to the network engineers about EtherChannel and how it looks when it is physically set up. The network engineers have difficulty envisioning how two switches could possibly be connected via several links that collectively act as one channel or connection. Your company is definitely considering implementing an EtherChannel network.

Therefore, you end the meeting with an assignment for the engineers. To prepare for the next day's meeting, they are to perform some research and bring to the meeting one graphic representation of an EtherChannel network connection. They are tasked with explaining how an EtherChannel network operates to the other engineers.

When researching EtherChannel, a good question to search for is "What does EtherChannel look like?" Prepare a few slides to demonstrate your research that will be presented to the network engineering group. These slides should provide a solid grasp of how EtherChannels are physically created within a network topology. Your goal is to ensure that everyone leaving the next meeting will have a good idea as to why they would consider moving to a network topology using EtherChannel as an option.

Refer to
Interactive Graphic
in online course.

3.1   Link Aggregation Concepts

3.1.1   Link Aggregation

3.1.1.1   Introduction to Link Aggregation

In the figure, traffic coming from several links (usually 100 or 1000 Mb/s) aggregates on the access switch and must be sent to distribution switches. Because of the traffic aggregation, links with higher bandwidth must be available between the access and distribution switches.

It may be possible to use faster links, such as 10 Gb/s, on the aggregated link between the access and distribution layer switches. However, adding faster links is expensive. Additionally, as the speed increases on the access links, even the fastest possible port on the aggregated link is no longer fast enough to aggregate the traffic coming from all access links.

It is also possible to multiply the number of physical links between the switches to increase the overall speed of switch-to-switch communication. However, by default, STP is enabled on switch devices. STP will block redundant links to prevent routing loops.

For these reasons, the best solution is to implement an EtherChannel configuration.

Refer to
Online Course
for Illustration

3.1.1.2   Advantages of EtherChannel

EtherChannel technology was originally developed by Cisco as a LAN switch-to-switch technique of grouping several Fast Ethernet or Gigabit Ethernet ports into one logical channel. When an EtherChannel is configured, the resulting virtual interface is called a port channel. The physical interfaces are bundled together into a port channel interface.

EtherChannel technology has many advantages:

- Most configuration tasks can be done on the EtherChannel interface instead of on each individual port, ensuring configuration consistency throughout the links.

- EtherChannel relies on existing switch ports. There is no need to upgrade the link to a faster and more expensive connection to have more bandwidth.

- Load balancing takes place between links that are part of the same EtherChannel. Depending on the hardware platform, one or more load-balancing methods can be implemented. These methods include source MAC to destination MAC load balancing, or source IP to destination IP load balancing, across the physical links.

- EtherChannel creates an aggregation that is seen as one logical link. When several EtherChannel bundles exist between two switches, STP may block one of the bundles to prevent switching loops. When STP blocks one of the redundant links, it blocks the entire EtherChannel. This blocks all the ports belonging to that EtherChannel link. Where there is only one EtherChannel link, all physical links in the EtherChannel are active because STP sees only one (logical) link.

- EtherChannel provides redundancy because the overall link is seen as one logical connection. Additionally, the loss of one physical link within the channel does not create a change in the topology; therefore a spanning tree recalculation is not required. Assuming at least one physical link is present; the EtherChannel remains functional, even if its overall throughput decreases because of a lost link within the EtherChannel.

Refer to
Online Course
for Illustration

3.1.2 EtherChannel Operation

3.1.2.1 Implementation Restrictions

EtherChannel can be implemented by grouping multiple physical ports into one or more logical EtherChannel links.

Note Interface types cannot be mixed; for example, Fast Ethernet and Gigabit Ethernet cannot be mixed within a single EtherChannel.

The EtherChannel provides full-duplex bandwidth up to 800 Mb/s (Fast EtherChannel) or 8 Gb/s (Gigabit EtherChannel) between one switch and another switch or host. Currently each EtherChannel can consist of up to eight compatibly-configured Ethernet ports. The Cisco IOS switch can currently support six EtherChannels. However, as new IOSs are developed and platforms change, some cards and platforms may support increased numbers of ports within an EtherChannel link, as well as support an increased number of Gigabit EtherChannels. The concept is the same no matter the speeds or number of links that are involved. When configuring EtherChannel on switches, be aware of the hardware platform boundaries and specifications.

The original purpose of EtherChannel is to increase speed capability on aggregated links between switches. However, this concept was extended as EtherChannel technology became more popular, and now many servers also support link aggregation with EtherChannel. EtherChannel creates a one-to-one relationship; that is, one EtherChannel link connects only two devices. An EtherChannel link can be created between two switches or an EtherChannel link can be created between an EtherChannel-enabled server and a switch. However, traffic cannot be sent to two different switches through the same EtherChannel link.

The individual EtherChannel group member port configuration must be consistent on both devices. If the physical ports of one side are configured as trunks, the physical ports of the other side must also be configured as trunks within the same native VLAN. Additionally, all ports in each EtherChannel link must be configured as Layer 2 ports.

Note Layer 3 EtherChannels can be configured on Cisco Catalyst multilayer switches, such as the Catalyst 3560, but these are not explored in this course. A Layer 3 EtherChannel has a single IP address associated with the logical aggregation of switch ports in the EtherChannel.

Each EtherChannel has a logical port channel interface, illustrated in the figure. A configuration applied to the port channel interface affects all physical interfaces that are assigned to that interface.

Refer to
Online Course
for Illustration

3.1.2.2 Port Aggregation Protocol

EtherChannels can be formed through negotiation using one of two protocols, PAgP or LACP. These protocols allow ports with similar characteristics to form a channel through dynamic negotiation with adjoining switches.

Note   It is also possible to configure a static or unconditional EtherChannel without PAgP or LACP.

PAgP

PAgP is a Cisco-proprietary protocol that aids in the automatic creation of EtherChannel links. When an EtherChannel link is configured using PAgP, PAgP packets are sent between EtherChannel-capable ports to negotiate the forming of a channel. When PAgP identifies matched Ethernet links, it groups the links into an EtherChannel. The EtherChannel is then added to the spanning tree as a single port.

When enabled, PAgP also manages the EtherChannel. PAgP packets are sent every 30 seconds. PAgP checks for configuration consistency and manages link additions and failures between two switches. It ensures that when an EtherChannel is created, all ports have the same type of configuration.

Note   In EtherChannel, it is mandatory that all ports have the same speed, duplex setting, and VLAN information. Any port modification after the creation of the channel also changes all other channel ports.

PAgP helps create the EtherChannel link by detecting the configuration of each side and ensuring that links are compatible so that the EtherChannel link can be enabled when needed. The figure shows the modes for PAgP.

- **On**- This mode forces the interface to channel without PAgP. Interfaces configured in the on mode do not exchange PAgP packets.

- **PAgP desirable**- This PAgP mode places an interface in an active negotiating state in which the interface initiates negotiations with other interfaces by sending PAgP packets.

- **PAgP auto**- This PAgP mode places an interface in a passive negotiating state in which the interface responds to the PAgP packets that it receives, but does not initiate PAgP negotiation.

The modes must be compatible on each side. If one side is configure to be in auto mode, it is placed in a passive state, waiting for the other side to initiate the EtherChannel negotiation. If the other side is also set to auto, the negotiation never starts and the EtherChannel does not form. If all modes are disabled by using the **no** command, or if no mode is configured, then the EtherChannel is disabled.

The on mode manually places the interface in an EtherChannel, without any negotiation. It works only if the other side is also set to on. If the other side is set to negotiate parameters through PAgP, no EtherChannel forms, because the side that is set to on mode does not negotiate.

Refer to
Online Course
for Illustration

3.1.2.3   Link Aggregation Control Protocol

LACP

LACP is part of an IEEE specification (802.3ad) that allows several physical ports to be bundled to form a single logical channel. LACP allows a switch to negotiate an automatic bundle by sending LACP packets to the peer. It performs a function similar to PAgP with Cisco EtherChannel. Because LACP is an IEEE standard, it can be used to facilitate EtherChannels in multivendor environments. On Cisco devices, both protocols are supported.

Note   LACP was originally defined as IEEE 802.3ad. However, LACP is now defined in the newer IEEE 802.1AX standard for local and metropolitan area networks.

LACP provides the same negotiation benefits as PAgP. LACP helps create the EtherChannel link by detecting the configuration of each side and making sure that they are compatible so that the EtherChannel link can be enabled when needed. The figure shows the modes for LACP.

- **On**- This mode forces the interface to channel without LACP. Interfaces configured in the on mode do not exchange LACP packets.

- **LACP active**- This LACP mode places a port in an active negotiating state. In this state, the port initiates negotiations with other ports by sending LACP packets.

- **LACP passive**- This LACP mode places a port in a passive negotiating state. In this state, the port responds to the LACP packets that it receives, but does not initiate LACP packet negotiation.

Just as with PAgP, modes must be compatible on both sides for the EtherChannel link to form. The on mode is repeated, because it creates the EtherChannel configuration unconditionally, without PAgP or LACP dynamic negotiation.

Refer to **Interactive Graphic** in online course.

3.1.2.4   Activity - Identify the PAgP and LACP Modes

Refer to **Online Course** for Illustration

3.2   Link Aggregation Configuration

3.2.1   Configuring EtherChannel

3.2.1.1   Configuration Guidelines

The following guidelines and restrictions are useful for configuring EtherChannel:

- **EtherChannel support**- All Ethernet interfaces on all modules must support EtherChannel with no requirement that interfaces be physically contiguous, or on the same module.

- **Speed and duplex**- Configure all interfaces in an EtherChannel to operate at the same speed and in the same duplex mode, as shown in the figure.

- **VLAN match**- All interfaces in the EtherChannel bundle must be assigned to the same VLAN, or be configured as a trunk (also shown in the figure).

- **Range of VLAN**- An EtherChannel supports the same allowed range of VLANs on all the interfaces in a trunking EtherChannel. If the allowed range of VLANs is not the same, the interfaces do not form an EtherChannel, even when set to `auto` or `desirable` mode.

If these settings must be changed, configure them in port channel interface configuration mode. After the port channel interface is configured, any configuration that is applied to the port channel interface also affects individual interfaces. However, configurations that are applied to the individual interfaces do not affect the port channel interface. Therefore, making configuration changes to an interface that is part of an EtherChannel link may cause interface compatibility issues.

Refer to
Online Course
for Illustration

3.2.1.2   Configuring Interfaces

Configuring EtherChannel with LACP is based on two steps:

Step 1.   Specify the interfaces that compose the EtherChannel group using the `interface range` interface global configuration mode command. The `range` keyword allows you to select several interfaces and configure them all together. A good practice is to start by shutting down those interfaces, so that any incomplete configuration does not create activity on the link.

Step 2.   Create the port channel interface with the `channel-group` identifier `mode active` command in interface range configuration mode. The identifier specifies a channel group number. The `mode active` keywords identify this as an LACP EtherChannel configuration.

Note   EtherChannel is disabled by default.

In Figure 1, FastEthernet0/1 and FastEthernet0/2 are bundled into EtherChannel interface port channel 1.

To change Layer 2 settings on the port channel interface, enter port channel interface configuration mode using the interface port-channel command, followed by the interface identifier. In the example, the EtherChannel is configured as a trunk interface with allowed VLANs specified. Also shown in Figure 1, interface port channel 1 is configured as a trunk with allowed VLANs 1, 2, and 20.

Use the Syntax Checker in Figure 2 to configure EtherChannel on switch S1.

Refer to **Packet Tracer Activity** for this chapter

3.2.1.3   Packet Tracer - Configuring EtherChannel

Background/Scenario

Three switches have just been installed. There are redundant uplinks between the switches. Usually, only one of these links could be used; otherwise, a bridging loop might occur. However, using only one link utilizes only half of the available bandwidth. EtherChannel allows up to eight redundant links to be bundled together into one logical link. In this lab, you will configure Port Aggregation Protocol (PAgP), a Cisco EtherChannel protocol, and Link Aggregation Control Protocol (LACP), an IEEE 802.3ad open standard version of EtherChannel.

Refer to
Lab Activity
for this chapter

3.2.1.4   Lab - Configuring EtherChannel

In this lab, you will complete the following objectives:

■ Part 1: Configure Basic Switch Settings

■ Part 2: Configure PAgP

■ Part 3: Configure LACP

Refer to
Online Course
for Illustration

3.2.2   Verifying and Troubleshooting EtherChannel

3.2.2.1   Verifying EtherChannel

There are a number of commands to verify an EtherChannel configuration. First, the `show interface port-channel` command displays the general status of the port channel interface. In Figure 1, the Port Channel 1 interface is up.

When several port channel interfaces are configured on the same device, use the `show etherchannel summary` command to simply display one line of information per port channel. In Figure 2, the switch has one EtherChannel configured; group 1 uses LACP.

The interface bundle consists of the FastEthernet0/1 and FastEthernet0/2 interfaces. The group is a Layer 2 EtherChannel and that it is in use, as indicated by the letters SU next to the port channel number.

Use the `show etherchannel port-channel` command to display information about a specific port channel interface, as shown in Figure 3. In the example, the Port Channel 1 interface consists of two physical interfaces, FastEthernet0/1 and FastEthernet0/2. It uses LACP in active mode. It is properly connected to another switch with a compatible configuration, which is why the port channel is said to be in use.

On any physical interface member of an EtherChannel bundle, the `show interfaces etherchannel` command can provide information about the role of the interface in the EtherChannel, as shown in Figure 4. The interface FastEthernet 0/1 is part of the EtherChannel bundle 1. The protocol for this EtherChannel is LACP.

Use the Syntax Checker in Figure 5 to verify EtherChannel on switch S1.

Refer to
Online Course
for Illustration

3.2.2.2   Troubleshooting EtherChannel

All interfaces within an EtherChannel must have the same configuration of speed and duplex mode, native and allowed VLANs on trunks, and access VLAN on access ports:

■ Assign all ports in the EtherChannel to the same VLAN, or configure them as trunks. Ports with different native VLANs cannot form an EtherChannel.

■ When configuring an EtherChannel from trunk ports, verify that the trunking mode is the same on all the trunks. Inconsistent trunk modes on EtherChannel ports can cause EtherChannel not to function and ports to be shut down (errdisable state).

- An EtherChannel supports the same allowed range of VLANs on all the ports. If the allowed range of VLANs is not the same, the ports do not form an EtherChannel even when PAgP is set to the `auto` or `desirable` mode.

- The dynamic negotiation options for PAgP and LACP must be compatibly configured on both ends of the EtherChannel.

Note   It is easy to confuse PAgP or LACP with DTP, because they both are protocols used to automate behavior on trunk links. PAgP and LACP are used for link aggregation (Ether-Channel). DTP is used for automating the creation of trunk links. When an EtherChannel trunk is configured, typically EtherChannel (PAgP or LACP) is configured first and then DTP.

In Figure 1, interfaces F0/1 and F0/2 on switches S1 and S2 are connected with an EtherChannel. The output indicates that the EtherChannel is down.

In Figure 2, more detailed output indicates that there are incompatible PAgP modes configured on S1 and S2.

In Figure 3, the PAgP mode on the EtherChannel is changed to desirable and the EtherChannel becomes active.

Note   EtherChannel and spanning tree must interoperate. For this reason, the order in which EtherChannel-related commands are entered is important, which is why (in Figure 3) you see interface Port-Channel 1 removed and then re-added with the `channel-group` command, as opposed to directly changed. If one tries to change the configuration directly, spanning tree errors cause the associated ports to go into blocking or errdisabled state.

Refer to **Packet Tracer Activity** for this chapter

3.2.2.3   Packet Tracer - Troubleshooting EtherChannel

Background/Scenario

Four switches were recently configured by a junior technician. Users are complaining that the network is running slow and would like you to investigate.

Refer to **Lab Activity** for this chapter

3.2.2.4   Lab - Troubleshooting EtherChannel

In this lab, you will complete the following objectives:

- Part 1: Build the Network and Load Device Configurations

- Part 2: Troubleshoot EtherChannel

Refer to
Online Course
for Illustration

Refer to
Lab Activity
for this chapter

3.3   Summary

3.3.1.1   Class Activity - Linking Up

Linking Up

Many bottlenecks occur on your small- to medium-sized business network, even though you have configured VLANs, STP, and other network traffic options on the company's switches.

Instead of keeping the switches as they are currently configured, you would like to try EtherChannel as an option for, at least, part of the network to see if it will decrease traffic congestion between your access and distribution layer switches.

Your company uses Catalyst 3560 switches at the distribution layer and Catalyst 2960 and 2950 switches at the access layer of the network. To verify if these switches can perform EtherChannel, you visit the System Requirements to Implement EtherChannel on Catalyst Switches. This site allows you to gather more information to determine if EtherChannel is a good option for the equipment and network currently in place.

After researching the models, you decide to use a simulation software program to practice configuring EtherChannel before implementing it live on your network. As a part of this procedure, you ensure that the equipment simulated in Packet Tracer will support these practice configurations.

Refer to **Packet
Tracer Activity**
for this chapter

3.3.1.2   Packet Tracer - Skills Integration Challenge

Background/Scenario

In this activity, two routers are configured to communicate with each other. You are responsible for configuring subinterfaces to communicate with the switches. You will configure VLANs, trunking, and EtherChannel with PVST. The Internet devices are all preconfigured.

Refer to
Online Course
for Illustration

3.3.1.3   Summary

EtherChannel aggregates multiple switched links together to load balance over redundant paths between two devices. All ports in one EtherChannel must have the same speed, duplex setting, and VLAN information on all interfaces on the devices at both ends. Settings configured in the port channel interface configuration mode will also be applied to the individual interfaces in that EtherChannel. Settings configured on individual interfaces will not be applied to the EtherChannel or to the other interfaces in the EtherChannel.

PAgP is a Cisco-proprietary protocol that aids in the automatic creation of EtherChannel links. PAgP modes are on, PAgP desirable, and PAgP auto. LACP is part of an IEEE specification that also allows multiple physical ports to be bundled into one logical channel. The LACP modes are on, LACP active and LACP passive. PAgP and LACP do not interoperate. The on mode is repeated in both PAgP and LACP because it creates an EtherChannel unconditionally, without the use of PAgP or LACP. The default for EtherChannel is that no mode is configured.

Go to the online course to take the quiz and exam.

Chapter 3 Quiz

This quiz is designed to provide an additional opportunity to practice the skills and knowledge presented in the chapter and to prepare for the chapter exam. You will be allowed multiple attempts and the grade does not appear in the gradebook.

Chapter 3 Exam

The chapter exam assesses your knowledge of the chapter content.

Your Chapter Notes

Wireless LANs

4.0 Introduction

4.0.1.1 Introduction

Wireless networks can provide client mobility, the ability to connect from any location and at any time, and the ability to roam while staying connected. A Wireless LAN (WLAN) is a classification of wireless network that is commonly used in homes, offices, and campus environments. Although it uses radio frequencies instead of cables, it is commonly implemented in a switched network environment and its frame format is similar to Ethernet.

This chapter covers WLAN technology, components, security, planning, implementation, and troubleshooting. The types of network attacks to which wireless networks are particularly susceptible are discussed.

Refer to **Lab Activity** for this chapter

4.0.1.2 Class Activity - Make Mine Wireless

Make Mine Wireless

As the network administrator for your small- to medium-sized business, you realize that your wireless network needs updating, both inside and outside of your building. Therefore, you decide to research how other businesses and educational and community groups set up their WLANs for better access to their employees and clients.

To research this topic, you visit the "Customer Case Studies and Research" website to see how other businesses use wireless technology. After viewing a few of the videos, or reading some of the case study PDFs, you decide to select two to show to your CEO to support upgrading to a more robust wireless solution for your company.

To complete this class modeling activity, open the accompanying PDF for further instructions on how to proceed.

Refer to **Interactive Graphic** in online course.

4.1 Wireless Concepts

4.1.1 Introduction to Wireless

4.1.1.1 Supporting Mobility

Business networks today are evolving to support people who are on the move. People are connected using multiple devices, including computers, laptops, tablets, and smart phones. This is the vision of mobility where people can take their connection to the network along with them on the road.

There are many different infrastructures (wired LAN, service provider networks) that make this type of mobility possible, but in a business environment, the most important is the wireless LAN (WLAN).

Productivity is no longer restricted to a fixed work location or a defined time period. People now expect to be connected at any time and place, from the office to the airport or the home. Traveling employees used to be restricted to pay phones for checking messages and returning a few phone calls between flights. Now employees can check email, voice mail, and the status of projects on smart phones.

Users now expect to be able to roam wirelessly. Roaming enables a wireless device to maintain Internet access without losing connection.

Play the video in the figure for an example of how wireless networks enable mobility.

Refer to
Online Course
for Illustration

4.1.1.2   Benefits of Wireless

There are many benefits to supporting wireless networking, both in the business environment and at home. Some of the benefits include increased flexibility, increased productivity, reduced costs, and the ability to grow and adapt to changing requirements.

Figure 1 provides examples of wireless flexibility for the mobile employee.

Most businesses rely on switch-based LANs for day-to-day operation within the office. However, employees are becoming more mobile and want to maintain access to their business LAN resources from locations other than their desks. Workers want to take their wireless devices to meetings, co-worker's offices, conference rooms, and even customer sites, all while maintaining access to office resources. Wireless networking provides this type of flexibility. Instead of spending a significant amount of time transporting necessary company material or locating wired connections to access network resources, using the wireless network, LAN resources can be easily made available to a varieties of wireless devices.

Although hard to measure, wireless access can result in increased productivity and more relaxed employees. With wireless networking, employees have the flexibility to work when they want, where they want. They can respond to customer inquiries whether at the office, or out to dinner. They can access email and other work-related resources quickly and easily, providing better management, better and faster results for customers, and increased profits.

Wireless networking can also reduce costs. In businesses with a wireless infrastructure already in place, savings are realized any time equipment changes or moves are required, such as when relocating an employee within a building, or reorganizing equipment or a lab, or moving to temporary locations or project sites.

Another important benefit of wireless networking is the ability to adapt to changing needs and technologies. Adding new equipment to the network is fairly seamless with wireless networking. Consider the wireless connectivity of the home. Users can surf the web from their kitchen table, living rooms, or even outdoors. Home users connect new devices, such as smart phones and smart pads, laptops, and smart televisions.

As shown in Figure 2, a wireless home router allows the user to connect to these devices without the additional cost or inconveniences of running cables to different locations in the home.

Refer to
Online Course
for Illustration

4.1.1.3   Wireless Technologies

Wireless communications are used in a variety of professions.

Although the mix of wireless technologies is continually expanding, the focus of this discussion is on wireless networks that allow users to be mobile. Wireless networks can be classified broadly as:

■ **Wireless Personal-Area Networks (WPAN)**- Operates in the range of a few feet. Bluetooth or Wi-Fi Direct-enabled devices are used in WPANs.

■ **Wireless LANs (WLANs)**- Operates in the range of a few hundred feet such as in a room, home, office, and even campus environment.

■ **Wireless Wide-Area Networks (WWANs)**- Operates in the range of miles such as a metropolitan area, cellular hierarchy, or even on intercity links through microwave relays.

Click each component in the figure to display more information about the various wireless technologies available to connect devices to these wireless networks:

■ **Bluetooth**- Originally an IEEE 802.15 WPAN standard that uses a device-pairing process to communicate over distances up to .05 mile (100m). Newer Bluetooth versions are standardized by the Bluetooth Special Interest Group (https://www.bluetooth. org/).

■ **Wi-Fi (wireless fidelity)**- An IEEE 802.11 WLAN standard commonly deployed to provide network access to home and corporate users, to include data, voice and video traffic, to distances up to 300m (0.18 mile).

■ **WiMAX (Worldwide Interoperability for Microwave Access)**- An IEEE 802.16 WWAN standard that provides wireless broadband access of up to 30 miles (50 km). WiMAX is an alternative to cable and DSL broadband connections. Mobility was added to WiMAX in 2005 and can now be used by service providers to provide cellular broadband.

■ **Cellular broadband**- Consists of various corporate, national, and international organizations using service provider cellular access to provide mobile broadband network connectivity. First available with 2nd generation cell phones in 1991 (2G) with higher speeds becoming available in 2001 and 2006 as part of the third (3G) and fourth (4G) generations of mobile communication technology.

■ **Satellite broadband**- Provides network access to remote sites through the use of a directional satellite dish that is aligned with a specific geostationary Earth orbit (GEO) satellite. It is usually more expensive and requires a clear line of sight.

There are many types of wireless technologies available. However, the focus of this chapter is on 802.11 WLANs.

Refer to
Online Course
for Illustration

4.1.1.4   Radio Frequencies

All wireless devices operate in the radio waves range of the electromagnetic spectrum. It is the responsibility of the International Telecommunication Union - Radiocommunication Sector (ITU-R) to regulate the allocation of the radio frequency (RF) spectrum. Ranges of frequencies, called bands, are allocated for various purposes. Some bands in the electro-magnetic spectrum are heavily regulated and are used for applications, such as air traffic control and emergency responder communications networks. Other bands are license free, such as the Industrial, Scientific, and Medical (ISM) and the national information infra-structure (UNII) frequency bands.

Note   WLAN networks operate in the ISM 2.4 GHz frequency band and the UNII 5 GHz band.

Wireless communication occurs in the radio waves range (i.e., 3 Hz to 300 GHz) of the electromagnetic spectrum, as shown in the figure. The radio waves range is subdivided into a radio frequencies section and a microwave frequencies section. Notice that WLANs, Bluetooth, cellular, and satellite communication all operate in the microwave UHF, SHF, and EHF ranges.

Wireless LAN devices have transmitters and receivers tuned to specific frequencies of the radio waves range. Specifically, the following frequency bands are allocated to 802.11 wire-less LANs:

- **2.4 GHz (UHF)** - 802.11b/g/n/ad

- **5 GHz (SHF)** - 802.11a/n/ac/ad

- **60 GHz (EHF)** - 802.11ad

4.1.1.5   802.11 Standards

Refer to
Online Course
for Illustration

The IEEE 802.11 WLAN standard defines how RF in the unlicensed ISM frequency bands is used for the physical layer and the MAC sublayer of wireless links.

Various implementation of the IEEE 802.11 standard have been developed over the years. The following highlights these standards:

- **802.11**- Released in 1997 and now obsolete, this is the original WLAN specifica-tion that operated in the 2.4 GHz band and offered speeds of up to 2 Mb/s. When it was released, wired LANs were operating at 10 Mb/s so the new wireless technology was not enthusiastically adopted. Wireless devices have one antenna to transmit and receive wireless signals.

- **IEEE 802.11a**- Released in 1999, it operates in the less crowded 5 GHz frequency band and offers speeds of up to 54 Mb/s. Because this standard operates at higher frequencies, it has a smaller coverage area and is less effective at penetrating building structures. Wireless devices have one antenna to transmit and receive wireless signals. Devices operating under this standard are not interoperable with the 802.11b and 802.11g standards.

- **IEEE 802.11b**- Released in 1999, it operates in the 2.4 GHz frequency band and offers speeds of up to 11 Mb/s. Devices implementing this standard have a longer range and are better able to penetrate building structures than devices based on 802.11a. Wireless devices have one antenna to transmit and receive wireless signals.

- **IEEE 802.11g**- Released in 2003, it operates in the 2.4 GHz frequency band and offers speeds of up to 54 Mb/s. Devices implementing this standard; therefore, operate at the same radio frequency and range as 802.11b, but with the bandwidth of 802.11a.

Wireless devices have one antenna to transmit and receive wireless signals. It is backward compatible with 802.11b. However, when supporting an 802.11b client, the overall bandwidth is reduced.

- **IEEE 802.11n**- Released in 2009, it operates in the 2.4 GHz and 5 GHz frequency bands and is referred to as a dual-band device. Typical data rates range from 150 Mb/s to 600 Mb/s with a distance range of up to 70 m (.5 mile). However, to achieve the higher speeds, APs and wireless clients require multiple antennas using the multiple-input and multiple-output (MIMO) technology. MIMO use multiple antennas as both the transmitter and receiver to improve communication performance. Up to four antennas can be supported. The 802.11n standard is backward compatible with 802.11a/b/g devices. However supporting a mixed environment limits the expected data rates.

- **IEEE 802.11ac**- Released in 2013, operates in the 5 GHz frequency band and provides data rates ranging from 450 Mb/s to 1.3 Gb/s (1300 Mb/s). It uses MIMO technology to improve communication performance. Up to eight antennas can be supported. The 802.11ac standard is backward compatible with 802.11a/n devices; however, supporting a mixed environment limits the expected data rates.

- **IEEE 802.11ad**- Scheduled for release in 2014 and also known as "WiGig", it uses a tri-band Wi-Fi solution using 2.4 GHz, 5 GHz, and 60 GHz, and offers theoretical speeds of up to 7 Gb/s. However, the 60 GHz band is a line-of-site technology and; therefore, cannot penetrate through walls. When a user is roaming, the device switches to the lower 2.4 GHz and 5 GHz bands. It is backward compatible with existing Wi-Fi devices. However supporting a mixed environment limits the expected data rates.

The figure summarizes each 802.11 standard.

4.1.1.6   Wi-Fi Certification

Refer to **Online Course** for Illustration

Standards ensure interoperability between devices made by different manufacturers. Internationally, the three organizations influencing WLAN standards are:

- **ITU-R**- Regulates the allocation of the RF spectrum and satellite orbits.

- **IEEE**- Specifies how RF is modulated to carry information. It maintains the standards for local and metropolitan area networks (MAN) with the IEEE 802 LAN/MAN family of standards. The dominant standards in the IEEE 802 family are 802.3 Ethernet and 802.11 WLAN. Although the IEEE has specified standards for RF modulation devices, it has not specified manufacturing standards; therefore, interpretations of the 802.11 standards by different vendors can cause interoperability problems between their devices.

- **Wi-Fi Alliance**- The Wi-Fi Alliance® (http://www.wi-fi.org) is a global, non-profit, industry trade association devoted to promoting the growth and acceptance of WLANs. It is an association of vendors whose objective is to improve the interoperability of products that are based on the 802.11 standard by certifying vendors for conformance to industry norms and adherence to standards.

The Wi-Fi Alliance certifies Wi-Fi and the following product compatibility:

- IEEE 802.11a/b/g/n/ac/ad compatible

- IEEE 802.11i secure using WPA2™ and Extensible Authentication Protocol (EAP)

- Wi-Fi Protected Setup (WPS) to simplify device connections

- Wi-Fi Direct to share media between devices

- Wi-Fi Passpoint to simplify securely connecting to Wi-Fi hotspot networks

- Wi-Fi Miracast to seamlessly display video between devices

Note   Other Wi-Fi certifications products are available such as WMM® (Wi-Fi Multimedia™), Tunneled Direct Link Setup (TDLS), and WMM-Power Save.

Figure 1 displays the Wi-Fi Alliance logos identifying specific feature compatibility. Devices displaying specific logos support the identified feature. A device may display a combination of these logos.

Click the Play button in Figures 2 to 4 to view playful videos of the Wi-Fi Direct, Wi-Fi Passpoint, and Wi-Fi Miracast features.

Refer to
Online Course
for Illustration

4.1.1.7   Comparing WLANs to a LAN

WLANs share a similar origin with Ethernet LANs. The IEEE has adopted the 802 LAN/MAN portfolio of computer network architecture standards. The two dominant 802 working groups are 802.3 Ethernet and 802.11 WLAN. However, there are important differences between the two.

WLANs use RF instead of cables at the physical layer and MAC sublayer of the data link layer. In comparison to cable, RF has the following characteristics:

- RF does not have boundaries, such as the limits of a wire in a sheath. This allows data frames traveling over the RF media to be available to anyone who can receive the RF signal.

- RF is unprotected from outside signals, whereas cable is in an insulating sheath. Radios operating independently in the same geographic area, but using the same or a similar RF can interfere with each other.

- RF transmission is subject to the same challenges inherent in any wave-based technology, such as consumer radio. For example, as the radio travels further away from the source, radio stations may start playing over each other and static noise increases. Eventually the signal is completely lost. Wired LANs have cables that are of an appropriate length to maintain signal strength.

- RF bands are regulated differently in various countries. The use of WLANs is subject to additional regulations and sets of standards that are not applied to wired LANs.

WLANs also differ from wired LANs as follows:

- WLANs connect clients to the network through a wireless access point (AP) or wireless router, instead of an Ethernet switch.

- WLANs connect mobile devices that are often battery powered, as opposed to plugged-in LAN devices. Wireless NICs tend to reduce the battery life of a mobile device.

- WLANs support hosts that contend for access on the RF media (frequency bands). 802.11 prescribes collision-avoidance (CSMA/CA) instead of collision-detection (CSMA/CD) for media access to proactively avoid collisions within the media.

- WLANs use a different frame format than wired Ethernet LANs. WLANs require additional information in the Layer 2 header of the frame.

- WLANs raise more privacy issues because radio frequencies can reach outside the facility.

Refer to
Interactive Graphic
in online course.

4.1.1.8 Activity - Identify the Wireless Technology

Refer to
Interactive Graphic
in online course.

4.1.1.9 Activity - Compare Wireless Standards

Refer to
Interactive Graphic
in online course.

4.1.1.10 Activity - Compare WLANs and LANs

Refer to
Online Course
for Illustration

4.1.2 Components of WLANs

4.1.2.1 Wireless NICs

The simplest wireless network requires a minimum of two devices. Each device must have a radio transmitter and a radio receiver tuned to the same frequencies.

However most wireless deployments require:

- End devices with wireless NICs

- Infrastructure device, such as a wireless router or wireless AP

To communicate wirelessly, end devices require a wireless NIC that incorporates a radio transmitter/receiver and the required software driver to make it operational. Laptops, tablets, smart phones now all include integrated wireless NICs. However, if a device does not have an integrated wireless NIC, then a USB wireless adapter can be used.

The figure displays two USB wireless adapters.

Refer to
Online Course
for Illustration

4.1.2.2 Wireless Home Router

The type of infrastructure device that an end device associates and authenticates with varies on the size and requirement of the WLAN.

For instance, a home user typically interconnects wireless devices using a small, integrated wireless router. These smaller, integrated routers serve as:

- **Access point**- Provides 802.11a/b/g/n/ac wireless access

- **Switch**- Provides a four-port, full-duplex, 10/100/1000 Ethernet switch to connect wired devices

- **Router**- Provides a default gateway for connecting to other network infrastructures

For example, the Cisco Linksys EA6500 router, shown in Figure 1, is commonly implemented as a small business or residential wireless access device. The wireless router connects to the ISP DLS modem and advertises its services by sending beacons containing its shared service set identifier (SSID). Internal devices wirelessly discover the router SSID and attempt to associate and authenticate with it to access the Internet.

The expected load on the Linksys EA6500 router, in this environment, is low enough that it should be able to manage the provision of WLAN, 802.3 Ethernet, and connect to an ISP. It also provides advanced features, such as high-speed access, optimized to support video streaming, IPv6 enabled, provide QoS, easy setup using Wi-Fi WPS, USB ports to connect printers or portable drives.

Additionally, for home users that want to extend their network services, both wireless and wired, wireless Powerline adapters can be implemented. With these devices, a device can connect directly to the network through electrical outlets, which is ideal for HD video streaming and online gaming. They are easy to set up: simply plug into wall outlet or power strip and connect the device with a push of a button.

Click the Play button in Figure 2 to see an overview of the Linksys Powerline adapters.

4.1.2.3 Business Wireless Solutions

Refer to **Online Course** for Illustration

Organizations providing wireless connectivity to their users require a WLAN infrastructure to provide additional connectivity options.

Note IEEE 802.11 refers to a wireless client as a station (STA). In this chapter, the term wireless client is used to describe any wireless capable device.

The small business network shown in Figure 1 is an 802.3 Ethernet LAN. Each client (i.e., PC1 and PC2) connects to a switch using a network cable. The switch is the point where the clients gain access to the network. Notice that the wireless AP also connects to the switch. In this example, either the Cisco WAP4410N AP or the WAP131 AP could be used to provide wireless network connectivity.

Wireless clients use their wireless NIC to discover nearby APs advertising their SSID. Clients then attempt to associate and authenticate with an AP, as shown in Figure 2. After being authenticated, wireless users have access to network resources.

Note Wireless needs of a small organization differ from those of a large organization. Large, wireless deployments require additional wireless hardware to simplify the installation and management of the wireless network.

4.1.2.4 Wireless Access Points

Refer to **Online Course** for Illustration

APs can be categorized as either autonomous APs or controller-based APs.

Autonomous APs

Autonomous APs, sometimes referred to as heavy APs, are standalone devices configured using the Cisco CLI or a GUI. Autonomous APs are useful in situations where only a couple of APs are required in the network. Optionally, multiple APs can be controlled using wireless domain services (WDS) and managed using CiscoWorks Wireless LAN Solution Engine (WLSE).

Note   A home router is an example of an autonomous AP because the entire AP configuration resides on the device.

Figure 1 displays an autonomous AP in a small network. If the wireless demands increase, more APs would be required. Each AP would operate independent of other APs and require manual configuration and management.

Controller-Based APs

Controller-based APs are server-dependent devices that require no initial configuration. Cisco offers two controller-based solutions. Controller-based APs are useful in situations where many APs are required in the network. As more APs are added, each AP is automatically configured and managed by a WLAN controller.

Figure 2 displays a controller-based AP in a small network. Notice how a WLAN controller is now required to manage the APs. The benefit of the controller is that it can be used to manage many APs.

Note   Some AP models can operate in either autonomous mode or in controller-based mode.

Refer to
Online Course
for Illustration

4.1.2.5   Small Wireless Deployment Solutions

For small wireless deployment requirements, Cisco offers the following wireless autonomous AP solutions:

- **Cisco WAP4410N AP**- This AP is ideal for small organization requiring two APs and supporting a small group of users.

- **Cisco WAP121 and WAP321 APs**- These APs are ideal for small organizations that want to simplify their wireless deployment using several APs.

- **Cisco AP541N AP**- This AP is ideal for small- to mid-sized organizations that want robust and an easily manageable cluster of APs.

Note   Most enterprise-level APs support PoE.

Figure 1 displays and summarizes the Cisco small business APs.

Figure 2 displays a sample topology for a small business network using the WAP4410N APs. Each AP is configured and managed individually. This can become a problem when several APs are required.

For this reason, the WAP121, WAP321, and AP541N APs support the clustering of APs without the use of a controller. The cluster provides a single point of administration and enables the administrator to view the deployment of APs as a single wireless network, rather than a series of separate wireless devices. The clustering capability makes it easy to set up, configure, and manage a growing wireless network. Multiple APs can be deployed and push a single configuration to all the devices within the cluster, managing the wireless network as a single system without worrying about interference between APs, and without configuring each AP as a separate device.

Specifically, the WAP121 and WAP321 support Single Point Setup (SPS), which makes AP deployment easier and faster, as shown in Figure 3. SPS helps to enable the wireless LAN to scale up to four WAP121 and up to eight WAP321 devices to provide broader coverage and support additional users as business needs change and grow. The Cisco AP541N AP can cluster up to 10 APs together and can support multiple clusters.

A cluster can be formed between two APs if the following conditions are met:

- Clustering mode is enabled on the APs.

- The APs joining the cluster have the same Cluster Name.

- The APs are connected on the same network segment.

- The APs use the same radio mode (i.e., both radios use 802.11n.).

Access an online AP541N emulator.

Refer to
Online Course
for Illustration

4.1.2.6 Large Wireless Deployment Solutions

Organizations requiring the clustering of multiple APs require a more robust and scalable solution. For larger organizations with many APs, Cisco provides controller-based managed solutions, including the Cisco Meraki Cloud Managed Architecture and the Cisco Unified Wireless Network Architecture.

Note   There are other controller-based solutions, such as the controllers using Flex mode. Visit http://www.cisco.com for more information.

Cisco Meraki Cloud Managed Architecture

The Cisco Meraki cloud architecture is a management solution used to simplify the wireless deployment. Using this architecture, APs are managed centrally from a controller in the cloud, as shown in Figure 1. Cloud networking and management provides centralized management, visibility, and control without the cost and complexity of controller appliances or overlay management software.

This process reduces costs and complexity. The controller pushes management settings, such as firmware updates, security settings, wireless network, and SSIDs settings to the Meraki APs.

Note   Only management data flows through the Meraki cloud infrastructure. No user traffic passes through Meraki's datacenters. Therefore, if the Cisco Meraki cannot access the cloud, the network continues to function normally. This means users can still authenticate, firewall rules remain in place, and traffic flows at full line rate. Only management functions, such as reports and configuration tools are interrupted.

The Cisco Meraki cloud managed architecture requires the following:

- **Cisco MR Cloud Managed Wireless APs**- Various models exist to address a broad range of wireless deployment.

- **Meraki Cloud Controller (MCC)-** The MCC provides centralized management, optimization, and monitoring of a Meraki WLAN system. The MCC is not an appliance that must be purchased and installed to manage wireless APs. Rather, the MCC is a cloud-based service that constantly monitors, optimizes, and reports the behavior of the network.

- **Web-based Dashboard-** Meraki's web-based Dashboard performs configuration and diagnostics remotely.

Click each component in Figure 2 to read more information about the Cisco Meraki architecture.

Refer to
Online Course
for Illustration

4.1.2.7   Large Wireless Deployment Solutions, Cont.

Cisco Unified Wireless Network Architecture

The Cisco Unified wireless network architecture solution, using a split MAC design, controls APs using a WLAN controller (WLC) and can be optionally managed using Cisco Wireless Control Systems (WCS). The lightweight APs communicate with the WLAN controller using the Lightweight Access Control Point Protocol (LWAPP). The controller has all of the intelligence for communication and the AP is a "dumb terminal" that simply processes packets.

The Cisco Unified wireless network architecture requires the following devices:

- **Lightweight APs-** Cisco Aironet 1600, 2600, or 3600 wireless APs models provide robust, dependable wireless network access for hosts.

- **Controllers for small and medium-sized businesses-** Cisco 2500 Series Wireless Controllers, Cisco Virtual Wireless Controller, or the Cisco Wireless Controller Module for Cisco ISR G2 provide small branch or single-site enterprise WLAN deployments with entry-level wireless for data.

Other WLAN controllers of greater capacity are also available. For example, the Cisco 5760 Wireless Controller and the Cisco 8500 Series Controller are designed to cost-effectively manage, secure, and optimize the performance of sizeable wireless networks, such as service provider and large campus deployments.

Figure 1 summarizes the lightweight APs.

Click each component in Figure 2 to display more information about the controllers for small and medium-sized businesses.

Refer to
Online Course
for Illustration

4.1.2.8   Wireless Antennas

Most business class APs require the use of external antennas to make them fully-functioning units. Cisco has developed antennas specifically designed for use with 802.11 APs while accommodating specific deployment conditions, including physical layout, distance, and aesthetics.

Cisco Aironet APs can use:

- **Omnidirectional Wi-Fi Antennas**- Factory Wi-Fi gear often uses basic dipole antennas, also referred to as "rubber duck" design, similar to those used on walkie-talkie radios. Omnidirectional antennas provide 360-degree coverage and are ideal in open office areas, hallways, conference rooms, and outside areas.

- **Directional Wi-Fi Antennas**- Directional antennas focus the radio signal in a given direction. This enhances the signal to and from the AP in the direction the antenna is pointing, providing stronger signal strength in one direction and less signal strength in all other directions.

- **Yagi antennas**- Type of directional radio antenna that can be used for long-distance Wi-Fi networking. These antennas are typically used to extend the range of outdoor hotspots in a specific direction, or to reach an outbuilding.

The figure displays various Cisco indoor and outdoor antennas.

IEEE 802.11n/ac/ad use MIMO technology to increase available bandwidth. Specifically, MIMO uses multiple antennas to exchange more data than it would be possible to do using a single antenna. Up to four antennas can be used to increase throughput.

Note   Not all wireless routers are the same. For instance, entry level 802.11n routers support 150 Mb/s bandwidth using one Wi-Fi radio, and one antenna attached to the unit. To support the higher data rates, an 802.11n router requires more radios and antennas to manage more channels of data in parallel. For example, two radios and two antennas on an 802.11n router support up to 300 Mb/s, while 450 and 600 Mb/s require three and four radios and antennas, respectively.

Refer to **Interactive Graphic** in online course.

4.1.2.9   Activity - Identify WLAN Component Terminology

Refer to **Lab Activity** for this chapter

4.1.2.10   Lab - Investigating Wireless Implementations
In this lab, you will complete the following objectives:

- Part 1: Explore Integrated Wireless Routers

- Part 2: Explore Wireless Access Points

Refer to **Online Course** for Illustration

4.1.3   802.11 WLAN Topologies

4.1.3.1   802.11 Wireless Topology Modes
Wireless LANs can accommodate various network topologies. The 802.11 standard identifies two main wireless topology modes:

- **Ad hoc mode**- When two devices connect wirelessly without the aid of an infrastructure device, such as a wireless router or AP. Examples include Bluetooth and Wi-Fi Direct.

- **Infrastructure mode**- When wireless clients interconnect via a wireless router or AP, such as in WLANs. APs connect to the network infrastructure using the wired distribution system (DS), such as Ethernet.

Figure 1 displays an example of ad hoc mode and Figure 2 displays an example of infrastructure mode.

4.1.3.2   Ad Hoc Mode

Refer to
Online Course
for Illustration

An ad hoc wireless network is when two wireless devices communicate in a peer-to-peer (P2P) manner without using APs or wireless routers. For example, a client workstation with wireless capability can be configured to operate in ad hoc mode enabling another device to connect to it. Bluetooth and Wi-Fi Direct are examples of ad hoc mode.

Note   The IEEE 802.11 standard refers to an ad hoc network as an independent basic service set (IBSS).

The figure displays a summary of ad hoc mode.

A variation of the ad hoc topology is when a smart phone or tablet with cellular data access is enabled to create a personal hotspot. This feature is sometimes referred to as Tethering. A hotspot is usually a temporary quick solution that enables a smart phone to provide the wireless services of a Wi-Fi router. Other devices can associate and authenticate with the smart phone to use the Internet connection. The Apple iPhone refers to this as the Personal Hotspot feature, while Android devices refer to as either Tethering or Portable Hotspot.

4.1.3.3   Infrastructure Mode

Refer to
Online Course
for Illustration

The IEEE 802.11 architecture consists of several components that interact to provide a WLAN that supports clients. It defines two infrastructure mode topology building blocks: a Basic Service Set (BSS) and an Extended Service Set (ESS).

Basic Service Set

A BSS consists of a single AP interconnecting all associated wireless clients. In Figure 1, two BSSs are displayed. The circles depict the coverage area within which the wireless clients of the BSS may remain in communication. This area is called the Basic Service Area (BSA). If a wireless client moves out of its BSA, it can no longer directly communicate with other wireless clients within the BSA. The BSS is the topology building block while the BSA is the actual coverage area (the terms BSA and BSS are often used interchangeably).

The Layer 2 MAC address of the AP is used to uniquely identify each BSS, which is called the Basic Service Set Identifier (BSSID). Therefore, the BSSID is the formal name of the BSS and is always associated with only one AP.

Extended Service Set

When a single BSS provides insufficient RF coverage, two or more BSSs can be joined through a common distribution system (DS) into an ESS. As shown in Figure 2, an ESS is the union of two or more BSSs interconnected by a wired DS. Wireless clients in one BSA can now communicate with wireless clients in another BSA within the same ESS. Roaming mobile wireless clients may move from one BSA to another (within the same ESS) and seamlessly connect.

The rectangular area depicts the coverage area within which members of an ESS may communicate. This area is called the Extended Service Area (ESA). An ESA typically involves several BSSs in overlapping and/or separated configurations.

Each ESS is identified by an SSID and in an ESS each BSS is identified by its BSSID. For security reasons, additional SSIDs can be propagated through the ESS to segregate the level of network access.

Note   The 802.11 standard refers to ad hoc mode as an IBSS.

Refer to
Interactive Graphic
in online course.

4.1.3.4   Activity - Identify WLAN Topology Terminology

Refer to
Online Course
for Illustration

4.2   Wireless LAN Operations

4.2.1   802.11 Frame Structure

4.2.1.1   Wireless 802.11 Frame

All Layer 2 frames consist of a header, payload, and FCS section as shown in Figure 1. The 802.11 frame format is similar to the Ethernet frame format, with the exception that it contains more fields.

As shown in Figure 2, all 802.11 wireless frames contain the following fields:

- **Frame Control**- Identifies the type of wireless frame and contains subfields for protocol version, frame type, address type, power management, and security settings.

- **Duration**- Typically used to indicate the remaining duration needed to receive the next frame transmission.

- **Address1**- Usually contains the MAC address of the receiving wireless device or AP.

- **Address2**- Usually contains the MAC address of the transmitting wireless device or AP.

- **Address3**- Sometimes contains the MAC address of the destination, such as the router interface (default gateway) to which the AP is attached.

- **Sequence Control**- Contains the Sequence Number and the Fragment Number subfields. The Sequence Number indicates the sequence number of each frame. The Fragment Number indicates the number of each frame sent of a fragmented frame.

- **Address4**- Usually missing because it is used only in ad hoc mode.

- **Payload**- Contains the data for transmission.

- **FCS**- Frame Check Sequence; used for Layer 2 error control.

Figure 3 displays a Wireshark capture of a WLAN beacon frame. Notice how the Frame Control field has also been expanded to display its subfields.

Note   The content of the Address fields vary depending on settings in the Frame Control field.

Refer to
Online Course
for Illustration

4.2.1.2   Frame Control Field

The Frame Control field contains multiple subfields as shown in Figure 1.

Specifically, the Frame Control field contains the following subfields:

- **Protocol Version**- Provides the current version of the 802.11 protocol used. Receiving devices use this value to determine if the version of the protocol of the received frame is supported.

- **Frame Type** and **Frame Subtype** - Determines the function of the frame. A wireless frame can either be a control frame, data frame, or a management frame. There are multiple subtype fields for each frame type. Each subtype determines the specific function to perform for its associated frame type.

- **ToDS** and **FromDS** - Indicates whether the frame is going to or exiting from the DS, and is only used in data frames of wireless clients associated with an AP.

- **More Fragments**- Indicates whether more fragments of the frame, either data or management type, are to follow.

- **Retry**- Indicates whether or not the frame, for either data or management frame types, is being retransmitted.

- **Power Management**- Indicates whether the sending device is in active mode or power-save mode.

- **More Data**- Indicates to a device in power-save mode that the AP has more frames to send. It is also used for APs to indicate that additional broadcast/multicast frames are to follow.

- **Security**- Indicates whether encryption and authentication are used in the frame. It can be set for all data frames and management frames, which have the subtype set to authentication.

- **Reserved**- Can indicate that all received data frames must be processed in order.

Figure 2 displays a Wireshark capture of a WLAN beacon frame. Notice that the Frame Type field and the Frame Subtype fields identify if the frame is a management frame, a control frame, or a data frame. In the example, the Frame Type is '0x0' identifying it as a management frame. The subtype value '8' identifies this as a beacon frame. The frame is specifically identified as '0x08'.

Refer to
Online Course
for Illustration

4.2.1.3   Wireless Frame Type

Note   The Frame Type and Frame Subtype fields are used to identify the type of wireless transmission. As shown in the figure, a wireless frame can be one of three frame types:

- **Management Frame**- Used in the maintenance of communication, such as finding, authenticating, and associating with an AP.

- **Control Frame**- Used to facilitate in the exchange of data frames between wireless clients.

- **Data Frame**- Used to carry the payload information such as web pages and files.

Refer to
Online Course
for Illustration

4.2.1.4   Management Frames

Management frames are used exclusively to find, authenticate, and associate with an AP.

Figure 1 displays the field value of common management frames including:

- **Association request frame** - (0x00) Sent from a wireless client, it enables the AP to allocate resources and synchronize. The frame carries information about the wireless connection including supported data rates and SSID of the network to the wireless client that wants to associate. If the request is accepted, the AP reserves memory and establishes an association ID for the device.

- **Association response frame** - (0x01) Sent from an AP to a wireless client containing the acceptance or rejection to an association request. If it is an acceptance, the frame contains information, such as an association ID and supported data rates.

- **Reassociation request frame** - (0x02) A device sends a reassociation request when it drops from range of the currently associated AP and finds another AP with a stronger signal. The new AP coordinates the forwarding of any information that may still be contained in the buffer of the previous AP.

- **Reassociation response frame** - (0x03) Sent from an AP containing the acceptance or rejection to a device reassociation request frame. The frame includes information required for association, such as the association ID and supported data rates.

- **Probe request frame** - (0x04) Sent from a wireless client when it requires information from another wireless client.

- **Probe response frame** - (0x05) Sent from an AP containing capability information, such as the supported data rates, after receiving a probe request frame.

- **Beacon frame** - (0x08) Sent periodically from an AP to announce its presence and provide the SSID and other preconfigured parameters.

- **Disassociation frame** - (0x0A) Sent from a device wanting to terminate a connection. Allows the AP to relinquish memory allocation and remove the device from the association table.

- **Authentication frame** - (0x0B) The sending device sends an authentication frame to the AP containing its identity.

- **Deauthentication frame** - (0x0C) Sent from a wireless client wanting to terminate connection from another wireless client.

Beacons are the only management frame that may regularly be broadcast by an AP. All other probing, authentication, and association frames are used only during the association (or reassociation) process.

Figure 2 displays a sample Wireshark screen capture of a management frame. The field values change to reflect the purpose of the frame.

Note   The example provided was captured using Wireshark. However, Wireshark must be specifically configured to capture WLAN traffic. The ability to capture traffic varies between operating systems and may require a special wireless NIC.

Refer to **Online Course** for Illustration

4.2.1.5 Control Frames

Control frames are used to manage the information exchange between a wireless client and an AP. They help prevent collisions from occurring on the wireless medium.

The figure displays the field value of common control frames including:

- **Request to Send (RTS) frame**- The RTS and CTS frames provide an optional collision reduction scheme for APs with hidden wireless clients. A wireless client sends an RTS frame as the first step in the two-way handshake, which is required before sending data frames.

- **Clear to Send (CTS) frame**- A wireless AP responds to an RTS frame with a CTS frame. It provides clearance for the requesting wireless client to send a data frame. The CTS contributes to collision control management by including a time value. This time delay minimizes the chance that other wireless clients will transmit while the requesting client transmits.

- **Acknowledgment (ACK) frame**- After receiving a data frame, the receiving wireless client sends an ACK frame to the sending client if no errors are found. If the sending client does not receive an ACK frame within a predetermined period of time, the sending client resends the frame.

Control frames are integral to wireless transmission and play a significant role in the media contention method used by wireless, known as Carrier Sense Multiple Access with Collision Avoidance (CSMA/CA).

Refer to **Interactive Graphic** in online course.

4.2.1.6 Activity - Identify the 802.11 Frame Control Fields

Refer to **Online Course** for Illustration

4.2.2 Wireless Operation

4.2.2.1 Carrier Sense Multiple Access with Collision Avoidance

Recall that the media contention method is the method in which devices determine how and when to access the media when traffic must be forwarded across the network. The IEEE 802.11 WLANs use the MAC protocol CSMA/CA. While the name is similar to the Ethernet CSMA/CD, the operating concept is completely different.

Wi-Fi systems are half-duplex, shared media configurations; therefore, wireless clients can transmit and receive on the same radio channel. This creates a problem because a wireless client cannot hear while it is sending; thus, making it impossible to detect a collision. To address this problem, the IEEE developed an additional collision avoidance mechanism called the Distributed Coordination Function (DCF). Using DCF, a wireless client transmits only if the channel is clear. All transmissions are acknowledged; therefore, if a wireless client does not receive an acknowledgment, it assumes a collision occurred and retries after a random waiting interval.

Wireless clients and APs use the RTS and CTS control frames to facilitate the actual data transfer.

As shown in Figure 1, when a wireless client sends data, it first senses the media to determine if other devices are transmitting. If not, it then sends an RTS frame to the AP. This frame is used to request dedicated access to the RF medium for a specified duration. The AP receives the frame and, if available, grants the wireless client access to the RF medium by sending a CTS frame of the same time duration. All other wireless devices observing the CTS frame relinquish the media to the transmitting node for transmission.

The CTS control frame includes the time duration that the transmitting node is allowed to transmit. Other wireless clients withhold transmissions for, at least, the specified duration.

Figure 2 displays a flowchart detailing the CSMA/CA process.

Refer to
Online Course
for Illustration

4.2.2.2   Wireless Clients and Access Point Association

For wireless devices to communicate over a network, they must first associate with an AP or wireless router. An important part of the 802.11 process is discovering a WLAN and subsequently connecting to it.

Management frames are used by wireless devices to complete the following three-stage process:

- Discover new wireless AP.
- Authenticate with AP.
- Associate with AP.

To associate, a wireless client and an AP must agree on specific parameters. Parameters must be configured on the AP and subsequently on the client to enable the negotiation of these processes.

Refer to
Online Course
for Illustration

4.2.2.3   Association Parameters

Figure 1 displays the wireless settings on a Linksys EA6500 wireless router. Common configurable wireless parameters include:

- **SSID**- An SSID is a unique identifier that wireless clients use to distinguish between multiple wireless networks in the same vicinity. The SSID name appears in the list of available wireless network on a client. Depending on the network configuration, several APs on a network can share an SSID. Names are usually 2 to 32 characters long.

- **Password**- Required from the wireless client to authenticate to the AP. A password is sometimes called the security key. It prevents intruders and other unwanted users from accessing the wireless network.

- **Network mode**- Refers to the 802.11a/b/g/n/ac/ad WLAN standards. APs and wireless routers can operate in a Mixed mode meaning that it can simultaneously use multiple standards.

- **Security mode**- Refers to the security parameter settings, such as WEP, WPA, or WPA2. Always enable the highest security level supported.

- **Channel settings**- Refers to the frequency bands being used to transmit wireless data. Wireless routers and AP can choose the channel setting or it can be set manually if there is interference with another AP or wireless device.

Notice that the Linksys EA6500 supports 2.4 GHz and 5 GHz radios.

Figure 2 displays the options for the 2.4 GHz radio Network mode. Notice that it can support Mixed, Wireless-N Only, or Wireless-G Only. The Mixed setting provides more flexibility, but it can also slow down communication. For example, if all the wireless clients connecting to the router are using 802.11n, then they all enjoy the better data rates provided. If 802.11g wireless client associate with the AP, then all of the faster wireless client contending for the channel must wait on 802.11g clients to clear the channel before transmitting. However, if all wireless client support 802.11n, then select Wireless-N Only for best performance.

Figure 3 displays the Network mode options for the 5 GHz radio. Notice that it also supports a Mixed setting, along with the Wireless-N Only and Wireless-AC Only settings.

Notice that the Linksys EA6500 does not support 802.11ad.

The Security options listed in Figure 4 are choices of security protocols available on the Linksys EA6500 wireless router. Home users should choose WPA2/WPA Mixed Personal, while business users would typically choose WPA2/WPA Mixed Enterprise. The 5 GHz radio offers the identical choices. The wireless end device must also support the selected security option to associate.

Note   All wireless routers and APs should be secured using the highest available settings. The None or WEP options should be avoided and only used in situations where security is of no concern.

Figure 5 displays the Channel settings for the 2.4 GHz radio. The preferred option to use is Auto; however, a specific channel could be selected if there were other APs or other devices nearby interfering with the channel selected by the router. Although the 5GHz radio also has the Auto option, in the example, it lists a specific channel (153) and channel width.

Refer to
Online Course
for Illustration

4.2.2.4   Discovering APs

Wireless devices must discover and connect to an AP or wireless router. Wireless clients connect to the AP using a scanning (probing) process. This process can be:

- **Passive mode**- The AP openly advertises its service by periodically sending broadcast beacon frames containing the SSID, supported standards, and security settings. The primary purpose of the beacon is to allow wireless clients to learn which networks and APs are available in a given area, thereby allowing them to choose which network and AP to use.

- **Active mode**- Wireless clients must know the name of the SSID. The wireless client initiates the process by broadcasting a probe request frame on multiple channels. The probe request includes the SSID name and standards supported. Active mode may be required if an AP or wireless router is configured to not broadcast beacon frames.

Figure 1 illustrates how passive mode works with the AP broadcasting a beacon frame every so often.

Figure 2 illustrates how active mode works with a wireless client broadcasting a probe request for a specific SSID. The AP with that SSID responds with a probe response frame.

A wireless client could also send a probe request without an SSID name to discover nearby WLAN networks. APs configured to broadcast beacon frames would respond to the wireless client with a probe response and provide the SSID name. APs with the broadcast SSID feature disabled do not respond.

Refer to
Online Course
for Illustration

4.2.2.5   Authentication

The 802.11 standard was originally developed with two authentication mechanisms:

■ **Open authentication**- Fundamentally a NULL authentication where the wireless client says "authenticate me" and the AP responds with "yes". Open authentication provides wireless connectivity to any wireless device and should only be used in situations where security is of no concern.

■ **Shared key authentication**- Technique is based on a key that is pre-shared between the client and the AP.

Figure 1 provides a simple overview of the authentication process. However, in most shared key authentication installations, the exchange is as follows:

1. The wireless client sends an authentication frame to the AP.

2. The AP responds with a challenge text to the client.

3. The client encrypts the message using its shared key and returns the encrypted text back to the AP.

4. The AP then decrypts the encrypted text using its shared key.

5. If the decrypted text matches the challenge text, the AP authenticates the client. If the messages do not match, the wireless client is not authenticated and wireless access is denied.

After a wireless client has been authenticated, the AP proceeds to the association stage. As shown in Figure 2, the association stage finalizes settings and establishes the data link between the wireless client and the AP.

As part of this stage:

■ The wireless client forwards an Association Request frame that includes its MAC address.

■ The AP responds with an Associate Response that includes the AP BSSID, which is the AP MAC address.

■ The AP maps a logical port known as the association identifier (AID) to the wireless client. The AID is equivalent to a port on a switch and allows the infrastructure switch to keep track of frames destined for the wireless client to be forwarded.

After a wireless client has associated with an AP, traffic is now able to flow between the client and the AP.

Refer to
Interactive Graphic
in online course.

4.2.2.6   Activity - Order the Steps in the Client and AP Association Process

Refer to
Online Course
for Illustration

4.2.3   Channel Management

4.2.3.1   Frequency Channel Saturation

As previously explained, wireless LAN devices have transmitters and receivers tuned to specific frequencies of radio waves to communicate. A common practice is for frequencies to be allocated as ranges. Such ranges are then split into smaller ranges called channels.

If the demand for a specific channel is too high, that channel is likely to become oversaturated. The saturation of the wireless medium degrades the quality of the communication. Over the years, a number of techniques have been created to improve wireless communication and alleviate saturation. The techniques listed below mitigate channel saturation by using the channels in a more efficient way:

- **Direct-sequence spread spectrum (DSSS)**- DSSS is a spread-spectrum modulation technique. Spread-spectrum is designed to spread a signal over a larger frequency band making it more resistant to interference. With DSSS the signal is multiplied by a "crafted noise" known as a spreading code. Because the receiver knows about the spreading code and when it was added, it can mathematically remove it and re-construct the original signal. In effect, this creates redundancy in the transmitted signal in an effort to counter quality loss in the wireless medium. DSSS is used by 802.11b. Also used by cordless phones operating in the 900 MHz, 2.4 GHz, 5.8 GHz bands, CDMA cellular, and GPS networks. (Figure 1)

- **Frequency-hopping spread spectrum (FHSS)**- FHSS also relies on spread-spectrum methods to communicate. It is similar to DSSS but transmits radio signals by rapidly switching a carrier signal among many frequency channels. With the FHSS, sender and receiver must be synchronized to "know" which channel to jump. This channel hopping process allows for a more efficient usage of the channels, decreasing channel congestion. Walkie-talkies and 900 MHz cordless phones also use FHSS, and Bluetooth uses a variation of FHSS. FHSS is also used by the original 802.11 standard. (Figure 2)

- **Orthogonal frequency-division multiplexing (OFDM)**- OFDM is a subset of frequency division multiplexing in which a single channel utilizes multiple sub-channels on adjacent frequencies. Sub-channels in an OFDM system are precisely orthogonal to one another which allow the sub-channels to overlap without interfering. As a result, OFDM systems are able to maximize spectral efficiency without causing adjacent channel interference. In effect, this makes it easier for a receiving station to "hear" the signal. Because OFDM uses sub-channels, channel usage is very efficient. OFDM is used by a number of communication systems including 802.11a/g/n/ac. (Figure 3)

Refer to
Online Course
for Illustration

4.2.3.2   Selecting Channels

The IEEE 802.11b/g/n all operate in the microwaves frequencies of the radio spectrum. The IEEE 802.11b/g/n standards operate in the 2.4 GHz to 2.5 GHz spectrum while 802.11a/n/ac standards operate in the more heavily regulated 5 GHz band. Figure 1 highlights which 802.11 standard operates in the 2.4 GHz, 5 GHz, and 60 GHz bands. Each spectrum is subdivided into channels with a center frequency and bandwidth, analogous to the way radio bands are subdivided.

The 2.4 GHz band is subdivided into multiple channels. The overall, combined channel bandwidth is 22 MHz with each channel separated by 5 MHz. The 802.11b standard identifies 11 channels for North America. The 22 MHz bandwidth, combined with the 5 MHz separation between frequencies, results in an overlap between successive channels, as shown in Figure 2.

Note   In Europe, there are 13 802.11b channels.

Interference occurs when an undesired signal overlaps a channel reserved for a desired signal, causing possible distortion. The solution to interference is to use non-overlapping channels. Specifically, channels 1, 6, and 11 are non-overlapping 802.11b channels, as shown in Figure 3.

A best practice for WLANs requiring multiple APs is to use non-overlapping channels. If there are three adjacent APs, use channels 1, 6, and 11. If there are just two, select any two that are five channels apart, such as channels 5 and 10. Most APs can automatically select a channel based on adjacent channels used. Some products continuously monitor the radio space to adjust the channel settings dynamically in response to environmental changes.

As enterprise WLANs migrate to 802.11n, they can use channels in the larger, less-crowded 5 GHz band, reducing "accidental denial of service (DoS)". For instance, the 802.11n standard uses OFDM and can support four non-overlapping channels, as shown in Figure 4.

802.11n can also use channel bonding, which combines two 20 MHz channel into on 40 MHz channels, as shown in Figure 5. Channel bonding increase throughput by using two channels at one time to deliver data.

Most modern APs can auto-adjust channels to circumvent interference.

Note   IEEE 802.11ac uses OFDM with channels widths of 80,160, and 80+80.

Refer to
Online Course
for Illustration

4.2.3.3   Planning a WLAN Deployment

Implementing a WLAN that takes the best advantage of resources and delivers the best service can require careful planning. WLANs can range from relatively simple installations to very complex and intricate designs. There should be a well-documented plan before a wireless network can be implemented.

The number of users a WLAN can support is not a straightforward calculation. The number or users depends on the geographical layout of the facility, including the number of bodies and devices that can fit in a space, the data rates users expect, the use of non-overlapping channels by multiple APs in an ESS, and transmit power settings.

Refer to the floor plan in Figure 1. When planning the location of APs, the administrator cannot simply draw coverage area circles and drop them over a plan. The approximate circular coverage area is important, but there are some additional recommendations:

- If APs are to use existing wiring or if there are locations where APs cannot be placed, note these locations on the map.

- Position APs above obstructions.

- Position APs vertically near the ceiling in the center of each coverage area, if possible.

- Position APs in locations where users are expected to be. For example, conference rooms are typically a better location for APs than a hallway.

When these points have been addressed, estimate the expected coverage area of an AP. This value varies depending on the WLAN standard or mix of standards that are deployed, the nature of the facility, the transmit power that the AP is configured for, and so on. Always consult the specifications for the AP when planning for coverage areas.

BSAs represent the coverage area provided by a single channel. An ESS should have 10 to 15 percent overlap between BSAs in an ESS. With a 15 percent overlap between BSAs, an SSID, and non-overlapping channels (i.e., one cell on channel 1 and the other on channel 6), roaming capability can be created.

Figure 2 provides a sample of how the BSAs could overlap.

Other factors include site surveys, which is a detailed analysis of where to locate the various APs.

*Refer to
Interactive Graphic
in online course.*

4.2.3.4   Activity - Identify Channel Management Terminology

*Refer to
Interactive Graphic
in online course.*

4.2.3.5   Activity - Cisco Wireless Explorer Game

*Refer to
Online Course
for Illustration*

4.3   Wireless LAN Security

4.3.1   WLAN Threats

4.3.1.1   Securing Wireless

The difficulties in keeping a wired network secure are amplified with a wireless network. Security should be a priority for anyone who uses or administers networks.

A WLAN is open to anyone within range of an AP and the appropriate credentials to associate to it. With a wireless NIC and knowledge of cracking techniques, an attacker may not have to physically enter the workplace to gain access to a WLAN.

Security concerns are even more significant when dealing with business networks, because the livelihood of the business relies on the protection of its information. Security breaches for a business can have major repercussions, especially if the business maintains financial information associated with its customers. Wireless networks are increasingly being deployed in enterprises and, in many cases have evolved from a convenience to a mission critical part of the network. Although WLANs have always been a target for attacks with their rise in popularity increasing, it is now a major target.

Attacks can be generated by outsiders, disgruntled employees, and even unintentionally by employees. Wireless networks are specifically susceptible to several threats, including:

- Wireless intruders

- Rogue apps

- Interception of data

- DoS attacks

On the figure, click each threat for more information.

Note   Other threats, such as AP/wireless client MAC spoofing, cracking, and infrastructure attacks are outside the scope of this chapter.

Refer to
Online Course
for Illustration

4.3.1.2   DoS Attack

Wireless DoS attacks can be the result of:

- **Improperly configured devices**- Configuration errors can disable the WLAN. For instance, an administrator could accidently alter a configuration and disable the network, or an intruder with administrator privileges could intentionally disable a WLAN.

- **A malicious user intentionally interfering with the wireless communication**- Their goal is to disable the wireless network completely or to the point where no legitimate device can access the medium.

- **Accidental interference**- WLANs operate in the unlicensed frequency bands and; therefore, all wireless networks, regardless of security features, are prone to interference from other wireless devices. Accidental interference may occur from such devices as microwave ovens, cordless phones, baby monitors, and more. The 2.4 GHz band is more prone to interference than the 5 GHz band.

To minimize the risk of a DoS attack due to improperly configured devices and malicious attack, harden all devices, keep passwords secure, create backups, and ensure that all configuration changes are incorporated off-hours.

Accidental interference only happens when another wireless device is introduced. The best solution is to monitor the WLAN for any interference problem and address them as they appear. Because the 2.4 GHz band is more prone to interference, the 5 GHz could be used in areas prone to interference. Some WLAN solutions enable APs to automatically adjust channels and use the 5 GHz band to compensate for interference. For instance, some 802.11n/ac/ad solutions automatically adjust to counter interference.

The figure illustrates how a cordless phone, or even a microwave, can interfere with WLAN communication.

The Cisco CleanAir technology enables devices to identify and locate non-802.11 interference sources. It creates a network that has the ability to adjust automatically to changes in its environment.

Refer to
Online Course
for Illustration

4.3.1.3   Management Frame DoS Attacks

Although unlikely, a malicious user could intentionally initiate a DoS attack using RF jamming devices that produce accidental interference. It is likelier that they will attempt to manipulate management frames to consume the AP resources and keep channels too busy to service legitimate user traffic.

Management frames can be manipulated to create various types of DoS attacks. Two common management frame attacks include:

- **A spoofed disconnect attack**- This occurs when an attacker sends a series of "disassociate" commands to all wireless clients within a BSS. These commands cause all clients to disconnect. When disconnected, the wireless clients immediately try to re-associate, which creates a burst of traffic. The attacker continues sending disassociate frames and the cycle repeats itself.

- **A CTS flood**- This occurs when an attacker takes advantage of the CSMA/CA contention method to monopolize the bandwidth and deny all other wireless clients access to the AP. To accomplish this, the attacker repeatedly floods the BSS with Clear to Send (CTS) frames to a bogus STA. All other wireless clients sharing the RF medium receive the CTS and withhold their transmissions until the attacker stops transmitting the CTS frames.

Figure 1 displays how a wireless client and an AP normally use CSMA/CA to access the medium.

Figure 2 illustrates how a CTS flood is created by an attacker sending out CTS frames to a bogus wireless client. All other clients must now wait the specified duration in the CTS frame. However, the attacker keeps sending CTS frames; thus, making the other clients wait indefinitely. The attacker now has control of the medium.

Note   This is only one example of a management frame attack. There are many others that exist.

To mitigate many of these attacks, Cisco has developed a variety of solutions, including the Cisco Management Frame Protection (MFP) feature, which also provides complete proactive protection against frame and device spoofing. The Cisco Adaptive Wireless IPS contributes to this solution by an early detection system where the attack signatures are matched.

The IEEE 802.11 committee has also released two standards in regards to wireless security. The 802.11i standard, which is based on Cisco MFP, specifies security mechanisms for wireless networks while the 802.11w management frame protection standard addresses the problem of manipulating management frames.

4.3.1.4   Rogue Access Points

Refer to **Online Course** for Illustration

A rogue AP is an AP or wireless router that has either been:

- Connected to a corporate network without explicit authorization and against corporate policy. Anyone with access to the premises can install (maliciously or non-maliciously) an inexpensive wireless router that can potentially allow access to a secure network resources.

- Connected or enabled by an attacker to capture client data such as the MAC addresses of clients (both wireless and wired), or to capture and disguise data packets, to gain access to network resources, or to launch man-in-the-middle attack.

Another consideration is how easy it is to create a personal network hotspot. For example, a user with secure network access enables their authorized Windows host to become a Wi-Fi AP. Doing so circumvents the security measures and other unauthorized devices can now access network resources as a shared device.

To prevent the installation of rogue APs, organizations must use monitoring software to actively monitor the radio spectrum for unauthorized APs. For example, the sample Cisco Prime Infrastructure network management software screenshot in the figure displays an RF map identifying the location of an intruder with a spoofed MAC address detected.

Note   Cisco Prime is network management software that works with other management software to provide a common look and central location for all network information. It is usually deployed in very large organizations.

Refer to
Online Course
for Illustration

4.3.1.5   Man-in-the-Middle Attack

One of the more sophisticated attacks a malicious user can use is called a man-in-the-middle (MITM) attack. There are many ways in which to create a MITM attack.

A popular wireless MITM attack is called the "evil twin AP" attack, where an attacker introduces a rogue AP and configures it with the same SSID as a legitimate AP. Locations offering free Wi-Fi, such as airports, cafes, and restaurants, are hotbeds for this type of attack due to the open authentication.

Connecting wireless clients would see two APs offering wireless access. Those near the rogue AP find the stronger signal and most likely associate with the evil twin AP. User traffic is now sent to the rogue AP, which in turn captures the data and forwards it to the legitimate AP. Return traffic from the legitimate AP is sent to the rogue AP, captured, and then forwarded to the unsuspecting STA. The attacker can steal the user password, personal information, gain network access, and compromise the user system.

For example, in Figure 1, a malicious user is in "Bob's Latte" coffee shop and wants to capture traffic from unsuspecting wireless clients. The attacker launches software, which enables their laptop to become an evil twin AP matching the same SSID and channel as the legitimate wireless router.

In Figure 2, a user sees two wireless connections available, but chooses and associates with the evil twin AP. The attacker captures the user data and forwards to the legitimate AP, which in turn directs the return traffic back to the evil twin AP. The evil twin AP captures the return traffic and forwards the information to the unsuspecting user.

Defeating an attack like an MITM attack depends on the sophistication of the WLAN infrastructure and the vigilance in monitoring activity on the network. The process begins with identifying legitimate devices on the WLAN. To do this, users must be authenticated. After all of the legitimate devices are known, the network can be monitored for abnormal devices or traffic.

Enterprise WLANs that use state-of-the-art WLAN devices provide administrators with tools that work together as a wireless intrusion prevention system (IPS). These tools include scanners that identify rogue APs and ad hoc networks, and radio resource management (RRM), which monitors the RF band for activity and AP load. An AP that is busier than normal alerts the administrator of possible unauthorized traffic.

Refer to
Online Course
for Illustration

4.3.2   Securing WLANs

4.3.2.1   Wireless Security Overview

Security has always been a concern with Wi-Fi because the network boundary has moved. Wireless signals can travel through solid matter, such as ceilings, floors, walls, outside of the home, or office space. Without stringent security measures in place, installing a WLAN can be the equivalent of putting Ethernet ports everywhere, even outside.

To address the threats of keeping wireless intruders out and protecting data, two early security features were used:

- **SSID cloaking**- APs and some wireless routers allow the SSID beacon frame to be disabled. Wireless clients must manually identify the SSID to connect to the network.

- **MAC addresses filtering**- An administrator can manually allow or deny clients wireless access based on their physical MAC hardware address.

Although these two features would deter most users, the reality is that neither SSID cloaking nor MAC address filtering would deter a crafty intruder. SSIDs are easily discovered even if APs do not broadcast them and MAC addresses can be spoofed. The best way to secure a wireless network is to use authentication and encryption systems, as shown in Figure 1.

Two types of authentication were introduced with the original 802.11 standard:

- **Open system authentication**- Any wireless client should easily be able to connect, and should only be used in situations where security is of no concern, such as in locations providing free Internet access like cafes, hotels, and in remote areas.

- **Shared key authentication**- Provides mechanisms, such as WEP, WPA, or WPA2 to authenticate and encrypt data between a wireless client and AP. However, the password must be pre-shared between both parties to connect.

The chart in Figure 2 summarizes the various types of authentication.

Refer to
Online Course
for Illustration

4.3.2.2   Shared Key Authentication Methods

As shown in Figure 1, there are three shared key authentication techniques available:

- **Wired Equivalent Privacy (WEP)**- Original 802.11 specification designed to provide privacy similar to connecting to a network using a wired connection. The data is secured using the RC4 encryption method with a static key. However, the key never changes when exchanging packets making it easy to hack.

- **Wi-Fi Protected Access (WPA)**- A Wi-Fi Alliance standard that uses WEP, but secures the data with the much stronger Temporal Key Integrity Protocol (TKIP) encryption algorithm. TKIP changes the key for each packet making it much more difficult to hack.

- **IEEE 802.11i/WPA2**- IEEE 802.11i is the industry standard for securing wireless networks. The Wi-Fi alliance version is called WPA2. 802.11i and WPA2; both use the Advanced Encryption Standard (AES) for encryption. AES is currently considered the strongest encryption protocol.

WEP is no longer recommended. Its shared WEP keys have proven to be flawed and; therefore, should never be used. To counteract shared WEP key weakness, the very first approach by companies was to try techniques, such as cloaking SSIDs and filtering MAC addresses. These techniques have also proven to be too weak.

Following the weakness of WEP-based security, there was a period of interim security measures. Vendors like Cisco, wanting to meet the demand for better security, developed their own systems while simultaneously helping to evolve the 802.11i standard. On the way to 802.11i, the TKIP encryption algorithm was created, which was linked to the Wi-Fi Alliance WPA security method.

Modern wireless networks should always use the 802.11i/WPA2 standard. WPA2 is the Wi-Fi version of 802.11i and; therefore, the terms WPA2 and 802.11i are often used interchangeably.

Since 2006, any device that bears the Wi-Fi Certified logo is WPA2 certified.

Note   Wireless-N networks should use the WPA2-Personal security mode for best performance.

The table in Figure 2 summarizes the three types of shared key authentication methods.

Refer to
Online Course
for Illustration

4.3.2.3   Encryption Methods

Encryption is used to protect data. If an intruder has captured encrypted data, they would not be able to decipher it in any reasonable amount of time.

The IEEE 802.11i and the Wi-Fi Alliance WPA and WPA2 standards use the following encryption protocols:

■ **Temporal Key Integrity Protocol (TKIP)**- TKIP is the encryption method used by WPA. It provides support for legacy WLAN equipment by addressing the original flaws associated with the 802.11 WEP encryption method. It makes use of WEP, but encrypts the Layer 2 payload using TKIP, and carries out a Message Integrity Check (MIC) in the encrypted packet to ensure the message has not been tampered with.

■ **Advanced Encryption Standard (AES)**- AES is the encryption method used by WPA2. It is the preferred method because it aligns with the industry standard IEEE 802.11i. AES performs the same functions as TKIP, but it is a far stronger method of encryption. It uses the Counter Cipher Mode with Block Chaining Message Authentication Code Protocol (CCMP) that allows destination hosts to recognize if the encrypted and non-encrypted bits have been tampered with.

Note   Always choose WPA2 with AES when possible.

Refer to
Online Course
for Illustration

4.3.2.4   Authenticating a Home User

The figure displays the security mode choices of the Linksys EA6500 wireless router. Notice how the **Security mode** for the 2.4 GHz network uses open authentication (i.e., None) and no password is required, while the **Security mode** 5 GHz network uses WPA2/ WPA Mixed Personal authentication and a password is required.

Note Typically both 2.4 GHz and 5 GHz networks would be configured with the same security modes. The example in the figure is for demonstration purposes only.

The **Security mode** drop-down list of the 2.4 GHz network displays the security methods available on the Linksys EA6500 router. It lists the weakest (i.e., None) to the strongest (i.e., WPA2/WPA Mixed Enterprise). The 5 GHz network includes the same drop-down list.

WPA and WPA2 support two types of authentication:

- **Personal**- Intended for home or small office networks, users authenticate using a pre-shared key (PSK). Wireless clients authenticate with the AP using a pre-shared password. No special authentication server is required.

- **Enterprise**- Intended for enterprise networks but requires a Remote Authentication Dial-In User Service (RADIUS) authentication server. Although more complicated to set up, it provides additional security. The device must be authenticated by the RADIUS server and then users must authenticate using 802.1X standard, which uses the Extensible Authentication Protocol (EAP) for authentication.

Refer to **Online Course** for Illustration

4.3.2.5   Authentication in the Enterprise

In networks that have stricter security requirements, an additional authentication or login is required to grant wireless clients such access. The Enterprise security mode choices require an Authentication, Authorization, and Accounting (AAA) RADIUS server.

Refer to the example in the figure. Notice the new fields displayed when choosing an Enterprise version of WPA or WPA2. These fields are necessary to supply the AP with the required information to contact the AAA server:

- **RADIUS Server IP address**- This is the reachable address of the RADIUS server.

- **UDP port numbers**- Officially assigned UDP ports 1812 for RADIUS Authentication and 1813 for RADIUS Accounting, but could also operate using UDP ports 1645 and 1646.

- **Shared key**- Used to authenticate the AP with the RADIUS server.

The shared key is not a parameter that must be configured on a STA. It is only required on the AP to authenticate with the RADIUS server.

Note There is no Password field listed, because the actual user authentication and authorization is handled by the 802.1X standard, which provides a centralized, server-based authentication of end users.

The 802.1X login process uses EAP to communicate with the AP and RADIUS server. EAP is a framework for authenticating network access. It can provide a secure authentication mechanism and negotiate a secure private key that can then be used for a wireless encryption session utilizing TKIP or AES encryption.

Refer to **Interactive Graphic** in online course.

4.3.2.6   Activity - Identify the WLAN Authentication Characteristics

Refer to
Online Course
for Illustration

4.4   Wireless LAN Configuration

4.4.1   Configure a Wireless Router

4.4.1.1   Configuring a Wireless Router

Modern wireless routers offer a variety of features and most are designed to be functional right out of the box with the default settings. However, it is good practice to change initial, default configurations.

Home wireless routers are configured using a GUI web interface.

The basic approach to wireless implementation, as with any basic networking, is to configure and test incrementally. For example, before implementing any wireless devices, verify that the existing wired network is operational and wired hosts can access Internet services.

After the wired network operation has been confirmed, the implementation plan consists of the following:

Step 1.   Start the WLAN implementation process with a single AP and a single wireless client, without enabling wireless security.

Step 2.   Verify that the client has received a DHCP IP address and can ping the local wired default router and then browse to the external Internet.

Step 3.   Configure wireless security using WPA2/WPA Mixed Personal. Never use WEP unless no other options exist.

Step 4.   Back up the configuration.

Before installing a wireless router, consider the following settings:

- **SSID Name**- Name of the WLAN network.

- **Network Password (if required)**- If prompted, this is the password required to associate and access the SSID.

- **Router Password**- This is a management router password equivalent to the `enable secret` privileged EXEC mode password.

- **Guest Network SSID Name**- For security reasons, guests can be isolated to a different SSID.

- **Guest Network Password**- This is the password to access the guest SSID.

- **Linksys Smart Wi-Fi Username**- Internet account required to access the router remotely over the Internet.

- **Linksys Smart Wi-Fi Password**- Password to access the router remotely.

The table in the figure outlines example settings used to configure the Linksys EA6500 wireless router.

Refer to
Online Course
for Illustration

4.4.1.2   Setting Up and Installed Initial Linksys EAS6500

The Linksys EA6500 wireless router is packaged with a Setup CD.

To set up and install the Linksys EA6500 router software, perform the following steps:

Step 1.   Insert the CD into the CD or DVD drive and the Setup should start automatically. If the Setup CD is not available, download the Setup program from http://Linksys.com/support.Figure 1 displays the initial Connect your Linksys EA6500 window with instructions to connect the router power and the Internet connection.

Note   In our example, the wireless router will not be connected to the Internet.

Step 2.   Click **Next** to begin the installation.

The Setup program begins the installation and displays a status window (Figure 2). During this time, the Setup program attempts to configure and enable the Internet connection. In the example, the Internet connection is unavailable, and after a few prompts to connect to the Internet, the option to skip this step displays.

The Linksys router settings window displays (Figure 3). This is where the SSID, wireless password, and administrative password is configured.

Step 3.   Click **Next** to display the summary router settings screen (Figure 4). Record these settings if the initial table was not previously completed.

Step 4.   Click **Next** to display the option to configure the Linksys Smart Wi-Fi account window (Figure 5).

This window enables you to manage the router remotely over the Internet. In this example, the Linksys Smart Wi-Fi account is not setup because there is no Internet access.

Step 5.   Click **Continue** to display the Sign In window (Figure 6). Because the Internet connection has not been configured, the administrative router password is required.

Step 6.   When the password is entered, click **Log in** to display the Linksys Smart Wi-Fi home page (Figure 7).

Refer to
Online Course
for Illustration

4.4.1.3   Configuring the Linksys Smart Wi-Fi Homepage

As shown in Figures 1 to 3, the Linksys Smart-Wi-Fi Home page is divided into the following three main sections:

- **Smart Wi-Fi Router Settings**- Use this section to alter settings for connectivity, troubleshooting, wireless, and security.

- **Smart Wi-Fi Tools**- Use this section to see who is currently connected to the network, create a separate network for guests, configure parental control to keep kids safe, prioritize bandwidth to specific devices and applications, test the Internet connection speed, and control access to shared files.

- **Smart Wi-Fi Widgets**- Provides a quick summary of the Smart Wi-Fi Tools section.

Click the Play button in Figure 4 to see a short video on the Smart Wi-Fi interface.

Refer to
Online Course
for Illustration

4.4.1.4   Smart Wi-Fi Settings

As shown in Figures 1 to 4, the Smart Wi-Fi settings enable you to:

- Configure the router's basic settings for the local network. This tool can be used to configure a DHCP Reservation, change the router's administration password, change the IP address of the Linksys router, set up the Linksys routers with a Static route, set up the router with Cable Internet service, and configure the MTU Settings of the Linksys router.

- Diagnose and troubleshoot connectivity issues on the network. It contains the current status of the router and connected devices. It can also be used to perform a Ping test and a traceroute, to back up and restore the router's current settings, to check the WAN IP Address, to reboot and reset the router to factory defaults, and to maintain of the router's status.

- Secure and personalize the wireless network. It can also be used to enable and configure wireless MAC filter and connect devices easily using WPS.

- Keep the network safe from Internet threats by configuring the DMZ feature.

- View connected computers and devices on the network, and set up port forwarding.

Refer to
Online Course
for Illustration

4.4.1.5   Smart Wi-Fi Tools

As shown in Figures 1 to 6, the Smart Wi-Fi tools provide additional services including:

- **Device List**- View to see who is connected to the WLAN. Device names and icons can be personalized. Devices can also be connected with this service.

- **Guest Access**- Create a separate network for up to 50 guests at home while keeping network files safe with the Guest Access Tool.

- **Parental Controls**- Protect kids and family members by restricting access to potentially harmful websites. This tool is used to restrict Internet access on specific devices, control the time and days of specific devices that can access the Internet, block specific websites for certain devices, disable restrictions on Internet access, and disable the Parental Controls feature.

- **Media Prioritization**- Prioritize bandwidth to specific devices and applications. With this tool, optimize the online experience by prioritizing bandwidth on applications and devices that need it the most. This tool can be used to utilize the Settings feature of the Media Prioritization Tool, add more applications to be assigned with a specific bandwidth, and allocate higher bandwidth to an application, device, or online game by setting the bandwidth priority.

- **Speed Test**- Tool used to test the upload and download speed of the Internet link. Useful for baselining.

- **USB Storage**- Controls access to shared files. Configures how users can access shared files. With this tool, users can access USB storage in the local network, create shares on a USB storage device, configure the Folder Access settings, configure how devices and computers within the network can access the FTP server, and configure the access to a Media Server.

Refer to
Online Course
for Illustration

4.4.1.6   Backing Up a Configuration

Just like the IOS of a Cisco router should be backed up in case of failure, so should the configuration of a home router. If a home router is left to its default configuration, then backing up the configuration is not really warranted. However, if many of the Smart Wi-Fi tools have been customized, then it may be advantageous to back up the configuration.

Backing up the configuration is easy to do with the Linksys EA6500 wireless router:

Step 1.   Log in to the Smart Wi-Fi Home page. Click the **Troubleshooting** icon to display the Troubleshooting Status window (Figure 1).

Step 2.   Click the **Diagnostic** tab to open the Diagnostic Troubleshooting window (Figure 2).

Step 3.   Under the Router configuration title, click **Backup** and save the file to an appropriate folder.

Note   To upload a previously saved backup, click **Restore**, locate the file, and start the restore process.

Refer to
Online Course
for Illustration

4.4.2   Configuring Wireless Clients

4.4.2.1   Connecting Wireless Clients

When the AP or wireless router has been configured, the wireless NIC on the client must be configured to allow it to connect to the WLAN. The user should also verify that the client has successfully connected to the correct wireless network, especially because there may be many WLANs available with which to connect.

Click the Play button in Figure 1 to see a short video on how to connect a Windows computer to the WLAN.

Click the Play button in Figure 2 to see a short video on connecting an iPod, iPhone, and iPad to the WLAN.

Refer to **Packet Tracer Activity** for this chapter

4.4.2.2   Packet Tracer - Configuring Wireless LAN Access

Background/Scenario

In this activity, you will configure a Linksys wireless router, allowing for remote access from PCs, as well as wireless connectivity with WPA2 security. You will manually configure PC wireless connectivity by entering the Linksys router SSID and password.

Refer to
Lab Activity
for this chapter

4.4.2.3   Lab - Configuring a Wireless Router and Client

In this lab, you will complete the following objectives:

- Part 1: Configure Basic Settings on a Linksys EA Series Router

- Part 2: Secure the Wireless Network

- Part 3: Review Additional Features on a Linksys EA Series Router

- Part 4: Connect a Wireless Client

Refer to
Online Course
for Illustration

4.4.3 Troubleshoot WLAN Issues

4.4.3.1 Troubleshooting Approaches

Troubleshooting any sort of network problem should follow a systematic approach. Logical networking models, such as the OSI and TCP/IP models, separate network functionality into modular layers.

When troubleshooting, these layered models can be applied to the physical network to isolate network problems. For example, if the symptoms suggest a physical connection problem, the network technician can focus on troubleshooting the circuit that operates at the physical layer. If that circuit functions properly, the technician looks at areas in another layer that could be causing the problem.

There are three main troubleshooting approaches used to resolve network problems:

- **Bottom-up**- Start at Layer 1 and work up. (Figure 1)

- **Top-down**- Start at the top layer and work down. (Figure 2)

- **Divide-and-conquer**- Ping the destination. If the pings fail, verify the lower layers. If the pings are successful, verify the upper layers. (Figure 3)

Refer to
Online Course
for Illustration

4.4.3.2 Wireless Client Not Connecting

When troubleshooting a WLAN, a process of elimination is recommended.

In the figure, a wireless client is not connecting to the WLAN. If there is no connectivity, check the following:

- Confirm the network configuration on the PC using the `ipconfig` command. Verify that the PC has received an IP address via DHCP or is configured with a static IP address.

- Confirm that the device can connect to the wired network. Connect the device to the wired LAN and `ping` a known IP address.

- If necessary, reload drivers as appropriate for the client. It may be necessary to try a different wireless NIC.

- If the wireless NIC of the client is working, check the security mode and encryption settings on the client. If the security settings do not match, the client cannot gain access to the WLAN.

If the PC is operational but the wireless connection is performing poorly, check the following:

- How far is the PC from an AP? Is the PC out of the planned coverage area (BSA)?

- Check the channel settings on the wireless client. The client software should detect the appropriate channel as long as the SSID is correct.

- Check for the presence of other devices in the area that may be interfering with the 2.4 GHz band. Examples of other devices are cordless phones, baby monitors, microwave ovens, wireless security systems, and potentially rogue APs. Data from these devices can cause interference in the WLAN and intermittent connection problems between a wireless client and AP.

Next, ensure that all the devices are actually in place. Consider a possible physical security issue. Is there power to all devices and are they powered on?

Finally, inspect links between cabled devices looking for bad connectors or damaged or missing cables. If the physical plant is in place, verify the wired LAN by pinging devices, including the AP. If connectivity still fails at this point, perhaps something is wrong with the AP or its configuration.

When the user PC is eliminated as the source of the problem, and the physical status of devices is confirmed, begin investigating the performance of the AP. Check the power status of the AP.

<table>
<tr><td>Refer to
Online Course
for Illustration</td></tr>
</table>

4.4.3.3 Troubleshooting When the Network Is Slow

To optimize and increase the bandwidth of 802.11n/ac dual-band routers, either:

- **Upgrade your wireless clients**- Older 802.11b and even 802.11g devices can slow the entire WLAN. For the best performance, all wireless devices should support the same highest acceptable standard.

- **Split the traffic**- The easiest way to improve wireless performance is to split the wireless traffic between the 802.11n 2.4 GHz band and the 5 GHz band. Therefore, 802.11n (or better) can use the two bands as two separate wireless networks to help manage the traffic. For example, use the 2.4 GHz network for basic Internet tasks, such as web browsing, email, and downloads, and use the 5 GHz band for streaming multimedia, as shown in Figure 1.

There are several reasons for using a split-the-traffic approach:

- The 2.4 GHz band may be suitable for basic Internet traffic that is not time-sensitive.

- The bandwidth may still be shared with other nearby WLANs.

- The 5 GHz band is much less crowded than the 2.4 GHz band; ideal for streaming multimedia.

- The 5 GHz band has more channels; therefore, the channel chosen is likely interference-free.

By default, dual-band routers use the same network name on both the 2.4 GHz band and the 5 GHz band. The simplest way to segment traffic is to rename one of the wireless networks, as shown in Figure 2. With a separate, descriptive name, it is easier to connect to the right network.

To improve the range of a wireless network, ensure the physical wireless router location is free of obstructions, such as furniture, fixtures, and tall appliances. These block the signal, which shortens the range of the WLAN. If this still does not solve the problem, then a Wi-Fi Range Extender or deploying the Powerline wireless technology may be used.

Refer to
Online Course
for Illustration

4.4.3.4 Updating Firmware

The IOS of the Linksys EA6500 router is called firmware. The firmware may need to be upgraded if there is a problem with the device or there is a new feature included with a new firmware update. Regardless of the reason, most modern wireless home routers offer upgradable firmware.

You can easily upgrade the Linksys EA6500 Smart Wi-Fi router firmware by performing the following steps:

Step 1. Access the Linksys Smart Wi-Fi Home page.

Step 2. Click the **Connectivity** icon to open the Connectivity window (Figure 1).

Step 3. Under the Firmware Update label, click **Check for Updates**.

The router either responds with `No updates found` or it prompts to download and install the new firmware.

Note Some routers require that the firmware file be downloaded ahead of time and then manually uploaded. To do so, select **Choose File**. If a firmware upgrade fails or makes the situation worse, then the router can load the previous firmware by clicking **Troubleshooting**, **Diagnostics**, and then selecting **Restore previous firmware** (Figure 2).

Caution Do not upgrade the firmware unless there are problems with the AP or the new firmware has a desired feature.

Refer to
Interactive Graphic
in online course.

4.4.3.5 Activity - Identify the Troubleshooting Solution

Refer to
Online Course
for Illustration

Refer to
Lab Activity
for this chapter

4.5 Summary

4.5.1.1 Class Activity - Inside and Outside Control

Inside and Outside Control

An assessment has been completed to validate the need for an upgrade to your small- to medium-sized wireless network. Approved for purchase are indoor and outdoor access points and one wireless controller. You must compare equipment models and their specifications before you purchase.

Therefore, you visit the "Wireless Compare Products and Services" web site and see a features chart for indoor and outdoor wireless access points and controller devices. After reviewing the chart, you note there is some terminology with which you are unfamiliar:

- Federal Information Processing Standard (FIPS)

- MIMO

- Cisco CleanAir Technology

- Cisco FlexConnect
- Band Select

Research the above terms. Prepare your own chart with your company's most important requirements listed for purchasing the indoor and outdoor wireless access points and wireless controller. This chart will assist in validating your purchase order to your accounting manager and CEO.

Refer to **Packet Tracer Activity** for this chapter

4.5.1.2   Packet Tracer - Skills Integration Challenge

Background/Scenario

In this challenge activity, you will configure VLANs and inter-VLAN routing, DHCP, and Rapid PVST+. You will also be required to configure a Linksys router for wireless connectivity with wireless security. At the end of the activity, the PCs will not be able to ping each other but should be able to ping the outside host.

Refer to **Online Course** for Illustration

4.5.1.3   Summary

WLANs are often implemented in homes, offices, and campus environments. Only the 2.4 GHz, 5.0 GHz, and 60 GHz frequencies are used for 802.11 WLANs. The ITU-R regulates the allocation of the RF spectrum, while IEEE provides the 802.11 standards to define how these frequencies are used for the physical and MAC sublayer of wireless networks. The Wi-Fi Alliance certifies that vendor products conform to industry standards and norms.

A wireless client uses a wireless NIC to connect to an infrastructure device, such as a wireless router or wireless AP. Wireless clients connect using an SSID. APs can be implemented as standalone devices, in small clusters, or in a larger controller-base network.

A Cisco Aironet AP can use an omnidirectional antenna, a directional antenna, or a Yagi antenna to direct signals. IEEE 802.11n/ac/ad use MIMO technology to improve throughput and support up to four antennas simultaneously.

In ad hoc mode or IBSS, two wireless devices connect to each other in a P2P manner.

In infrastructure mode, APs connect to network infrastructure using the wired DS. Each AP defines a BSS and is uniquely identified by its BSSID. Multiple BSSs can be joined into an ESS. Using a particular SSID in an ESS provides seamless roaming capabilities among the BSSs in the ESS. Additional SSIDs can be used to segregate the level of network access defined by which SSID is in use.

A wireless client first authenticates with an AP, and then associates with that AP. The 802.11i/WPA2 authentication standard should be used. AES is the encryption method that should be used with WPA2.

When planning a wireless network, non-overlapping channels should be used when deploying multiple APs to cover a particular area. There should be a 10-15 percent overlap between BSAs in an ESS. Cisco APs support PoE to simplify installation.

Wireless networks are specifically susceptible to threats, such as wireless intruders, rogue APs, data interception, and DoS attacks. Cisco has developed a range of solutions to mitigate against these types of threats.

Go to the online course to take the quiz and exam.

Chapter 4 Quiz

This quiz is designed to provide an additional opportunity to practice the skills and knowledge presented in the chapter and to prepare for the chapter exam. You will be allowed multiple attempts and the grade does not appear in the gradebook.

Chapter 4 Exam

The chapter exam assesses your knowledge of the chapter content.

Your Chapter Notes

Adjust and Troubleshoot Single-Area OSPF

5.0 Adjust and Troubleshoot Single-Area OSPF

5.0.1.1 Introduction

OSPF is a popular link state routing protocol that can be fine-tuned in many ways. Some of the most common methods of fine tuning include manipulating the Designated Router/Backup Designated Router (DR/BDR) election process, propagating default routes, fine-tuning the OSPFv2 and OSPFv3 interfaces, and enabling authentication.

This chapter of OSPF describes these tuning features, the configuration mode commands to implement these features for both IPv4 and IPv6, and the components and commands used to troubleshoot OSPFv2 and OSPFv3.

Refer to
Lab Activity
for this chapter

5.0.1.2 Class Activity - DR and BDR Election

DR and BDR Elections

You are trying to decide how to influence the selection of the designated router and backup designated router for your OSPF network. This activity simulates that process.

Three separate designated-router election scenarios will be presented. The focus is on electing a DR and BDR for your group. Refer to the PDF for this activity for the remaining instructions.

If additional time is available, two groups can be combined to simulate DR and BDR elections.

Refer to
Interactive Graphic
in online course.

5.1 Advanced Single-Area OSPF Configurations

5.1.1 Routing in the Distribution and Core Layers

5.1.1.1 Routing versus Switching

A scalable network requires a hierarchical network design. The focus of the preceding chapters was on the access and distribution layers. As shown in Figure 1, Layer 2 switches, link aggregation, LAN redundancy, and wireless LANs are all technologies that provide or enhance user access to network resources.

Scalable networks also require optimal reachability between sites. Remote network reachability is provided by routers and Layer 3 switches which operate in the distribution and core layers as shown in Figure 2. Routers and Layer 3 switches learn about remote networks in one of two ways:

- **Manually**- Remote networks are manually entered into the route table using static routes.

- **Dynamically**- Remote routes are automatically learned using a dynamic routing protocol such as Enhanced Interior Gateway Routing Protocol (EIGRP) or Open Shortest Path First (OSPF).

<table>
<tr><td>Refer to
Online Course
for Illustration</td></tr>
</table>

5.1.1.2   Static Routing

Static Routing

The example in the figure provides a sample scenario of static routing. A network administrator can manually configure a static route to reach a specific network. Unlike a dynamic routing protocol, static routes are not automatically updated and must be manually reconfigured any time the network topology changes. A static route does not change until the administrator manually reconfigures it.

Static routing has three primary uses:

- Providing ease of routing table maintenance in smaller networks that are not expected to grow significantly.

- Routing to and from stub networks. A stub network is a network accessed by a single route, and the router has only one neighbor.

- Using a single default route to represent a path to any network that does not have a more specific match with another route in the routing table. Default routes are used to send traffic to any destination beyond the next upstream router.

<table>
<tr><td>Refer to
Online Course
for Illustration</td></tr>
</table>

5.1.1.3   Dynamic Routing Protocols

Dynamic Routing

Routing protocols allow routers to dynamically share information about remote networks as shown in the figure. Routers receiving the update automatically add this information to their own routing tables. The routing protocols then determine the best path, or route, to each network. A primary benefit of dynamic routing protocols is that routers exchange routing information when there is a topology change. This exchange allows routers to automatically learn about new networks and also to find alternate paths when there is a link failure to a current network.

Compared to static routing, dynamic routing protocols require less administrative overhead. However, the expense of using dynamic routing protocols is dedicating part of a router's resources for protocol operation, including CPU time and network link bandwidth. Despite the benefits of dynamic routing, static routing still has its place. There are times when static routing is more appropriate and other times when dynamic routing is the better choice. However, it is important to understand that static and dynamic routing are not mutually exclusive. Rather, most networks use a combination of dynamic routing protocols and static routes.

The two most common dynamic routing protocols are EIGRP and OSPF. The focus of this chapter is on OSPF.

Note   All dynamic routing protocols are capable of advertising and propagating static routes in their routing updates.

Refer to
Online Course
for Illustration

5.1.1.4   Open Shortest Path First

OSPF is a commonly implemented link-state routing protocol. It was developed as a replacement for the distance vector routing protocol, RIP. However, OSPF has significant advantages over RIP in that it offers faster convergence and scales to much larger network implementations.

OSPF features, as shown in the figure, include:

- **Classless**- It is classless by design; therefore, it supports VLSM and CIDR.

- **Efficient**- Routing changes trigger routing updates (no periodic updates). It uses the SPF algorithm to choose the best path.

- **Fast convergence**- It quickly propagates network changes.

- **Scalable**- It works well in small and large network sizes. Routers can be grouped into areas to support a hierarchical system.

- **Secure**- It supports Message Digest 5 (MD5) authentication. When enabled, OSPF routers only accept encrypted routing updates from peers with the same pre-shared password.

Refer to
Online Course
for Illustration

5.1.1.5   Configuring Single-Area OSPF

The focus of this chapter is to adjust and troubleshoot OSPF. However, it is a good idea to review a basic implementation of the OSPF routing protocol.

The example in Figure 1 displays the topology used for configuring OSPFv2. The routers in the topology have a starting configuration, including enabled interface addresses. There is currently no static routing or dynamic routing configured on any of the routers. All interfaces on routers R1, R2, and R3 (except the loopback on R2) are within the OSPF backbone area. The ISP router is used as the routing domain's gateway to the Internet.

In Figure 2, the Gigabit Ethernet 0/0 interface of R1 is configured to reflect its true bandwidth of 1,000,000 kilobits (i.e.1,000,000,000 b/s). Next, from OSPF router configuration mode, the router ID is assigned, the reference bandwidth is adjusted to account for fast interfaces, and the three networks attached to R1 are advertised. Notice how the wildcard mask is used to identify the specific networks.

In Figure 3, the Gigabit Ethernet 0/0 interface of R2 is also configured to reflect its true bandwidth, the router ID is assigned, the reference bandwidth is adjusted to account for fast interfaces, and the three networks attached to R2 are advertised. Notice how the use of the wildcard mask can be avoided by identifying the actual router interface with a quad zero mask. This effectively makes OSPF use the subnet mask assigned to the router interface as the advertised network mask.

Use the Syntax Checker in Figure 4 to adjust the bandwidth on the R3 G0/0 interface, enter OSPF router configuration mode, assign the correct router ID, adjust the reference bandwidth, and advertise the three directly connected networks using the router interfaces and quad zero wildcard mask.

Notice the informational messages displaying that R3 has established a full neighbor adjacency with R1 with router ID 1.1.1.1 and R2 with router ID 2.2.2.2. The OSPF network has converged.

Refer to
Online Course
for Illustration

5.1.1.6   Verifying Single-Area OSPF

Useful commands to verify OSPF include the following:

- `show ip ospf neighbor`- Command to verify that the router has formed an adjacency with its neighboring routers. If the router ID of the neighboring router is not displayed, or if it does not show as being in a state of FULL, the two routers have not formed an OSPF adjacency.

- `show ip protocols`- Command provides a quick way to verify vital OSPF configuration information. This includes the OSPF process ID, the router ID, networks the router is advertising, the neighbors the router is receiving updates from, and the default administrative distance, which is 110 for OSPF.

- `show ip ospf`- Command is used to display the OSPF process ID and router ID as well as the OSPF SPF and OSPF area information.

- `show ip ospf interface`- Command provides a detailed list for every OSPF-enabled interface and is very useful to determine whether the `network` statements were correctly composed.

- `show ip ospf interface brief`- Command is useful to display a summary and status of OSPF-enabled interfaces.

Figures 1 to 5 display the corresponding output each verification command entered on R1.

Use the Syntax Checker in Figure 6 to verify the neighbor adjacency, vital OSPF configuration information, and to display a summary of OSPF enabled interfaces on R2.

Use the Syntax Checker in Figure 7 to verify the neighbor adjacency, vital OSPF configuration information, and to display a summary of OSPF enabled interfaces on R3.

Refer to
Online Course
for Illustration

5.1.1.7   Configuring Single-Area OSPFv3

The following is a review of a basic implementation of the OSPFv3 routing protocol for IPv6.

The example in Figure 1 displays the topology used for configuring OSPFv3. The routers in the topology have a starting configuration, including enabled interface IPv6 addresses. There is currently no static routing or dynamic routing configured on any of the routers. All interfaces on routers R1, R2, and R3 (except the loopback on R2) are within the OSPF backbone area.

In Figure 2, from OSPFv3 router configuration mode on R1, the router ID is manually assigned and the reference bandwidth is adjusted to account for fast interfaces. Next the interfaces participating in OSPFv3 are configured. The Gigabit Ethernet 0/0 is also configured to reflect its true bandwidth. Notice how there is no wildcard mask require when configuring OSPFv3.

In Figure 3, from OSPFv3 router configuration mode on R2, the router ID is manually assigned and the reference bandwidth is adjusted to account for fast interfaces. Next the interfaces participating in OSPFv3 are configured. Again, the Gigabit Ethernet 0/0 is also configured to reflect its true bandwidth.

Use the Syntax Checker in Figure 4 to manually assign the router ID and adjust the reference bandwidth. Next configure the interfaces accordingly starting with interface Gigabit Ethernet 0/0. Also assign the true bandwidth to that interface.

Notice the informational messages displaying that R3 has established a full neighbor adjacency with R1 with router ID 1.1.1.1 and R2 with router ID 2.2.2.2. The OSPFv3 network has converged.

Refer to **Online Course** for Illustration

5.1.1.8   Verifying Single-Area OSPFv3

Useful commands to verify OSPFv3 include the following:

- `show ipv6 ospf neighbor`- Command to verify that the router has formed an adjacency with its neighboring routers. If the router ID of the neighboring router is not displayed, or if it does not show as being in a state of FULL, the two routers have not formed an OSPF adjacency.

- `show ipv6 protocols`- Command provides a quick way to verify vital OSPFv3 configuration information, including the OSPF process ID, the router ID, and the interfaces enabled for OSPFv3.

- `show ipv6 route ospf`- Command provides specifics about OSPFv3 routes in the routing table.

- `show ipv6 ospf interface brief`- Command is useful to display a summary and status of OSPFv3 enabled interfaces.

Figures 1 through 4 displays the corresponding output each verification command entered on R1.

Refer to **Lab Activity** for this chapter

5.1.1.9   Lab - Configuring Basic Single-Area OSPFv2

In this lab, you will complete the following objectives:

- Part 1: Build the Network and Configure Basic Device Settings
- Part 2: Configure and Verify OSPF Routing
- Part 3: Change Router ID Assignments
- Part 4: Configure OSPF Passive Interfaces
- Part 5: Change OSPF Metrics

Refer to **Online Course** for Illustration

5.1.2   OSPF in Multiaccess Networks

5.1.2.1   OSPF Network Types

To configure OSPF adjustments, start with a basic implementation of the OSPF routing protocol.

OSPF defines five network types, as shown in Figures 1 to 5:

- **Point-to-point**- Two routers interconnected over a common link. No other routers are on the link. This is often the configuration in WAN links. (Figure 1)

- **Broadcast multiaccess**- Multiple routers interconnected over an Ethernet network. (Figure 2)

- **Nonbroadcast multiaccess (NBMA)**- Multiple routers interconnected in a network that does not allow broadcasts, such as Frame Relay. (Figure 3)

- **Point-to-multipoint**- Multiple routers interconnected in a hub-and-spoke topology over an NBMA network. Often used to connect branch sites (spokes) to a central site (hub). (Figure 4)

- **Virtual links**- Special OSPF network used to interconnect distant OSPF areas to the backbone area. (Figure 5)

A multiaccess network is a network with multiple devices on the same shared media, which are sharing communications. Ethernet LANs are the most common example of broadcast multiaccess networks. In broadcast networks, all devices on the network see all broadcast and multicast frames. They are multiaccess networks because there may be numerous hosts, printers, routers, and other devices that are all members of the same network.

Refer to **Online Course** for Illustration

5.1.2.2   Challenges in Multiaccess Networks

Multiaccess networks can create two challenges for OSPF regarding the flooding of LSAs:

- **Creation of multiple adjacencies**- Ethernet networks could potentially interconnect many OSPF routers over a common link. Creating adjacencies with every router is unnecessary and undesirable. This would lead to an excessive number of LSAs exchanged between routers on the same network.

- **Extensive flooding of LSAs**- Link-state routers flood their link-state packets when OSPF is initialized, or when there is a change in the topology. This flooding can become excessive.

The following formula can be used to calculate the number of required adjacencies. The number of adjacencies required for any number of routers (designated as n) on a multiaccess network is:

$n (n - 1) / 2$

Figure 1 shows a simple topology of four routers, all of which are attached to the same multiaccess Ethernet network. Without some type of mechanism to reduce the number of adjacencies, collectively these routers would form six adjacencies: 4 (4 - 1) / 2 = 6, as shown in Figure 2. Figure 3 shows that as routers are added to the network, the number of adjacencies increases dramatically.

Refer to **Online Course** for Illustration

5.1.2.3   OSPF Designated Router

The solution to managing the number of adjacencies and the flooding of LSAs on a multiaccess network is the DR. On multiaccess networks, OSPF elects a DR to be the collection and distribution point for LSAs sent and received. A BDR is also elected in case the DR fails. The BDR listens passively to this exchange and maintains a relationship with all the routers. If the DR stops producing Hello packets, the BDR promotes itself and assumes the role of DR.

All other non-DR or BDR routers become DROTHER (a router that is neither the DR nor the BDR).

In Figure 1, R1 has been elected as the designated router for the Ethernet LAN interconnecting R2, R3, and R4. Notice how the number of adjacencies has been reduced to 3.

Routers on a multiaccess network elect a DR and BDR. DROTHERs only form full adjacencies with the DR and BDR in the network. Instead of flooding LSAs to all routers in the network, DROTHERs only send their LSAs to the DR and BDR using the multicast address 224.0.0.6 (all DR routers).

Click the Play button in Figure 2 to see the animation of the role of DR. In the animation, R1 sends LSAs to the DR. The BDR also listens. The DR is responsible for forwarding the LSAs from R1 to all other routers. The DR uses the multicast address 224.0.0.5 (all OSPF routers). The end result is that there is only one router doing all of the flooding of all LSAs in the multiaccess network.

Note   DR/BDR elections only occur in multiaccess networks and do not occur in point-to-point networks.

Refer to
Online Course
for Illustration

5.1.2.4   Verifying DR/BDR Roles

In the multiaccess topology shown in Figure 1, there are three routers interconnected over a common Ethernet multiaccess network, 192.168.1.0/28. Each router is configured with the indicated IP address on the Gigabit Ethernet 0/0 interface.

Because the routers are connected over a common multiaccess broadcast network, OSPF has automatically elected a DR and BDR. In this example, R3 has been elected as the DR because its router ID is 3.3.3.3, which is the highest in this network. R2 is the BDR because it has the second highest router ID in the network.

To verify the roles of the router, use the `show ip ospf interface` command (Figure 2). The output generated by R1 confirms that:

- R1 is not the DR or BDR, but is a DROTHER with a default priority of 1. (1)

- The DR is R3 with router ID 3.3.3.3 at IP address 192.168.1.3, while the BDR is R2 with router ID 2.2.2.2 at IP address 192.168.1.2. (2)

- R1 has two adjacencies: one with the BDR and one with the DR. (3)

The output generated by R2 in Figure 3 confirms that:

- R2 is the BDR with a default priority of 1. (1)

- The DR is R3 with router ID 3.3.3.3 at IP address 192.168.1.3, while the BDR is R2 with router ID 2.2.2.2 at IP address 192.168.1.2. (2)

- R2 has two adjacencies; one with a neighbor with router ID 1.1.1.1 (R1) and the other with the DR. (3)

The output generated by R3 in Figure 4 confirms that:

- R3 is the DR with a default priority of 1. (1)

- The DR is R3 with router ID 3.3.3.3 at IP address 192.168.1.3, while the BDR is R2 with router ID 2.2.2.2 at IP address 192.168.1.2. (2)

- R3 has two adjacencies: one with a neighbor with router ID 1.1.1.1 (R1) and the other with the BDR. (3)

Refer to
Online Course
for Illustration

5.1.2.5   Verifying DR/BDR Adjacencies

To verify the OSPF adjacencies, use the `show ip ospf neighbor` command as shown in Figure 1.

Unlike serial links that only display a state of FULL/-, the state of neighbors in multiaccess networks can be:

- FULL/DROTHER - This is a DR or BDR router that is fully adjacent with a non-DR or BDR router. These two neighbors can exchange Hello packets, updates, queries, replies, and acknowledgments.

- FULL/DR - The router is fully adjacent with the indicated DR neighbor. These two neighbors can exchange Hello packets, updates, queries, replies, and acknowledgments.

- FULL/BDR - The router is fully adjacent with the indicated BDR neighbor. These two neighbors can exchange Hello packets, updates, queries, replies, and acknowledgments.

- 2-WAY/DROTHER - The non-DR or BDR router has a neighbor relationship with another non-DR or BDR router. These two neighbors exchange Hello packets.

The normal state for an OSPF router is usually FULL. If a router is stuck in another state, it is an indication that there are problems in forming adjacencies. The only exception to this is the 2-WAY state, which is normal in a multiaccess broadcast network.

In multiaccess networks, DROTHERs only form FULL adjacencies with the DR and BDR. However, DROTHERs will still form a 2-WAY neighbor adjacency with any DROTHERs that join the network. This means that all DROTHER routers in the multiaccess network still receive Hello packets from all other DROTHER routers. In this way, they are aware of all routers in the network. When two DROTHER routers form a neighbor adjacency, the neighbor state displays as 2-WAY/DROTHER.

The output generated by R1 confirms that R1 has adjacencies with router:

- R2 with router ID 2.2.2.2 is in a Full state and the role of R2 is BDR. (1)

- R3 with router ID 3.3.3.3 is in a Full state and the role of R3 is DR. (2)

The output generated by R2 in Figure 2 confirms that R2 has adjacencies with router:

- R1 with router ID 1.1.1.1 is in a Full state and R1 is neither the DR nor BDR. (1)

- R3 with router ID 3.3.3.3 is in a Full state and the role of R3 is DR. (2)

The output generated by R3 in Figure 3 confirms that R3 has adjacencies with router:

- R1 with router ID 1.1.1.1 is in a Full state and R1 is neither the DR nor BDR. (1)

- R2 with router ID 2.2.2.2 is in a Full state and the role of R2 is BDR. (2)

Refer to
Online Course
for Illustration

5.1.2.6 Default DR/BDR Election Process

How do the DR and BDR get elected? The OSPF DR and BDR election decision is based on the following criteria, in sequential order:

1. The routers in the network elect the router with the highest interface priority as the DR. The router with the second highest interface priority is elected as the BDR. The priority can be configured to be any number between 0 – 255. The higher the priority, the likelier the router will be selected as the DR. If the priority is set to 0, the router is not capable of becoming the DR. The default priority of multiaccess broadcast interfaces is 1. Therefore, unless otherwise configured, all routers have an equal priority value and must rely on another tie breaking method during the DR/BDR election.

2. If the interface priorities are equal, then the router with the highest router ID is elected the DR. The router with the second highest router ID is the BDR.

Recall that the router ID is determined in one of three ways:

- The router ID can be manually configured.

- If no router IDs are configured, the router ID is determined by the highest loopback IP address.

- If no loopback interfaces are configured, the router ID is determined by the highest active IPv4 address.

Note In an IPv6 network, if there are no IPv4 addresses configured on the router, then the router ID must be manually configured with the `router-id` rid command; otherwise, OSPFv3 does not start.

In the figure, all Ethernet router interfaces have a default priority of 1. As a result, based on the selection criteria listed above, the OSPF router ID is used to elect the DR and BDR. R3 with the highest router ID becomes the DR; and R2, with the second highest router ID, becomes the BDR.

Note Serial interfaces have default priorities set to 0; therefore, they do not elect DR and BDRs.

The DR and BDR election process takes place as soon as the first router with an OSPF-enabled interface is active on the multiaccess network. This can happen when the routers are powered on, or when the OSPF `network` command for that interface is configured. The election process only takes a few seconds. If all of the routers on the multiaccess network have not finished booting, it is possible that a router with a lower router ID becomes the DR. (This can be a lower-end router that takes less time to boot.)

Refer to
Online Course
for Illustration

5.1.2.7 DR/BDR Election Process

OSPF DR and BDR elections are not preemptive. If a new router with a higher priority or higher router ID is added to the network after the DR and BDR election, the newly added router does not take over the DR or the BDR role. This is because those roles have already been assigned. The addition of a new router does not initiate a new election process.

After the DR is elected, it remains the DR until one of the following events occurs:

- The DR fails
- The OSPF process on the DR fails or is stopped
- The multiaccess interface on the DR fails or is shutdown

If the DR fails, the BDR is automatically promoted to DR. This is the case even if another DROTHER with a higher priority or router ID is added to the network after the initial DR/BDR election. However, after a BDR is promoted to DR, a new BDR election occurs and the DROTHER with the higher priority or router ID is elected as the new BDR.

Figures 1 to 4 illustrate various scenarios relating to the DR and BDR election process.

In Figure 1, the current DR (R3) fails; therefore, the pre-elected BDR (R2) assumes the role of DR. Subsequently, an election is held to choose a new BDR. Because R1 is the only DROTHER, it is elected as the BDR.

In Figure 2, R3 has re-joined the network after several minutes of being unavailable. Because the DR and BDR already exist, R3 does not take over either role; instead, it becomes a DROTHER.

In Figure 3, a new router (R4) with a higher router ID is added to the network. DR (R2) and BDR (R1) retain the DR and BDR roles. R4 automatically becomes a DROTHER.

In Figure 4, R2 has failed. The BDR (R1) automatically becomes the DR and an election process selects R4 as the BDR because it has the higher router ID.

Refer to
Online Course
for Illustration

5.1.2.8 The OSPF Priority

The DR becomes the focal point for the collection and distribution of LSAs; therefore, this router must have sufficient CPU and memory capacity to handle the workload. It is possible to influence the DR/BDR election process through configurations.

If the interface priorities are equal on all routers, the router with the highest router ID is elected the DR. It is possible to configure the router ID to manipulate the DR/BDR election. However, this process only works if there is a stringent plan for setting the router ID on all routers. In large networks, this can be cumbersome.

Instead of relying on the router ID, it is better to control the election by setting interface priorities. Priorities are an interface-specific value, which means it provides better control on a multiaccess network. This also allows a router to be the DR in one network and a DROTHER in another.

To set the priority of an interface, use the following commands:

- `ip ospf priority` value - OSPFv2 interface command
- `ipv6 ospf priority` value - OSPFv3 interface command

The value can be:

■ **0**- Does not become a DR or BDR.

■ **1 – 255** - The higher the priority value, the more likely the router becomes the DR or BDR on the interface.

In the figure, all routers have an equal OSPF priority because the priority value defaults to 1 for all router interfaces. Therefore, the router ID is used to determine the DR (R3) and BDR (R2). Changing the priority value on an interface from 1 to a higher value, would enable the router to become a DR or BDR router during the next election.

If the interface priority is configured after OSPF is enabled, the administrator must shut down the OSPF process on all routers, and then re-enable the OSPF process, to force a new DR/BDR election.

Refer to
Online Course
for Illustration

5.1.2.9   Changing the OSPF Priority

In the topology in Figure 1, R3 is the DR and R2 is the BDR. It has been decided that:

■ R1 should be the DR and will be configured with a priority of 255.

■ R2 should be the BDR and will be left with the default priority of 1.

■ R3 should never be a DR or BDR and will be configured with a priority of 0.

Figure 2 changes the R1 interface Gigabit 0/0 priority from 1 to 255.

Figure 3 changes the R3 interface Gigabit 0/0 priority from 1 to 0.

The changes do not automatically take effect because the DR and BDR are already elected. Therefore, the OSPF election must be negotiated using one of the following methods:

■ Shutdown the router interfaces and then re-enable them starting with the DR, then the BDR, and then all other routers.

■ Reset the OSPF process using the `clear ip ospf process` privileged EXEC mode command on all routers.

Figure 4 displays how to clear the OSPF process on R1. Assume that the `clear ip ospf process` privileged EXEC mode command has been also been configured on R2 and R3. Notice the OSPF state information generated.

The output displayed in Figure 5 confirms that R1 is now the DR with a priority of 255 and identifies the new neighbor adjacencies of R1.

Use the Syntax Checker in Figure 6 to verify the role and adjacencies of R2 and R3.

Refer to
Interactive Graphic
in online course.

5.1.2.10   Activity - Identify OSPF Network Type Terminology

Refer to
Interactive Graphic
in online course.

5.1.2.11   Activity - Select the Designated Router

Refer to **Packet
Tracer Activity**
for this chapter

5.1.2.12   Packet Tracer - Determining the DR and BDR

Background/Scenario

In this activity, you will examine DR and BDR roles and watch the roles change when there is a change in the network. You will then modify the priority to control the roles and force a new election. Finally, you will verify routers are filling the desired roles.

Refer to
Lab Activity
for this chapter

5.1.2.13   Lab - Configuring OSPFv2 on a Multiaccess Network

In this lab, you will complete the following objectives:

- Part 1: Build the Network and Configure Basic Device Settings

- Part 2: Configure and Verify OSPFv2 on the DR, BDR, and DROther

- Part 3: Configure OSPFv2 Interface Priority to Determine the DR and BDR

Refer to
Online Course
for Illustration

5.1.3   Default Route Propagation

5.1.3.1   Propagating a Default Static Route in OSPFv2

Propagating a Default Static Route

With OSPF, the router connected to the Internet is used to propagate a default route to other routers in the OSPF routing domain. This router is sometimes called the edge, the entrance, or the gateway router. However, in OSPF terminology, the router located between an OSPF routing domain and a non-OSPF network is also called the autonomous system boundary router (ASBR).

In Figure 1, R2 is single-homed to a service provider. Therefore, all that is required for R2 to reach the Internet is a default static route to the service provider.

Note   In this example, a loopback interface with IP address 209.165.200.225 is used to simulate the connection to the service provider.

To propagate a default route, the edge router (R2) must be configured with:

- A default static route using the `ip route 0.0.0.0 0.0.0.0` {ip-address | exit-intf} command.

- The `default-information originate` router configuration mode command. This instructs R2 to be the source of the default route information and propagate the default static route in OSPF updates.

Figure 2 shows how to configure a fully-specified default static route to the service provider.

Refer to
Online Course
for Illustration

5.1.3.2   Verifying the Propagated Default Route

Verify the default route settings on R2 using the `show ip route` command, as shown in Figure 1.

Use the Syntax Checker in Figure 2 to verify that the default route has been propagated to R1 and R3. Notice that the route source is `O*E2`, signifying that it was learned using OSPF.

The asterisk identifies this as a good candidate for the default route. The E2 designation identifies that it is an external route.

External routes are either external type 1 or external type 2. The difference between the two is in the way the cost (metric) of the route is being calculated. The cost of a type 2 route is always the external cost, regardless of the interior cost to reach that route. A type 1 cost is the addition of the external cost and the internal cost used to reach that route. A type 1 route is always preferred over a type 2 route for the same destination.

Refer to **Online Course** for Illustration

5.1.3.3   Propagating a Default Static Route in OSPFv3

The process of propagating a default static route in OSPFv3 is almost identical to OSPFv2.

In Figure 1, R2 is single-homed to a service provider. Therefore, all that is required for R2 to reach the Internet is a default static route to the service provider.

Note   In this example, a loopback interface with the IP address of 2001:DB8:FEED:1::1/64 is used to simulate the connection to the service provider.

Figure 2 displays the current IPv6 routing table of R1. Notice that it has no knowledge of the route to the Internet.

To propagate a default route, the edge router (R2) must be configured with:

■ A default static route using the `ipv6 route ::/0` {ipv6-address | exit-intf} command.

■ The `default-information originate` router configuration mode command. This instructs R2 to be the source of the default route information and propagate the default static route in OSPF updates.

The example in Figure 3 configures a fully-specified default static route to the service provider.

Refer to **Online Course** for Illustration

5.1.3.4   Verifying the Propagated IPv6 Default Route

Verify the default static route setting on R2 using the `show ipv6 route` command, as shown in Figure 1.

Use the Syntax Checker in Figure 2 to verify that the default route has been propagated to R1 and R3. Notice that the route source is `OE2` signifying that it was learned using OSPFv3. The E2 designation identifies that it is external route.

Unlike the IPv4 routing table, IPv6 does not use the asterisk to signify that the route is a good candidate for the default route.

Refer to **Packet Tracer Activity** for this chapter

5.1.3.5   Packet Tracer - Propagating a Default Route in OSPFv2

Background/Scenario

In this activity, you will configure an IPv4 default route to the Internet and propagate that default route to other OSPF routers. You will then verify the default route is in downstream routing tables and that hosts can now access a web server on the Internet.

Refer to
Online Course
for Illustration

5.1.4   Fine-tuning OSPF Interfaces

5.1.4.1   OSPF Hello and Dead Intervals

The OSPF Hello and Dead intervals are configurable on a per-interface basis. The OSPF intervals must match or a neighbor adjacency does not occur.

To verify the currently configured interface intervals, use the `show ip ospf interface` command, as shown in Figure 1. The Serial 0/0/0 Hello and Dead intervals are set to the default 10 seconds and 40 seconds respectively.

Figure 2 provides an example of using a filtering technique to display the OSPF intervals for the OSPF enabled interface Serial 0/0/0 on R1.

In Figure 3, the `show ip ospf neighbor` command is used on R1 to verify that R1 is adjacent to R2 and R3. Notice in the output that the Dead Time is counting down from 40 seconds. By default, this value is refreshed every 10 seconds when R1 receives a Hello from the neighbor.

Refer to
Online Course
for Illustration

5.1.4.2   Modifying OSPFv2 Intervals

It may be desirable to change the OSPF timers so that routers detect network failures in less time. Doing this increases traffic, but sometimes the need for quick convergence is more important than the extra traffic it creates.

Note   The default Hello and Dead intervals are based on best practices and should only be altered in rare situations.

OSPF Hello and Dead intervals can be modified manually using the following interface configuration mode commands:

■   `ip ospf hello-interval` seconds

■   `ip ospf dead-interval` seconds

Use the `no ip ospf hello-interval` and `no ip ospf dead-interval` commands to reset the intervals to their default.

The example in Figure 1 modifies the Hello interval to 5 seconds. Immediately after changing the Hello interval, the Cisco IOS automatically modifies the Dead interval to four times the Hello interval. However, it is always good practice to explicitly modify the timer instead of relying on an automatic IOS feature so that modifications are documented in the configuration. Therefore, the Dead interval is also manually set to 20 seconds on the R1 Serial 0/0/0 interface.

As displayed by the highlighted OSPFv2 adjacency message in Figure 1, when the Dead Timer on R1 expires, R1 and R2 lose adjacency. The reason is because the values have only been altered on one side of the serial link between R1 and R2. Recall that the OSPF Hello and Dead intervals must match between neighbors.

Use the `show ip ospf neighbor` command on R1 to verify the neighbor adjacencies, as shown in Figure 2. Notice that the only neighbor listed is the 3.3.3.3 (R3) router and that R1 is no longer adjacent with the 2.2.2.2 (R2) neighbor. The timers set on Serial 0/0/0 do not affect the neighbor adjacency with R3.

To restore adjacency between R1 and R2, the R2 Serial 0/0/0 interface Hello interval is set to `5` seconds, as shown in Figure 3. Almost immediately, the IOS displays a message that adjacency has been established with a state of `FULL`.

Verify the interface intervals using the `show ip ospf interface` command, as shown in Figure 4. Notice that the Hello time is 5 seconds and that the Dead Time was automatically set to 20 seconds instead of the default 40 seconds. Remember that the OSPF automatically sets the Dead interval to four times the Hello interval.

5.1.4.3   Modifying OSPFv3 Intervals

Refer to
Online Course
for Illustration

Like OSPFv2, OSPFv3 intervals can also be adjusted.

OSPFv3 Hello and Dead intervals can be modified manually using the following interface configuration mode commands:

- `ipv6 ospf hello-interval` seconds

- `ipv6 ospf dead-interval` seconds

Note   Use the `no ipv6 ospf hello-interval` and `no ipv6 ospf dead-interval` commands to reset the intervals to their default.

Refer to the IPv6 topology in Figure 1. Assume that the network has converged using OSPFv3.

The example in Figure 2 modifies the OSPFv3 Hello interval to `5` seconds. Immediately after changing the Hello interval, the Cisco IOS automatically modifies the Dead interval to four times the Hello interval. However, as with OSPFv2, it is always good practice to explicitly modify the timer instead of relying on an automatic IOS feature so that modifications are documented in the configuration. Therefore, the Dead interval is also manually set to `20` seconds on the R1 Serial 0/0/0 interface.

Once the Dead Timer on R1 expires, R1 and R2 lose adjacency, as displayed by the highlighted OSPFv3 adjacency message in Figure 2, because the values have only been altered on one side of the serial link between R1 and R2. Recall that the OSPFv3 Hello and Dead intervals must be equivalent between neighbors.

Use the `show ipv6 ospf neighbor` command on R1 to verify the neighbor adjacencies (Figure 3). Notice that R1 is no longer adjacent with the 2.2.2.2 (R2) neighbor.

To restore adjacency between R1 and R2, the R2 Serial 0/0/0 interface Hello interval is set to `5` seconds (Figure 4). Almost immediately, the IOS displays a message that adjacency has been established with a state of `FULL`.

Verify the interface intervals using the `show ipv6 ospf interface` command (Figure 5). Notice that the Hello time is `5` seconds and that the Dead Time was automatically set to `20` seconds instead of the default `40` seconds. Remember that the OSPF automatically sets the Dead interval to four times the Hello interval.

Refer to
Online Course
for Illustration

5.1.5 Secure OSPF

5.1.5.1 Routers are Targets

The role of routers in a network is so crucial that they are often the targets of network attacks. Network administrators must be aware that routers are at risk from attack just as much as end-user systems.

In general, routing systems can be attacked by disrupting the routing peers or by falsifying the information carried within the routing protocol. Falsified routing information may generally be used to cause systems to misinform (lie to) each other, cause a denial-of-service (DoS) attack, or cause traffic to follow a path it would not normally follow. The consequences of falsifying routing information are:

- Redirecting traffic to create routing loops
- Redirecting traffic so it can be monitored on an insecure link
- Redirecting traffic to discard it

Click the Play button in the animation to see an example of an attack that creates a routing loop. An attacker has been able to connect directly to the link between routers R1 and R2. The attacker injects false routing information destined to router R1 only, indicating that R2 is the preferred destination to the 192.168.10.10/32 host route. Although R1 has a routing table entry to the directly connected 192.168.10.0/24 network, it adds the injected route to its routing table because of the longer subnet mask. A route with a longer matching subnet mask is considered to be superior to a route with a shorter subnet mask. Consequently, when a router receives a packet, it selects the longer subnet mask, because it is a more precise route to the destination.

When PC3 sends a packet to PC1 (192.168.10.10/24), R1 does not forward the packet to the PC1 host. Instead, it routes the packet to router R2, because the apparent best path to 192.168.10.10/32 is through R2. When R2 gets the packet, it looks in its routing table and forwards the packet back to R1, which creates the loop.

To mitigate against routing protocol attacks, configure OSPF authentication.

Refer to
Online Course
for Illustration

5.1.5.2 Secure Routing Updates

When neighbor authentication has been configured on a router, the router authenticates the source of each routing update packet that it receives. This is accomplished by the exchange of an authenticating key (sometimes referred to as a password) that is known to both the sending and the receiving router.

To exchange routing update information in a secure manner, enable OSPF authentication. OSPF authentication can either be none (or null), simple, or Message Digest 5 (MD5).

OSPF supports 3 types of authentication:

- **Null**- This is the default method and means that no authentication is used for OSPF.
- **Simple password authentication**- This is also referred to as plaintext authentication because the password in the update is sent in plaintext over the network. This is considered to be a legacy method of OSPF authentication.

■ **MD5 authentication**- This is the most secure and recommended method of authentication. MD5 authentication provides higher security because the password is never exchanged between peers. Instead it is calculated using the MD5 algorithm. Matching results authenticate the sender.

Click the Play button in the animation to see how MD5 authentication is used to authenticate neighboring peer messages.

Note RIPv2, EIGRP, OSPF, IS-IS, and BGP all support various forms of MD5 authentication.

Refer to **Online Course** for Illustration

5.1.5.3   MD5 Authentication

The following example illustrates how MD5 authentication is used to authenticate two neighboring OSPF routers.

In Figure 1, R1 combines the routing message with the pre-shared secret key and calculates the signature using the MD5 algorithm. The signature is also known as a hash value.

In Figure 2, R1 adds the signature to the routing message and sends it to R2.

MD5 does not encrypt the message; therefore, the content is easily readable.

In Figure 3, R2 opens the packet, combines the routing message with the pre-shared secret key and calculates the signature using the MD5 algorithm.

■ If the signatures match, then R2 accepts the routing update.

■ If the signatures do not match, then R2 discards the update.

OSPFv3 (OSPF for IPv6) does not include any authentication capabilities of its own. Instead it relies entirely on IPSec to secure communications between neighbors using the `ipv6 ospf authentication ipsec spi` interface configuration mode command. This is beneficial in simplifying the OSPFv3 protocol and standardizing its authentication mechanism.

Refer to **Online Course** for Illustration

5.1.5.4   Configuring OSPF MD5 Authentication

OSPF supports routing protocol authentication using MD5. MD5 authentication can be enabled globally for all interfaces or on a per-interface basis.

To enable OSPF MD5 authentication globally, configure:

■ `ip ospf message-digest-key` key `md5` password interface configuration mode command.

■ `area` area-id `authentication message-digest` router configuration mode command.

This method forces authentication on all OSPF enabled interfaces. If an interface is not configured with the `ip ospf message-digest-key` command, it will not be able to form adjacencies with other OSPF neighbors.

To provide more flexibility, authentication is now supported on a per-interface basis. To enable MD5 authentication on a per-interface basis, configure:

- `ip ospf message-digest-key` key `md5` password interface configuration mode command.

- `ip ospf authentication message-digest` interface configuration mode command.

Global and per-interface OSPF MD5 authentication can be used on the same router. However, the interface setting overrides the global setting. MD5 authentication passwords do not have to be the same throughout an area; however, they do need to be the same between neighbors.

For example, assume that all routers in the figure have converged using OSPF and routing is functioning properly. OSPF authentication will be implemented on all routers.

Refer to **Online Course** for Illustration

5.1.5.5   OSPF MD5 Authentication Example

The example in Figure 1 configures R1 to enable OSPF MD5 authentication on all interfaces. Notice the informational messages stating that the OSPF neighbor adjacencies with R2 and R3 have changed to the Down state, because R2 and R3 have not yet been configured to support MD5 authentication.

As an alternative to globally enabling MD5 authentication, the example in Figure 2 demonstrates how to configure R1 to enable OSPF MD5 authentication on a per-interface basis. Again, notice how the OSPF neighbor adjacencies have changed to the Down state.

Use the Syntax Checker in Figure 3 to enable OSPF MD5 authentication globally on R2 and per interface on R3.

Again, informational messages appear. The first message is because the neighbor adjacency with R1 has been re-established. However, the adjacency with R3 has transitioned to the Down state, because R3 is still not configured

After R3 is configured, all neighbor adjacencies have been re-established.

Refer to **Online Course** for Illustration

5.1.5.6   Verifying OSPF MD5 Authentication

To verify that OSPF MD5 authentication is enabled, use the **show ip ospf interface** privileged EXEC mode command. By verifying that the routing table is complete successful authentication can be confirmed.

Figure 1 verifies the OSPF MD5 authentication on the serial 0/0/0 interface on R1.

Figure 2 confirms that the authentication is successful.

Use the Syntax Checker in Figure 3 to verify the OSPF MD5 authentication on R2 and R3.

Refer to **Packet Tracer Activity** for this chapter

5.1.5.7   Packet Tracer - Configuring OSPFv2 Advance Features

Background/Scenario

In this activity, OSPF is already configured and all end devices currently have full connectivity. You will modify the default OSPF routing configuration by changing the Hello and Dead timers, adjusting the bandwidth of a link, and enabling OSPF authentication. Then you will verify that full connectivity is restored for all end devices.

Refer to
Lab Activity
for this chapter

5.1.5.8   Lab - Configuring OSPFv2 Advance Features

In this lab, you will complete the following objectives:

- Part 1: Build the Network and Configure Basic Device Settings

- Part 2: Configure and Verify OSPF Routing

- Part 3: Change OSPF Metrics

- Part 4: Configure and Propagate a Static Default Route

- Part 5: Configure OSPF Authentication

Refer to
Online Course
for Illustration

5.2   Troubleshooting Single-Area OSPF Implementations

5.2.1   Components of Troubleshooting Single-Area OSPF

5.2.1.1   Overview

OSPF is a popularly implemented routing protocol used in large enterprise networks. Troubleshooting problems related to the exchange of routing information is one of the most essential skills for a network professional that is involved in the implementation and maintenance of large, routed enterprise networks that use OSPF as the IGP.

Issues with forming OSPF adjacencies are listed in the figure.

Refer to
Online Course
for Illustration

5.2.1.2   OSPF States

To troubleshoot OSPF, it is important to understand how OSPF routers traverse different OSPF states when adjacencies are being established.

The figure lists the OSPF states and provides a summary of functions of each state.

When troubleshooting OSPF neighbors, be aware that the FULL or 2WAY states are normal. All other states are transitory; that is, the router should not remain in those states for extended periods of time.

Refer to
Online Course
for Illustration

5.2.1.3   OSPF Troubleshooting Commands

There are many different OSPF commands that can be used to help in the troubleshooting process. The following summarizes the most common of these commands:

- `show ip protocols` (Figure 1) - Used to verify vital OSPF configuration information, including the OSPF process ID, the router ID, networks the router is advertising, the neighbors the router is receiving updates from, and the default administrative distance, which is 110 for OSPF.

- `show ip ospf neighbor` (Figure 2) - Used to verify that the router has formed an adjacency with its neighboring routers. Displays the neighbor router ID, neighbor priority, OSPF state, Dead timer, neighbor interface IP address, and interface that the neighbor is accessible through. If the router ID of the neighboring router is not displayed, or if it does not show as a state of FULL or 2WAY, the two routers have not formed an OSPF adjacency. If two routers do not establish adjacency, link-state information will not be exchanged. Incomplete link-state databases can cause inaccurate SPF trees and routing tables. Routes to destination networks may not exist or may not be the most optimum path.

■ `show ip ospf interface` (Figure 3) - Used to display the OSPF parameters configured on an interface, such as the OSPF process ID that the interface is assigned to, the area that the interfaces are in, the cost of the interface, and the Hello and Dead intervals. Adding the interface name and number to the command displays output for a specific interface.

■ `show ip ospf` (Figure 4) - Used to examine the OSPF process ID and router ID. Additionally, this command displays the OSPF area information, as well as the last time the SPF algorithm was calculated.

■ `show ip route ospf` (Figure 5) - Used to display only the OSPF learned routes in the routing table. The output shows that R1 has learned about four remote networks through OSPF.

■ `clear ip ospf` [process-id] `process` - Used to reset the OSPFv2 neighbor adjacencies.

5.2.1.4 Components of Troubleshooting OSPF

Refer to **Online Course** for Illustration

As shown in the figure, OSPF problems usually relate to:

■ Neighbor adjacencies

■ Missing routes

■ Path selection

When troubleshooting neighbor issues, verify if the router has established adjacencies with neighboring routers using the `show ip ospf neighbors` command. If there is no adjacency, then the routers cannot exchange routes. Verify if interfaces are operational and enabled for OSPF using the `show ip interface brief` and the `show ip ospf interface` commands. If the interfaces are operational and enabled for OSPF, ensure that interfaces on both routers are configured for the same OSPF area and the interfaces are not configured as passive interfaces.

If adjacency between two routers is established, verify that there are OSPF routes in the routing table using the `show ip route ospf` command. If there are no OSPF routes, verify that there are no other routing protocols with lower administrative distances running in the network. Verify if all of the required networks are advertised into OSPF. Also verify if an access list is configured on a router that would filter either incoming or outgoing routing updates.

If all of the required routes are in the routing table, but the path that traffic takes is not correct, verify the OSPF cost on interfaces on the path. Also be careful in cases where the interfaces are faster than 100 Mb/s, because all interfaces above this bandwidth have the same OSPF cost, by default.

Refer to **Interactive Graphic** in online course.

5.2.1.5   Activity - Identify the Troubleshooting Command

Refer to **Online Course** for Illustration

5.2.2   Troubleshoot Single-Area OSPFv2 Routing Issues

5.2.2.1   Troubleshooting Neighbor Issues

This example will highlight how to troubleshoot neighbor problems. In the topology in Figure 1, all of the routers have been configured to support OSPF routing.

A quick look at the R1 routing table, as shown in Figure 2, reveals that it is not adding any OSPF routes. There are multiple reasons why this could be. However, a prerequisite for the neighbor relationship to form between two routers is OSI Layer 3 connectivity.

The output in Figure 3 confirms that the S0/0/0 interface is up and active. The successful ping also confirms that the R2 serial interface is active. A successful ping does not mean an adjacency will form because it is possible to have overlapping subnets. You still have to verify that interfaces on the connected devices share the same subnet. If the ping was not successful, check the cabling and verify that interfaces on connected devices are configured correctly and operational.

For an interface to be enabled for OSPF, a matching `network` command must be configured under the OSPF routing process. Active OSPF interfaces can be verified using the `show ip ospf interface` command. The output in Figure 4 verifies that the Serial 0/0/0 interface is enabled for OSPF. If connected interfaces on two routers are not enabled for OSPF, the neighbors will not form an adjacency.

Verify the OSPF settings using the `show ip protocols` command. The output displayed in Figure 5 verifies that OSPF is enabled and also lists the networks being advertised as enabled by the `network` command. If an IP address on an interface falls within a network that has been enabled for OSPF, the interface will be enabled for OSPF.

However, notice that the Serial 0/0/0 interface is listed as passive. Recall that the `passive-interface` command stops both outgoing and incoming routing updates because the effect of the command causes the router to stop sending and receiving Hello packets over an interface. For this reason, the routers will not become neighbors.

To disable the interface as passive, use the `no passive-interface` router configuration mode command as shown in Figure 6. After you disable the passive interface, the routers become adjacent as indicated by automatically generated information message.

A quick verification of the routing table as shown in Figure 7 confirms that OSPF is now exchanging routing information.

Another problem that may arise is when two neighboring routers have mismatched MTU sizes on their connecting interfaces. The MTU size is the largest network layer packet that the router will forward out each interface. Routers default to an MTU size of 1500 bytes. However, this value can be changed for IPv4 packets using the `ip mtu` size interface configuration command or the `ipv6 mtu` size interface command for IPv6 packets. If two connecting routers had mismatched MTU values, they would still attempt to form an adjacency but they would not exchange their LSDBs and the neighbor relationship would fail.

Refer to
Online Course
for Illustration

5.2.2.2 Troubleshooting OSPF Routing Table Issues

In the topology in Figure 1, all of the routers have been configured to support OSPF routing.

A quick look at the R1 routing table (Figure 2) reveals that it receives default route information, the R2 LAN (172.16.2.0/24) and the link between R2 and R3 (192.168.10.8/30). However, it does not receive the R3 LAN OSPF route.

The output in Figure 3 verifies the OSPF settings on R3. Notice that R3 only advertises the link between R3 and R2. It does not advertise the R3 LAN (192.168.1.0/24).

For an interface to be enabled for OSPF, a matching `network` command must be configured under the OSPF routing process. The output in Figure 4 confirms that the R3 LAN is not advertised in OSPF.

The example in Figure 5 adds a `network` command for the R3 LAN. R3 should now advertise the R3 LAN to its OSPF neighbors.

The output in Figure 6 verifies that the R3 LAN is now in the routing table of R1.

Refer to **Packet Tracer Activity** for this chapter

5.2.2.3 Packet Tracer - Troubleshooting Single-Area OSPFv2

Background/Scenario

In this activity, you will troubleshoot OSPF routing issues using `ping` and `show` commands to identify errors in the network configuration. Then, you will document the errors you discover and implement an appropriate solution. Finally, you will verify end-to-end connectivity is restored.

Refer to
Online Course
for Illustration

5.2.3 Troubleshoot Single-Area OSPFv3 Routing Issues

5.2.3.1 OSPFv3 Troubleshooting Commands

Refer to Figure 1 for the OSPFv3 reference topology.

Troubleshooting OSPFv3 is almost identical to OSPFv2; therefore, many OSPFv3 commands and troubleshooting criteria also apply to OSPFv3.

For example, the following are the equivalent commands used with OSPFv3:

- `show ipv6 protocols` (Figure 2) - This command is used to verify vital OSPFv3 configuration information, including the OSPFv3 process ID, the router ID, and the interfaces the router is receiving updates from.

- `show ipv6 ospf neighbor` (Figure 3) - Used to verify that the router has formed an adjacency with its neighboring routers. This output displays the neighbor router ID, the neighbor priority, OSPFv3 state, dead timer, neighbor interface ID, and the interface that the neighbor is accessible through. If the router ID of the neighboring router is not displayed, or if it does not show as a state of `FULL` or `2WAY`, the two routers have not formed an OSPFv3 adjacency. If two routers do not establish adjacency, link-state information will not be exchanged. Incomplete link-state databases can cause inaccurate SPF trees and routing tables. Routes to destination networks may not exist, or they may not be the most optimum paths.

- **`show ipv6 ospf interface`** (Figure 4) - Used to display the OSPFv3 parameters configured on an interface, such as the OSPFv3 process ID that the interface is assigned to, area that the interfaces are in, and cost of the interface, and the Hello and Dead intervals. Adding the interface name and number to the command displays output for a specific interface.

- **`show ipv6 ospf`** (Figure 5) - Used to examine the OSPF process ID and router ID, as well as information about the LSA transmissions.

- **`show ipv6 route ospf`** (Figure 6) - Used to display only the OSPFv3 learned routes in the routing table. The output shows that R1 has learned about four remote networks through OSPFv3.

- **`clear ipv6 ospf`** [process-id] **`process`** - Used to reset the OSPFv3 neighbor adjacencies.

Refer to
Online Course
for Illustration

5.2.3.2   Troubleshooting OSPFv3

In the topology in Figure 1, all of the routers have been configured to support OSPFv3 routing.

A quick look at the R1 IPv6 routing table (Figure 2) reveals that it receives the default route, the R2 LAN (2001:DB8:CAFE:2::/64) and the link between R2 and R3 (2001:DB8:CAFE:A002::/64). However, it does not receive the R3 LAN OSPFv3 route (2001:DB8:CAFE:3::/64).

The output in Figure 3 verifies the OSPFv3 settings on R3. Notice that OSPF is only enabled on the Serial 0/0/1 interface. It appears that it is not enabled on the G0/0 R3 interface.

Unlike OSPFv2, OSPFV3 does not use the **`network`** command. Instead OSPFv3 is enabled directly on the interface. The output in Figure 4 confirms that the R3 interface is not enabled for OSPFv3.

The example in Figure 5 enables OSPFv3 on the R3 Gigabit Ethernet 0/0 interface. R3 should now advertise the R3 LAN to its OSPFv3 neighbors.

The output in Figure 6 verifies that the R3 LAN is now in the routing table of R1.

Refer to
Lab Activity
for this chapter

5.2.3.3   Lab - Troubleshooting Basic Single-Area OSPFv2 and OSPFv3

In this lab, you will complete the following objectives:

- Part 1: Build the Network and Load Device Configurations

- Part 2: Troubleshoot Layer 3 Connectivity

- Part 3: Troubleshoot OSPFv2

- Part 4: Troubleshoot OSPFv3

Refer to **Lab Activity** for this chapter

5.2.3.4 Lab - Troubleshooting Advanced Single-Area OSPFv2

In this lab, you will complete the following objectives:

- Part 1: Build the Network and Load Device Configurations
- Part 2: Troubleshoot OSPF

Refer to **Online Course** for Illustration

5.3 Summary

Refer to **Lab Activity** for this chapter

5.3.1.1 Class Activity - OSPF Troubleshooting Mastery

OSPF Troubleshooting Mastery

You have decided to change your routing protocol from RIPv2 to OSPFv2. Your small- to medium-sized business network topology will not change from its original physical settings. Use the diagram on the PDF for this activity as your company's small- to medium-sized business network design.

Your addressing design is complete and you then configure your routers with IPv4 and VLSM. OSPF has been applied as the routing protocol. However, some routers are sharing routing information with each other and some are not.

Open the PDF file that accompanies this modeling activity and follow the directions to complete the activity.

When the steps in the directions are complete, regroup as a class and compare recorded activity correction times. The group taking the shortest time to find and fix the configuration error will be declared the winner only after successfully explaining how they found the error, fixed it, and proved that the topology is now working.

Refer to **Packet Tracer Activity** for this chapter

5.3.1.2 Packet Tracer - Skills Integration Challenge

Background/Scenario

In this Skills Integration Challenge, your focus is OSPFv2 advanced configurations. IP addressing has been configured for all devices. You will configure OSPFv2 routing with passive interfaces and default route propagation. You will modify the OSPFv2 configuration by adjusting timers and establishing MD5 authentication. Finally, you will verify your configurations and test connectivity between end devices.

Refer to **Online Course** for Illustration

5.3.1.3 Summary

OSPF defines five network types: point-to-point, broadcast multiaccess, nonbroadcast multiaccess, point-to-multipoint, and virtual links.

Multiaccess networks can create two challenges for OSPF regarding the flooding of LSAs: creation of multiple adjacencies and extensive flooding of LSAs. The solution to managing the number of adjacencies and the flooding of LSAs on a multiaccess network is the DR and BDR. If the DR stops producing Hellos, the BDR promotes itself and assumes the role of DR.

The routers in the network elect the router with the highest interface priority as DR. The router with the second highest interface priority is elected the BDR. The higher the priority, the likelier the router will be selected as the DR. If set to 0, the router is not capable of becoming the DR. The default priority of multiaccess broadcast interfaces is 1. Therefore, unless otherwise configured, all routers have an equal priority value and must rely on another tie breaking method during the DR/BDR election. If the interface priorities are equal, then the router with the highest router ID is elected the DR. The router with the second highest router ID is the BDR. The addition of a new router does not initiate a new election process.

To propagate a default route in OSPF, the router must be configured with a default static route and the `default-information originate` command must be added to the configuration. Verify routes with the `show ip route` or `show ipv6 route` command.

To assist OSPF in making the correct path determination, the reference bandwidth must be changed to a higher value to accommodate networks with links faster than 100 Mb/s. To adjust the reference bandwidth, use the `auto-cost reference-bandwidth` Mbps router configuration mode command. To adjust the interface bandwidth, use the `bandwidth` kilobits interface configuration mode command. The cost can be manually configured on an interface using the `ip ospf cost` value interface configuration mode command.

The OSPF Hello and Dead intervals must match or a neighbor adjacency does not occur. To modify these intervals, use the following interface commands:

- `ip ospf hello-interval` seconds

- `ip ospf dead-interval` seconds

- `ipv6 ospf hello-interval` seconds

- `ipv6 ospf dead-interval` seconds

OSPF supports 3 types of authentication: null, simple password authentication, and MD5 authentication. OSPF MD5 authentication can be configured globally or per interface. To verify OSPF MD5 implementation is enabled, use the `show ip ospf interface` privileged EXEC mode command.

When troubleshooting OSPF neighbors, be aware that the FULL or 2WAY states are normal. The following commands summarize IPv4 OSPF troubleshooting:

- `show ip protocols`

- `show ip ospf neighbor`

- `show ip ospf interface`

- `show ip ospf`

- `show ip route ospf`

- `clear ip ospf` [process-id] `process`

Troubleshooting OSPFv3 is similar to OSPFv2. The following commands are the equivalent commands used with OSPFv3: `show ipv6 protocols`, `show ipv6 ospf neighbor`, `show ipv6 ospf interface`, `show ipv6 ospf`, `show ipv6 route ospf`, and `clear ipv6 ospf` [process-id] `process`.

Go to the online course to take the quiz and exam.

Chapter 5 Quiz

This quiz is designed to provide an additional opportunity to practice the skills and knowledge presented in the chapter and to prepare for the chapter exam. You will be allowed multiple attempts and the grade does not appear in the gradebook.

Chapter 5 Exam

The chapter exam assesses your knowledge of the chapter content.

Your Chapter Notes

6.0   Multiarea OSPF

6.0.1.1   Introduction

Multiarea OSPF is used to divide a large OSPF network. Too many routers in one area increase the load on the CPU and create a large link-state database. In this chapter, directions are provided to effectively partition a large single area into multiple areas. Area 0 used in a single-area OSPF is known as the backbone area.

Discussion is focused on the LSAs exchanged between areas. In addition, activities for configuring OSPFv2 and OSPFv3 are provided. The chapter concludes with the `show` commands used to verify OSPF configurations.

Refer to
Lab Activity
for this chapter

6.0.1.2   Class Activity - Leaving on a Jet Plane
Leaving on a Jet Plane

You and a classmate are starting a new airline to serve your continent.

In addition to your core area or headquarters airport, you will locate and map four intra-continental airport service areas and one transcontinental airport service area that can be used for additional source and destination travel.

Use the blank world map provided to design your airport locations. Additional instructions for completing this activity can be found in the accompanying PDF.

Refer to
Interactive Graphic
in online course.

6.1   Multiarea OSPF Operation

6.1.1   Why Multiarea OSPF?

6.1.1.1   Single-Area OSPF
Single-area OSPF is useful in smaller networks where the web of router links is not complex, and paths to individual destinations are easily deduced.

However, if an area becomes too big, the following issues must be addressed (see the figure for illustration):

- **Large routing table**- OSPF does not perform route summarization by default. If the routes are not summarized, the routing table can become very large, depending on the size of the network.

- **Large link-state database (LSDB)**- Because the LSDB covers the topology of the entire network, each router must maintain an entry for every network in the area, even if not every route is selected for the routing table.

- **Frequent SPF algorithm calculations**- In a large network, changes are inevitable, so the routers spend many CPU cycles recalculating the SPF algorithm and updating the routing table.

To make OSPF more efficient and scalable, OSPF supports hierarchical routing using areas. An OSPF area is a group of routers that share the same link-state information in their link-state databases.

Refer to **Online Course** for Illustration

6.1.1.2   Multiarea OSPF

When a large OSPF area is divided into smaller areas, this is called multiarea OSPF. Multiarea OSPF is useful in larger network deployments to reduce processing and memory overhead.

For instance, any time a router receives new information about the topology, as with additions, deletions, or modifications of a link, the router must rerun the SPF algorithm, create a new SPF tree, and update the routing table. The SPF algorithm is CPU-intensive and the time it takes for calculation depends on the size of the area. Too many routers in one area make the LSDB larger and increase the load on the CPU. Therefore, arranging routers into areas effectively partitions one potentially large database into smaller and more manageable databases.

Multiarea OSPF requires a hierarchical network design. The main area is called the backbone area (area 0) and all other areas must connect to the backbone area. With hierarchical routing, routing still occurs between the areas (interarea routing); while many of the tedious routing operations, such as recalculating the database, are kept within an area.

As illustrated in Figure 1, the hierarchical-topology possibilities of multiarea OSPF have these advantages:

- **Smaller routing tables**- There are fewer routing table entries as network addresses can be summarized between areas. For example, R1 summarizes the routes from area 1 to area 0 and R2 summarizes the routes from area 51 to area 0. R1 and R2 also propagate a default static route to area 1 and area 51.

- **Reduced link-state update overhead**- Minimizes processing and memory requirements, because there are fewer routers exchanging LSAs.

- **Reduced frequency of SPF calculations**- Localizes impact of a topology change within an area. For instance, it minimizes routing update impact, because LSA flooding stops at the area boundary.

In Figure 2, assume a link fails between two internal routers in area 51. Only the routers in area 51 exchange LSAs and rerun the SPF algorithm for this event. R1 does not receive LSAs from area 51 and does not recalculate the SPF algorithm.

Refer to
Online Course
for Illustration

6.1.1.3   OSPF Two-Layer Area Hierarchy

Multiarea OSPF is implemented in a two-layer area hierarchy:

- **Backbone (Transit) area**- An OSPF area whose primary function is the fast and efficient movement of IP packets. Backbone areas interconnect with other OSPF area types. Generally, end users are not found within a backbone area. The backbone area is also called OSPF area 0. Hierarchical networking defines area 0 as the core to which all other areas directly connect. (Figure 1)

- **Regular (Non-backbone) area** - Connects users and resources. Regular areas are usually set up along functional or geographical groupings. By default, a regular area does not allow traffic from another area to use its links to reach other areas. All traffic from other areas must cross a transit area. (Figure 2)

Note   A regular area can have a number of subtypes, including a standard area, stub area, totally stubby area, and not-so-stubby area (NSSA). Stub, totally stubby, and NSSAs are beyond the scope of this chapter.

OSPF enforces this rigid two-layer area hierarchy. The underlying physical connectivity of the network must map to the two-layer area structure, with all non-backbone areas attaching directly to area 0. All traffic moving from one area to another area must traverse the backbone area. This traffic is referred to as interarea traffic.

The optimal number of routers per area varies based on factors such as network stability, but Cisco recommends the following guidelines:

- An area should have no more than 50 routers.

- A router should not be in more than three areas.

- Any single router should not have more than 60 neighbors.

Refer to
Online Course
for Illustration

6.1.1.4   Types of OSPF Routers

OSPF routers of different types control the traffic that goes in and out of areas. The OSPF routers are categorized based on the function they perform in the routing domain.

There are four different types of OSPF routers:

- **Internal router** – This is a router that has all of its interfaces in the same area. All internal routers in an area have identical LSDBs. (Figure 1)

- **Backbone router** – This is a router in the backbone area. Generally, the backbone area is set to area 0. (Figure 2)

- **Area Border Router (ABR)** – This is a router that has interfaces attached to multiple areas. It must maintain separate LSDBs for each area it is connected to, and can route between areas. ABRs are exit points for the area, which means that routing information destined for another area can get there only via the ABR of the local area. ABRs can be configured to summarize the routing information from the LSDBs of their attached areas. ABRs distribute the routing information into the backbone. The backbone routers then forward the information to the other ABRs. In a multiarea network, an area can have one or more ABRs. (Figure 3)

■ **Autonomous System Boundary Router (ASBR)** – This is a router that has at least one interface attached to an external internetwork (another autonomous system), such as a non-OSPF network. An ASBR can import non-OSPF network information to the OSPF network, and vice versa, using a process called route redistribution. (Figure 4)

Redistribution in multiarea OSPF occurs when an ASBR connects different routing domains (e.g., EIGRP and OSPF) and configures them to exchange and advertise routing information between those routing domains.

A router can be classified as more than one router type. For example, if a router connects to area 0 and area 1, and in addition, maintains routing information for another, non-OSPF network, it falls under three different classifications: a backbone router, an ABR, and an ASBR.

Refer to
Interactive Graphic
in online course.

6.1.1.5 Activity - Identify the Multiarea OSPF Terminology

Refer to
Online Course
for Illustration

6.1.2 Multiarea OSPF LSA Operation

6.1.2.1 OSPF LSA Types

LSAs are the building blocks of the OSPF LSDB. Individually, they act as database records and provide specific OSPF network details. In combination, they describe the entire topology of an OSPF network or area.

The RFCs for OSPF currently specify up to 11 different LSA types (Figure 1). However, any implementation of multiarea OSPF must support the first five LSAs: LSA 1 to LSA 5 (Figure 2). The focus of this topic is on these first five LSAs.

Each router link is defined as an LSA type. The LSA includes a link ID field that identifies, by network number and mask, the object to which the link connects. Depending on the type, the link ID has different meanings. LSAs differ on how they are generated and propagated within the routing domain.

Note OSPFv3 includes additional LSA types.

Refer to
Online Course
for Illustration

6.1.2.2 OSPF LSA Type 1

As shown in the figure, all routers advertise their directly connected OSPF-enabled links in a type 1 LSA and forward their network information to OSPF neighbors. The LSA contains a list of the directly connected interfaces, link types, and link states.

Type 1 LSAs are also referred to as router link entries.

Type 1 LSAs are flooded only within the area in which they originated. ABRs subsequently advertise the networks learned from the type 1 LSAs to other areas as type 3 LSAs.

The type 1 LSA link ID is identified by the router ID of the originating router.

Refer to
Online Course
for Illustration

6.1.2.3 OSPF LSA Type 2

A type 2 LSA only exists for multiaccess and non-broadcast multiaccess (NBMA) networks where there is a DR elected and at least two routers on the multiaccess segment. The type 2 LSA contains the router ID and IP address of the DR, along with the router ID of all other routers on the multiaccess segment. A type 2 LSA is created for every multiaccess network in the area.

The purpose of a type 2 LSA is to give other routers information about multiaccess networks within the same area.

The DR floods type 2 LSAs only within the area in which they originated. Type 2 LSAs are not forwarded outside of an area.

Type 2 LSAs are also referred to as network link entries.

As shown in the figure, ABR1 is the DR for the Ethernet network in area 1. It generates the type 2 LSA and forwards it into area 1. ABR2 is the DR for the multiaccess network in area 0. There are no multiaccess networks in area 2 and therefore, no type 2 LSAs are ever propagated in that area.

The link-state ID for a network LSA is the IP interface address of the DR that advertises it.

Refer to **Online Course** for Illustration

6.1.2.4   OSPF LSA Type 3

Type 3 LSAs are used by ABRs to advertise networks from other areas. ABRs collect type 1 LSAs in the LSDB. After an OSPF area has converged, the ABR creates a type 3 LSA for each of its learned OSPF networks. Therefore, an ABR with many OSPF routes must create type 3 LSAs for each network.

As shown in the figure, ABR1 and ABR2 floods type 3 LSAs from one area to other areas. The ABRs propagate the type 3 LSAs into other areas. In a large OSPF deployment with many networks, propagating type 3 LSAs can cause significant flooding problems. For this reason, it is strongly recommended that manual route summarization be configured on the ABR.

The link-state ID is set to the network number and the mask is also advertised.

Receiving a type 3 LSA into its area does not cause a router to run the SPF algorithm. The routes being advertised in the type 3 LSAs are appropriately added to or deleted from the router's routing table, but a full SPF calculation is not necessary.

Refer to **Online Course** for Illustration

6.1.2.5   OSPF LSA Type 4

Type 4 and type 5 LSAs are used collectively to identify an ASBR and advertise external networks into an OSPF routing domain.

A type 4 summary LSA is generated by an ABR only when an ASBR exists within an area. A type 4 LSA identifies the ASBR and provides a route to it. All traffic destined to an external autonomous system requires routing table knowledge of the ASBR that originated the external routes.

As shown in the figure, the ASBR sends a type 1 LSA, identifying itself as an ASBR. The LSA includes a special bit known as the external bit (e bit) that is used to identify the router as an ASBR. When ABR1 receives the type 1 LSA, it notices the e bit, it builds a type 4 LSA, and then floods the type 4 LSA to the backbone (area 0). Subsequent ABRs flood the type 4 LSA into other areas.

The link-state ID is set to the ASBR router ID.

Refer to
Online Course
for Illustration

6.1.2.6   OSPF LSA Type 5

Type 5 external LSAs describe routes to networks outside the OSPF autonomous system. Type 5 LSAs are originated by the ASBR and are flooded to the entire autonomous system.

Type 5 LSAs are also referred to as autonomous system external LSA entries.

In the figure, the ASBR generates type 5 LSAs for each of its external routes and floods it into the area. Subsequent ABRs also flood the type 5 LSA into other areas. Routers in other areas use the information from the type 4 LSA to reach the external routes.

In a large OSPF deployment with many networks, propagating multiple type 5 LSAs can cause significant flooding problems. For this reason, it is strongly recommended that manual route summarization be configured on the ASBR.

The link-state ID is the external network number.

Refer to
Interactive Graphic
in online course.

6.1.2.7   Activity - Identify the OSPF LSA Type

Refer to
Online Course
for Illustration

6.1.3   OSPF Routing Table and Types of Routes

6.1.3.1   OSPF Routing Table Entries

Figure 1 provides a sample routing table for a multiarea OSPF topology with a link to an external non-OSPF network. OSPF routes in an IPv4 routing table are identified using the following descriptors:

- O- Router (type 1) and network (type 2) LSAs describe the details within an area. The routing table reflects this link-state information with a designation of **O**, meaning that the route is intra-area.

- O IA- When an ABR receives summary LSAs, it adds them to its LSDB and regenerates them into the local area. When an ABR receives external LSAs, it adds them to its LSDB and floods them into the area. The internal routers then assimilate the information into their databases. Summary LSAs appear in the routing table as IA (interarea routes).

- O E1 or O E2 - External LSAs appear in the routing table marked as external type 1 (E1) or external type 2 (E2) routes.

Figure 2 displays an IPv6 routing table with OSPF router, interarea, and external routing table entries.

Refer to
Online Course
for Illustration

6.1.3.2   OSPF Route Calculation

Each router uses the SPF algorithm against the LSDB to build the SPF tree. The SPF tree is used to determine the best paths.

As shown in the figure, the order in which the best paths are calculated is as follows:

1. All routers calculate the best paths to destinations within their area (intra-area) and add these entries to the routing table. These are the type 1 and type 2 LSAs, which are noted in the routing table with a routing designator of O. (1)

2. All routers calculate the best paths to the other areas within the internetwork. These best paths are the interarea route entries, or type 3 and type 4 LSAs, and are noted with a routing designator of O IA. (2)

3. All routers (except those that are in a form of stub area) calculate the best paths to the external autonomous system (type 5) destinations. These are noted with either an O E1 or an O E2 route designator, depending on the configuration. (3)

When converged, a router can communicate with any network within or outside the OSPF autonomous system.

Refer to **Interactive Graphic** in online course.

6.1.3.3   Activity - Order the Steps for OSPF Best Path Calculations

Refer to **Online Course** for Illustration

6.2   Configuring Multiarea OSPF

6.2.1   Configuring Multiarea OSPF

6.2.1.1   Implementing Multiarea OSPF

OSPF can be implemented as single-area or multiarea. The type of OSPF implementation chosen depends on the specific requirements and existing topology.

There are 4 steps to implementing multiarea OSPF, as displayed in the figure.

Steps 1 and 2 are part of the planning process.

Step 1.   **Gather the network requirements and parameters -** This includes determining the number of host and network devices, the IP addressing scheme (if already implemented), the size of the routing domain, the size of the routing tables, the risk of topology changes, and other network characteristics.

Step 2.   **Define the OSPF parameters -** Based on information gathered during Step 1, the network administrator must determine if single-area or multiarea OSPF is the preferred implementation. If multiarea OSPF is selected, there are several considerations the network administrator must take into account while determining the OSPF parameters, to include:

■ **IP addressing plan**- This governs how OSPF can be deployed and how well the OSPF deployment might scale. A detailed IP addressing plan, along with the IP subnetting information, must be created. A good IP addressing plan should enable the usage of OSPF multiarea design and summarization. This plan more easily scales the network, as well as optimizes OSPF behavior and the propagation of LSA.

■ **OSPF areas**- Dividing an OSPF network into areas decreases the LSDB size and limits the propagation of link-state updates when the topology changes. The routers that are to be ABRs and ASBRs must be identified, as are those that are to perform any summarization or redistribution.

■ **Network topology**- This consists of links that connect the network equipment and belong to different OSPF areas in a multiarea OSPF design. Network topology is important to determine primary and backup links. Primary and backup links are defined by the changing OSPF cost on interfaces. A detailed network topology plan should also be used to determine the different OSPF areas, ABR, and ASBR as well as summarization and redistribution points, if multiarea OSPF is used.

Step 3.   Configure the multiarea OSPF implementation based on the parameters.

Step 4.   Verify the multiarea OSPF implementation based on the parameters.

6.2.1.2   Configuring Multiarea OSPF

Refer to
Online Course
for Illustration

Figure 1 displays the reference multiarea OSPF topology. In this example:

■ R1 is an ABR because it has interfaces in area 1 and an interface in area 0.

■ R2 is an internal backbone router because all of its interfaces are in area 0.

■ R3 is an ABR because it has interfaces in area 2 and an interface in area 0.

There are no special commands required to implement this multiarea OSPF network. A router simply becomes an ABR when it has two `network` statements in different areas.

As shown in Figure 2, R1 is assigned the router ID 1.1.1.1. This example enables OSPF on the two LAN interfaces in area 1. The serial interface is configured as part of OSPF area 0. Because R2 has interfaces connected to two different areas, it is an ABR.

Use the Syntax Checker in Figure 3 to configure multiarea OSPF on R2 and R3. In this Syntax Checker, on R2, use the wildcard mask of the interface network address. On R3, use the 0.0.0.0 wildcard mask for all networks.

Upon completion of the R2 and R3 configuration, notice the informational messages informing of the adjacencies with R1 (1.1.1.1).

Upon completion of the R3 configuration, notice the informational messages informing of an adjacency with R1 (1.1.1.1) and R2 (2.2.2.2). Also notice how the IP addressing scheme used for the router ID makes it easy to identify the neighbor.

Note   The inverse wildcard masks used to configure R2 and R3 purposely differ to demonstrate the two alternatives to entering `network` statements. The method used for R3 is simpler because the wildcard mask is always `0.0.0.0` and does not need to be calculated.

6.2.1.3   Configuring Multiarea OSPFv3

Refer to
Online Course
for Illustration

Like OSPFv2, implementing the multiarea OSPFv3 topology in Figure 1 is simple. There are no special commands required. A router simply becomes an ABR when it has two interfaces in different areas.

For example in Figure 2, R1 is assigned the router ID 1.1.1.1. The example also enables OSPF on the two LAN interfaces in area 1 and the serial interface in area 0. Because R1 has interfaces connected to two different areas, it becomes an ABR.

Use the Syntax Checker in Figure 3 to configure multiarea OSPFv3 on R2 and on R3.

Upon completion of the R2 configuration, notice the message that there is an adjacency with R1 (1.1.1.1).

Upon completion of the R3 configuration, notice the message that there is an adjacency with R2 (2.2.2.2).

Refer to
Online Course
for Illustration

6.2.2   OSPF Route Summarization

6.2.2.1   OSPF Route Summarization

Summarization helps keep routing tables small. It involves consolidating multiple routes into a single advertisement, which can then be propagated into the backbone area.

Normally, type 1 and type 2 LSAs are generated inside each area, translated into type 3 LSAs, and sent to other areas. If area 1 had 30 networks to advertise, then 30 type 3 LSAs would be forwarded into the backbone. With route summarization, the ABR consolidates the 30 networks into one of two advertisements.

In Figure 1, R1 consolidates all of the network advertisements into one summary LSA. Instead of forwarding individual LSAs for each route in area 1, R1 forwards a summary LSA to the core router C1. C1 in turn, forwards the summary LSA to R2 and R3. R2 and R3 then forward it to their respective internal routers.

Summarization also helps increase the network's stability, because it reduces unnecessary LSA flooding. This directly affects the amount of bandwidth, CPU, and memory resources consumed by the OSPF routing process. Without route summarization, every specific-link LSA is propagated into the OSPF backbone and beyond, causing unnecessary network traffic and router overhead.

In Figure 2, a network link on R1a fails. R1a sends an LSA to R1. However, R1 does not propagate the update, because it has a summary route configured. Specific-link LSA flooding outside the area does not occur.

Refer to
Online Course
for Illustration

6.2.2.2   Interarea and External Route Summarization

In OSPF, summarization can only be configured on ABRs or ASBRs. Instead of advertising many specific networks, the ABR routers and ASBR routers advertise a summary route. ABR routers summarize type 3 LSAs and ASBR routers summarize type 5 LSAs.

By default, summary LSAs (type 3 LSAs) and external LSAs (type 5 LSAs) do not contain summarized (aggregated) routes; that is, by default, summary LSAs are not summarized.

As illustrated in Figures 1 and 2, route summarization can be configured as follows:

- **Interarea route summarization**- Interarea route summarization occurs on ABRs and applies to routes from within each area. It does not apply to external routes injected into OSPF via redistribution. To perform effective interarea route summarization, network addresses within areas should be assigned contiguously so that these addresses can be summarized into a minimal number of summary addresses.

- **External route summarization**- External route summarization is specific to external routes that are injected into OSPF via route redistribution. Again, it is important to ensure the contiguity of the external address ranges that are being summarized. Generally, only ASBRs summarize external routes. As shown in Figure 2, EIGRP external routes are summarized by ASBR R2 in a single LSA and sent to R1 and R3.

Note   External route summarization is configured on ASBRs using the `summary-address` address mask router configuration mode command.

Refer to
Online Course
for Illustration

6.2.2.3   Interarea Route Summarization

OSPF does not perform auto-summarization. Interarea summarization must be manually configured on ABRs.

Summarization of internal routes can only be done by ABRs. When summarization is enabled on an ABR, it injects into the backbone a single type 3 LSA describing the summary route. Multiple routes inside the area are summarized by the one LSA.

A summary route is generated if at least one subnet within the area falls in the summary address range. The summarized route metric is equal to the lowest cost of all subnets within the summary address range.

Note   An ABR can only summarize routes that are within the areas connected to the ABR.

Figure 1 shows a multiarea OSPF topology. The routing tables of R1 and R3 are examined to see the effect of the summarization.

Figure 2 displays the R1 routing table before summarization is configured, while Figure 3 displays the R3 routing table. Notice how R3 currently has two interarea entries to the R1 area 1 networks.

Refer to
Online Course
for Illustration

6.2.2.4   Calculating the Summary Route

The figure illustrates that summarizing networks into a single address and mask can be done in three steps:

Step 1.   List the networks in binary format. In the example, the two area 1 networks 10.1.1.0/24 and 10.1.2.0/24 are listed in binary format.

Step 2.   Count the number of far left matching bits to determine the mask for the summary route. As highlighted, the first 22 far left matching bits match. This results in the prefix **/22** or subnet mask **255.255.252.0**.

Step 3.   Copy the matching bits and then add zero bits to determine the summarized network address. In this example, the matching bits with zeros at the end result in a network address of 10.1.0.0/22. This summary address summarizes four networks: 10.1.0.0/24, 10.1.1.0/24, 10.1.2.0/24, and 10.1.3.0/24.

In the example the summary address matches four networks although only two networks exist.

Refer to
Online Course
for Illustration

6.2.2.5   Configuring Interarea Route Summarization

In Figure 1, to demonstrate the effect of route summarization, R1 is configured to summarize the internal area 1 routes.

To manually configure interarea route summarization on an ABR, use the **area** area-id **range** address mask router configuration mode command. This instructs the ABR to summarize routes for a specific area before injecting them into a different area, via the backbone as type 3 summary LSAs.

Note   In OSPFv3, the command is identical except for the IPv6 network address. The command syntax for OSPFv3 is **area** area-id **range** prefix/prefix-length.

Figure 2 summarizes the two internal area 1 routes into one OSPF interarea summary route on R1. The summarized route 10.1.0.0/22 actually summarizes four network addresses, 10.1.0.0/24 to 10.1.3.0/24.

Figure 3 displays the IPv4 routing table of R1. Notice how a new entry has appeared with a Null0 exit interface. The Cisco IOS automatically creates a bogus summary route to the Null0 interface when manual summarization is configured to prevent routing loops. A packet sent to a null interface is dropped.

For example, assume R1 received a packet destined for 10.1.0.10. Although it would match the R1 summary route, R1 does not have a valid route in area 1. Therefore, R1 would refer to the routing table for the next longest match, which would be the Null0 entry. The packet would get forwarded to the Null0 interface and dropped. This prevents the router from forwarding the packet to a default route and possibly creating a routing loop.

Figure 4 displays the updated R3 routing table. Notice how there is now only one interarea entry going to the summary route 10.1.0.0/22. Although this example only reduced the routing table by one entry, summarization could be implemented to summarize many networks. This would reduce the size of routing tables.

Use the Syntax Checker in Figure 5 to summarize the area 2 routes on R3.

Refer to
Online Course
for Illustration

6.2.3   Verifying Multiarea OSPF

6.2.3.1   Verifying Multiarea OSPF

The same verification commands used to verify single-area OSPF also can be used to verify the multiarea OSPF topology in the figure:

- `show ip ospf neighbor`

- `show ip ospf`

- `show ip ospf interface`

Commands that verify specific multiarea information include:

- `show ip protocols`

- `show ip ospf interface brief`

- `show ip route ospf`

- `show ip ospf database`

Note   For the equivalent OSPFv3 command, simply substitute `ip` with `ipv6`.

Refer to
Online Course
for Illustration

6.2.3.2   Verify General Multiarea OSPF Settings

Use the `show ip protocols` command to verify the OSPF status. The output of the command reveals which routing protocols are configured on a router. It also includes routing protocol specifics such as the router ID, number of areas in the router, and networks included within the routing protocol configuration.

Figure 1 displays the OSPF settings of R1. Notice that the command shows that there are two areas. The `Routing for Networks` section identifies the networks and their respective areas.

Use the `show ip ospf interface brief` command to display concise OSPF-related information of OSPF-enabled interfaces. This command reveals useful information, such as the OSPF process ID that the interface is assigned to, the area that the interfaces are in, and the cost of the interface.

Figure 2 verifies the OSPF-enabled interfaces and the areas to which they belong.

Use the Syntax Checker in Figure 3 to verify general settings on R2 and R3.

Refer to
Online Course
for Illustration

6.2.3.3   Verify the OSPF Routes

The most common command used to verify a multiarea OSPF configuration is the `show ip route` command. Add the `ospf` parameter to display only OSPF-related information.

Figure 1 displays the routing table of R1. Notice how the **O IA** entries in the routing table identify networks learned from other areas. Specifically, **O** represents OSPF routes, and **IA** represents interarea, which means that the route originated from another area. Recall that R1 is in area 0, and the 192.168.1.0 and 192.168.2.0 subnets are connected to R3 in area 2. The [110/1295] entry in the routing table represents the administrative distance that is assigned to OSPF (`110`) and the total cost of the routes (cost of `1295`).

Use the Syntax Checker in Figure 2 to verify the routing table of R2 and R3 using the `show ip route ospf` command.

Refer to
Online Course
for Illustration

6.2.3.4   Verify the Multiarea OSPF LSDB

Use the `show ip ospf database` command to verify the contents of the LSDB.

There are many command options available with the `show ip ospf database` command.

For example, Figure 1 displays the content of the LSDB of R1. Notice R1 has entries for area 0 and area 1, because ABRs must maintain a separate LSDB for each area to which they belong. In the output, `Router Link States` in area 0 identifies three routers. The `Summary Net Link States` section identifies networks learned from other areas and which neighbor advertised the network.

Use the Syntax Checker in Figure 2 to verify the LSDB of R2 and R3 using the `show ip ospf database` command. R2 only has interfaces in area 0; therefore, only one LSDB is required. Like R1, R3 contains two LSDBs.

Refer to
Online Course
for Illustration

6.2.3.5   Verify Multiarea OSPFv3

Like OSPFv2, OSPFv3 provides similar OSPFv3 verification commands. Refer to the reference OSPFv3 topology in Figure 1.

Figure 2 displays the OSPFv3 settings of R1. Notice that the command confirms that there are now two areas. It also identifies each interface enabled for the respective area.

Figure 3 verifies the OSPFv3-enabled interfaces and the area to which they belong.

Figure 4 displays the routing table of R1. Notice how the IPv6 routing table displays **OI** entries in the routing table to identify networks learned from other areas. Specifically, **O** represents OSPF routes, and **I** represents interarea, which means that the route originated from another area. Recall that R1 is in area 0, and the 2001:DB8:CAFE3::/64 subnet is connected to R3 in area 2. The [110/1295] entry in the routing table represents the administrative distance that is assigned to OSPF (`110`) and the total cost of the routes (cost of `1295`).

Figure 5 displays the content of the LSDB of R1. The command offers similar information to its OSPFv2 counterpart. However, the OSPFv3 LSDB contains additional LSA types not available in OSPFv2.

Refer to **Packet
Tracer Activity**
for this chapter

6.2.3.6   Packet Tracer - Configuring Multiarea OSPFv2

Background/Scenario

In this activity, you will configure multiarea OSPFv2. The network is already connected and interfaces are configured with IPv4 addressing. Your job is to enable multiarea OSPFv2, verify connectivity, and examine the operation of multiarea OSPFv2.

Refer to **Packet
Tracer Activity**
for this chapter

6.2.3.7   Packet Tracer - Configuring Multiarea OSPFv3

Background/Scenario

In this activity, you will configure multiarea OSPFv3. The network is already connected and interfaces are configured with IPv6 addressing. Your job is to enable multiarea OSPFv3, verify connectivity, and examine the operation of multiarea OSPFv3.

Refer to
Lab Activity
for this chapter

6.2.3.8   Lab - Configuring Multiarea OSPFv2

In this lab, you will complete the following objectives:

- Part 1: Build the Network and Configure Basic Device Settings
- Part 2: Configure a Multiarea OSPFv2 Network
- Part 3: Configure Interarea Summary Routes

Refer to
Lab Activity
for this chapter

6.2.3.9   Lab - Configuring Multiarea OSPFv3

In this lab, you will complete the following objectives:

- Part 1: Build the Network and Configure Basic Device Settings
- Part 2: Configure Multiarea OSPFv3 Routing
- Part 3: Configure Interarea Route Summarization

Refer to
Lab Activity
for this chapter

6.2.3.10   Lab - Troubleshooting Multiarea OSPFv2 and OSPFv3

In this lab, you will complete the following objectives:

■ Part 1: Build the Network and Load Device Configurations

■ Part 2: Troubleshoot Layer 3 Connectivity

■ Part 3: Troubleshoot OSPFv2

■ Part 4: Troubleshoot OSPFv3

Refer to
Online Course
for Illustration

Refer to
Lab Activity
for this chapter

6.3   Summary

6.3.1.1   Class Activity - Digital Trolleys

Digital Trolleys

Your city has an aging digital trolley system based on a one-area design. All communications within this one area are taking longer to process as trolleys are being added to routes serving the population of your growing city. Trolley departures and arrivals are also taking a little longer, because each trolley must check large routing tables to determine where to pick up and deliver residents from their source and destination streets.

A concerned citizen has come up with the idea of dividing the city into different areas for a more efficient way to determine trolley routing information. It is thought that if the trolley maps are smaller, the system might be improved because of faster and smaller updates to the routing tables.

Your city board approves and implements the new area-based, digital trolley system. But to ensure the new area routes are more efficient, the city board needs data to show the results at the next open board meeting.

Complete the directions found in the PDF for this activity. Share your answers with your class.

Refer to
Online Course
for Illustration

6.3.1.2   Summary

Single-area OSPF is useful in smaller networks but in larger networks multiarea OSPF is a better choice. Multiarea OSPF solves the issues of large routing table, large link-state database, and frequent SPF algorithm calculations, as shown in Figures 1 and 2.

The main area is called the backbone area (area 0) and all other areas must connect to the backbone area. Routing still occurs between the areas while many of the routing operations, such as recalculating the database, are kept within an area.

There are four different types of OSPF routers: Internal router, Backbone router, Area Border Router (ABR), and Autonomous System Boundary Router (ASBR). A router can be classified as more than one router type.

Link State Advertisements (LSAs) are the building blocks of OSPF. This chapter concentrated on LSA type 1 to LSA type 5. Type 1 LSAs are referred to as the router link entries. Type 2 LSAs are referred to as the network link entries and are flooded by a DR. Type 3 LSAs are referred to as the summary link entries and are created and propagated by ABRs. A type 4 summary LSA is generated by an ABR only when an ASBR exists within an area. Type 5 external LSAs describe routes to networks outside the OSPF autonomous system. Type 5 LSAs are originated by the ASBR and are flooded to the entire autonomous system.

OSPF routes in an IPv4 routing table are identified using the following descriptors: O, O IA, O E1 or O E2. Each router uses the SPF algorithm against the LSDB to build the SPF tree. The SPF tree is used to determine the best paths.

There are no special commands required to implement a multiarea OSPF network. A router simply becomes an ABR when it has two **network** statements in different areas.

An example of multiarea OSPF configuration:

```
R1(config)# router ospf 10
R1(config-router)# router-id 1.1.1.1
R1(config-router)# network 10.1.1.1 0.0.0.0 area 1
R1(config-router)# network 10.1.2.1 0.0.0.0 area 1
R1(config-router)# network 192.168.10.1 0.0.0.0 area 0
```

OSPF does not perform auto summarization. In OSPF, summarization can only be configured on ABRs or ASBRs. Interarea route summarization must be manually configured and occurs on ABRs and applies to routes from within each area. To manually configure interarea route summarization on an ABR, use the **area** area-id **range** address mask router configuration mode command.

External route summarization is specific to external routes that are injected into OSPF via route redistribution. Generally, only ASBRs summarize external routes. External route summarization is configured on ASBRs using the **summary-address** address mask router configuration mode command.

Commands that are used to verify OSPF configuration consist of the following:

- `show ip ospf neighbor`
- `show ip ospf`
- `show ip ospf interface`
- `show ip protocols`
- `show ip ospf interface brief`
- `show ip route ospf`
- `show ip ospf database`

Go to the online course to take the quiz and exam.

Chapter 6 Quiz

This quiz is designed to provide an additional opportunity to practice the skills and knowledge presented in the chapter and to prepare for the chapter exam. You will be allowed multiple attempts and the grade does not appear in the gradebook.

Chapter 6 Exam

The chapter exam assesses your knowledge of the chapter content.

Your Chapter Notes

7.0 EIGRP

7.0.1.1 Introduction

Enhanced Interior Gateway Routing Protocol (EIGRP) is an advanced distance vector routing protocol developed by Cisco Systems. As the name suggests, EIGRP is an enhancement of another Cisco routing protocol IGRP (Interior Gateway Routing Protocol). IGRP is an older classful, distance vector routing protocol, now obsolete since IOS 12.3.

EIGRP is a distance vector routing protocol that includes features found in link-state routing protocols. EIGRP is suited for many different topologies and media. In a well-designed network, EIGRP can scale to include multiple topologies and can provide extremely quick convergence times with minimal network traffic.

This chapter introduces EIGRP and provides basic configuration commands to enable it on a Cisco IOS router. It also explores the operation of the routing protocol and provides more detail on how EIGRP determines best path.

Refer to
Lab Activity
for this chapter

7.0.1.2 Class Activity - Classless EIGRP

Classless EIGRP

EIGRP was introduced as a distance vector routing protocol in 1992. It was originally designed to work as a proprietary protocol on Cisco devices only. In 2013, EIGRP became a multi-vendor routing protocol, meaning that it can be used by other device vendors in addition to Cisco devices.

Complete the reflection questions which accompany the PDF file for this activity. Save your work and be prepared to share your answers with the class.

Refer to
Interactive Graphic
in online course.

7.1 Characteristics of EIGRP

7.1.1 Basic Features of EIGRP

7.1.1.1 Features of EIGRP

EIGRP was initially released in 1992 as a proprietary protocol available only on Cisco devices. In 2013, Cisco released a basic functionality of EIGRP as an open standard to the IETF as an informational RFC. This means that other networking vendors can now implement EIGRP on their equipment to interoperate with both Cisco and non-Cisco routers running EIGRP. However, advanced features of EIGRP, such as EIGRP stub, needed for the Dynamic

Multipoint Virtual Private Network (DMVPN) deployment, will not be released to the IETF. As an informational RFC, Cisco will continue to maintain control of EIGRP.

EIGRP includes features of both link-state and distance vector routing protocols. However, EIGRP is still based on the key distance vector routing protocol principle, in which information about the rest of the network is learned from directly connected neighbors.

EIGRP is an advanced distance vector routing protocol that includes features not found in other distance vector routing protocols like RIP and IGRP.

Diffusing Update Algorithm

As the computational engine that drives EIGRP, the Diffusing Update Algorithm (DUAL) resides at the center of the routing protocol. DUAL guarantees loop-free and backup paths throughout the routing domain. Using DUAL, EIGRP stores all available backup routes for destinations so that it can quickly adapt to alternate routes when necessary.

Establishing Neighbor Adjacencies

EIGRP establishes relationships with directly connected routers that are also enabled for EIGRP. Neighbor adjacencies are used to track the status of these neighbors.

Reliable Transport Protocol

The Reliable Transport Protocol (RTP) is unique to EIGRP and provides delivery of EIGRP packets to neighbors. RTP and the tracking of neighbor adjacencies set the stage for DUAL.

Partial and Bounded Updates

EIGRP uses the terms, partial and bounded, when referring to its updates. Unlike RIP, EIGRP does not send periodic updates and route entries do not age out. The term partial means that the update only includes information about the route changes, such as a new link or a link becoming unavailable. The term bounded refers to the propagation of partial updates that are sent only to those routers that the changes affect. This minimizes the bandwidth that is required to send EIGRP updates.

Equal and Unequal Cost Load Balancing

EIGRP supports equal cost load balancing and unequal cost load balancing, which allows administrators to better distribute traffic flow in their networks.

Note   The term hybrid routing protocol is used in some older documentation to define EIGRP. However, this term is misleading because EIGRP is not a hybrid between distance vector and link-state routing protocols. EIGRP is solely a distance vector routing protocol; therefore, Cisco no longer uses this term to refer to it.

Refer to
Online Course
for Illustration

7.1.1.2   Protocol Dependent Modules

EIGRP has the capability for routing several different protocols including IPv4 and IPv6 using protocol-dependent modules (PDMs). Although now obsolete, EIGRP also used PDMs to route Novell's IPX and Apple Computer's AppleTalk network layer protocols.

PDMs are responsible for network layer protocol-specific tasks. An example is the EIGRP module that is responsible for sending and receiving EIGRP packets that are encapsulated in IPv4. This module is also responsible for parsing EIGRP packets and informing DUAL of the new information that is received. EIGRP asks DUAL to make routing decisions, but the results are stored in the IPv4 routing table.

PDMs are responsible for the specific routing tasks for each network layer protocol, including:

■ Maintaining the neighbor and topology tables of EIGRP routers that belong to that protocol suite

■ Building and translating protocol-specific packets for DUAL

■ Interfacing DUAL to the protocol-specific routing table

■ Computing the metric and passing this information to DUAL

■ Implementing filtering and access lists

■ Performing redistribution functions to and from other routing protocols

■ Redistributing routes that are learned by other routing protocols

When a router discovers a new neighbor, it records the neighbor's address and interface as an entry in the neighbor table. One neighbor table exists for each protocol-dependent module, such as IPv4. EIGRP also maintains a topology table. The topology table contains all destinations that are advertised by neighboring routers. There is also a separate topology table for each PDM.

Refer to
Online Course
for Illustration

7.1.1.3   Reliable Transport Protocol

EIGRP uses Reliable Transport Protocol (RTP) for the delivery and reception of EIGRP packets. EIGRP was designed as a network layer independent routing protocol; because of this design EIGRP cannot use the services of UDP or TCP. This allows EIGRP to be used for protocols other than those from the TCP/IP protocol suite, such as IPX and AppleTalk. The figure conceptually shows how RTP operates.

Although "reliable" is part of its name, RTP includes both reliable delivery and unreliable delivery of EIGRP packets, similar to TCP and UDP, respectively. Reliable RTP requires an acknowledgment to be returned by the receiver to the sender. An unreliable RTP packet does not require an acknowledgment. For example, an EIGRP update packet is sent reliably over RTP and requires an acknowledgment. An EIGRP Hello packet is also sent over RTP, but unreliably. This means that EIGRP Hello packets do not require an acknowledgment.

RTP can send EIGRP packets as unicast or multicast.

■ Multicast EIGRP packets for IPv4 use the reserved IPv4 multicast address 224.0.0.10.

■ Multicast EIGRP packets for IPv6 are sent to the reserved IPv6 multicast address FF02::A.

Refer to
Online Course
for Illustration

7.1.1.4   Authentication

Like other routing protocols, EIGRP can be configured for authentication. RIPv2, EIGRP, OSPF, IS-IS, and BGP can each be configured to authenticate their routing information.

It is a good practice to authenticate transmitted routing information. Doing so ensures that routers only accept routing information from other routers that have been configured with the same password or authentication information.

Note   Authentication does not encrypt the EIGRP routing updates.

Refer to **Online Course** for Illustration

7.1.2   Types of EIGRP Packets

7.1.2.1   EIGRP Packet Types

EIGRP uses five different packet types, some in pairs. EIGRP packets are sent using either RTP reliable or unreliable delivery and can be sent as a unicast, multicast, or sometimes both. EIGRP packet types are also called EIGRP packet formats or EIGRP messages.

As shown in Figure 1, the five EIGRP packet types include:

Hello packets - Used for neighbor discovery and to maintain neighbor adjacencies.

- Sent with unreliable delivery
- Multicast (on most network types)

Update packets - Propagates routing information to EIGRP neighbors.

- Sent with reliable delivery
- Unicast or multicast

Acknowledgment packets - Used to acknowledge the receipt of an EIGRP message that was sent using reliable delivery.

- Sent with unreliable delivery
- Unicast

Query packets - Used to query routes from neighbors.

- Sent with reliable delivery
- Unicast or multicast

Reply packets - Sent in response to an EIGRP query.

- Sent with unreliable delivery
- Unicast

Figure 2 shows that EIGRP messages are typically encapsulated in IPv4 or IPv6 packets. EIGRP for IPv4 messages use IPv4 as the network layer protocol. The IPv4 protocol field uses 88 to indicate the data portion of the packet is an EIGRP for IPv4 message. EIGRP for IPv6 messages are encapsulated in IPv6 packets using the next header field of 88. Similar, to the protocol field for IPv4, the IPv6 next header field indicates the type of data carried in the IPv6 packet.

Refer to
Online Course
for Illustration

7.1.2.2   EIGRP Hello Packets

EIGRP uses small Hello packets to discover other EIGRP-enabled routers on directly connected links. Hello packets are used by routers to form EIGRP neighbor adjacencies, also known as neighbor relationships.

EIGRP Hello packets are sent as IPv4 or IPv6 multicasts, and use RTP unreliable delivery. This means that the receiver does not reply with an acknowledgment packet.

- The reserved EIGRP multicast address for IPv4 is 224.0.0.10.

- The reserved EIGRP multicast address for IPv6 is FF02::A.

EIGRP routers discover neighbors and establish adjacencies with neighbor routers using the Hello packet. On most networks, EIGRP Hello packets are sent as multicast packets every five seconds. However, on multipoint, nonbroadcast multiple access (NBMA) networks, such as X.25, Frame Relay, and Asynchronous Transfer Mode (ATM) interfaces with access links of T1 (1.544 Mb/s) or slower, Hello packets are sent as unicast packets every 60 seconds.

EIGRP also uses Hello packets to maintain established adjacencies. An EIGRP router assumes that as long as it receives Hello packets from a neighbor, the neighbor and its routes remain viable.

EIGRP uses a Hold timer to determine the maximum time the router should wait to receive the next Hello before declaring that neighbor as unreachable. By default, the hold time is three times the Hello interval, or 15 seconds on most networks and 180 seconds on low-speed NBMA networks. If the hold time expires, EIGRP declares the route as down and DUAL searches for a new path by sending out queries.

Refer to
Online Course
for Illustration

7.1.2.3   EIGRP Update and Acknowledgment Packets

EIGRP Update Packets

EIGRP sends Update packets to propagate routing information. Update packets are sent only when necessary. EIGRP updates contain only the routing information needed and are sent only to those routers that require it.

Unlike RIP, EIGRP (another distance vector routing protocol) does not send periodic updates and route entries do not age out. Instead, EIGRP sends incremental updates only when the state of a destination changes. This may include when a new network becomes available, an existing network becomes unavailable, or a change occurs in the routing metric for an existing network.

EIGRP uses the terms *partial* and *bounded* when referring to its updates. The term partial means that the update only includes information about the route changes. The term bounded refers to the propagation of partial updates that are sent only to those routers that the changes affect.

By sending only the routing information that is needed, only to those routers that need it, EIGRP minimizes the bandwidth that is required to send EIGRP updates.

EIGRP update packets use reliable delivery, which means the sending router requires an acknowledgment. Update packets are sent as a multicast when required by multiple routers, or as a unicast when required by only a single router. In the figure, because the links are point-to-point, the updates are sent as unicasts.

EIGRP Acknowledgment Packets

EIGRP sends Acknowledgment (ACK) packets when reliable delivery is used. An EIGRP acknowledgment is an EIGRP Hello packet without any data. RTP uses reliable delivery for EIGRP update, query, and reply packets. EIGRP acknowledgment packets are always sent as an unreliable unicast. Unreliable delivery makes sense; otherwise, there would be an endless loop of acknowledgments.

In the figure, R2 has lost connectivity to the LAN attached to its Gigabit Ethernet interface. R2 immediately sends an update to R1 and R3 noting the downed route. R1 and R3 respond with an acknowledgment to let R2 know that they have received the update.

Note   Some documentation refers to the Hello and acknowledgment as a single type of EIGRP packet.

Refer to **Online Course** for Illustration

7.1.2.4   EIGRP Query and Reply Packets

EIGRP Query Packets

DUAL uses query and reply packets when searching for networks and other tasks. Queries and replies use reliable delivery. Queries can use multicast or unicast, whereas replies are always sent as unicast.

In the figure, R2 has lost connectivity to the LAN and it sends out queries to all EIGRP neighbors searching for any possible routes to the LAN. Because queries use reliable delivery, the receiving router must return an EIGRP acknowledgment. The acknowledgment informs the sender of the query that it has received the query message. To keep this example simple, acknowledgments were omitted in the graphic.

EIGRP Reply Packets

All neighbors must send a reply, regardless of whether or not they have a route to the downed network. Because replies also use reliable delivery, routers such as R2, must send an acknowledgment.

It may not be obvious why R2 would send out a query for a network it knows is down. Actually, only R2's interface that is attached to the network is down. Another router could be attached to the same LAN and have an alternate path to this same network. Therefore, R2 queries for such a router before completely removing the network from its topology table.

Refer to **Interactive Graphic** in online course.

7.1.2.5   Activity - Identify the EIGRP Packet Type

Refer to **Interactive Graphic** in online course.

7.1.2.6   Video Demonstration - Observing EIGRP Protocol Communications

Refer to **Online Course** for Illustration

7.1.3   EIGRP Messages

7.1.3.1   Encapsulating EIGRP Messages

The data portion of an EIGRP message is encapsulated in a packet. This data field is called type, length, value (TLV). The types of TLVs relevant to this course are EIGRP parameters, IP internal routes, and IP external routes.

The EIGRP packet header is included with every EIGRP packet, regardless of its type. The EIGRP packet header and TLV are then encapsulated in an IPv4 packet. In the IPv4 packet header, the protocol field is set to 88 to indicate EIGRP, and the IPv4 destination address is set to the multicast 224.0.0.10. If the EIGRP packet is encapsulated in an Ethernet frame, the destination MAC address is also a multicast address, 01-00-5E-00-00-0A.

Figures 1 to 4 show the Data Link Ethernet Frame. EIGRP for IPv4 is encapsulated in an IPv4 packet. EIGRP for IPv6 would use a similar type of encapsulation. EIGRP for IPv6 is encapsulated using an IPv6 header. The IPv6 destination address would be the multicast address FF02::A and the next header field would be set to 88.

Refer to
Online Course
for Illustration

7.1.3.2   EIGRP Packet Header and TLV

Every EIGRP message includes the header, as shown in Figure 1. Important fields include the Opcode field and the Autonomous System Number field. Opcode specifies the EIGRP packet type as follows:

- Update

- Query

- Reply

- Hello

The autonomous system number specifies the EIGRP routing process. Unlike RIP, multiple instances of EIGRP can run on a network; the autonomous system number is used to track each running EIGRP process.

Figure 2 shows the EIGRP parameter's TLV. The EIGRP parameter's message includes the weights that EIGRP uses for its composite metric. By default, only bandwidth and delay are weighted. Both are weighted equally; therefore, the K1 field for bandwidth and the K3 field for delay are both set to one (1). The other K values are set to zero (0).

The Hold Time is the amount of time the EIGRP neighbor receiving this message should wait before considering the advertising router to be down.

Figure 3 shows the IP Internal Routes TLV. The IP internal message is used to advertise EIGRP routes within an autonomous system. Important fields include the metric fields (delay and bandwidth), the subnet mask field (prefix length), and the destination field.

Delay is calculated as the sum of delays from source to destination in units of 10 microseconds. Bandwidth is the lowest configured bandwidth of any interface along the route.

The subnet mask is specified as the prefix length or the number of network bits in the subnet mask. For example, the prefix length for the subnet mask 255.255.255.0 is 24, because 24 is the number of network bits.

The Destination field stores the address of the destination network. Although only 24 bits are shown in this figure, this field varies based on the value of the network portion of the 32-bit network address. For example, the network portion of 10.1.0.0/16 is 10.1; therefore, the Destination field stores the first 16 bits. Because the minimum length of this field is 24 bits, the remainder of the field is padded with zeros. If a network address is longer than 24 bits (192.168.1.32/27, for example), then the Destination field is extended for another 32 bits (for a total of 56 bits) and the unused bits are padded with zeros.

Figure 4 shows the IP External Routes TLV. The IP external message is used when external routes are imported into the EIGRP routing process. In this chapter, we will import or redistribute a default static route into EIGRP. Notice that the bottom half of the IP External Routes TLV includes all the fields used by the IP Internal TLV.

Note   The maximum transmission unit (MTU) is not a metric used by EIGRP. The MTU is included in the routing updates, but it is not used to determine the routing metric.

Refer to **Online Course** for Illustration

7.2   Configuring EIGRP for IPv4

7.2.1   Configuring EIGRP with IPv4

7.2.1.1   EIGRP Network Topology

Figure 1 displays the topology that is used in this course to configure EIGRP for IPv4. The types of serial interfaces and their associated bandwidths may not necessarily reflect the more common types of connections found in today's networks. The bandwidths of the serial links used in this topology were chosen to help explain the calculation of the routing protocol metrics and the process of best path selection.

The routers in the topology have a starting configuration, including addresses on the interfaces. There is currently no static routing or dynamic routing configured on any of the routers.

Figures 2, 3, and 4 display the interface configurations for the three EIGRP routers in the topology. Only routers R1, R2, and R3 are part of the EIGRP routing domain. The ISP router is used as the routing domain's gateway to the Internet.

Refer to **Online Course** for Illustration

7.2.1.2   Autonomous System Numbers

EIGRP uses the `router eigrp` autonomous-system command to enable the EIGRP process. The autonomous system number referred to in the EIGRP configuration is not associated with the Internet Assigned Numbers Authority (IANA) globally assigned autonomous system numbers used by external routing protocols.

So what is the difference between the IANA globally assigned autonomous system number and the EIGRP autonomous system number?

An IANA globally assigned autonomous system is a collection of networks under the administrative control of a single entity that presents a common routing policy to the Internet. In the figure, companies A, B, C, and D are all under the administrative control of ISP1. ISP1 presents a common routing policy for all of these companies when advertising routes to ISP2.

The guidelines for the creation, selection, and registration of an autonomous system are described in RFC 1930. Global autonomous system numbers are assigned by IANA, the same authority that assigns IP address space. The local regional Internet registry (RIR) is responsible for assigning an autonomous system number to an entity from its block of assigned autonomous system numbers. Prior to 2007, autonomous system numbers were

16-bit numbers ranging from 0 to 65,535. Today, 32-bit autonomous system numbers are assigned increasing the number of available autonomous system numbers to over 4 billion.

Usually Internet Service Providers (ISPs), Internet backbone providers, and large institutions connecting to other entities require an autonomous system number. These ISPs and large institutions use the exterior gateway routing protocol, Border Gateway Protocol (BGP), to propagate routing information. BGP is the only routing protocol that uses an actual autonomous system number in its configuration.

The vast majority of companies and institutions with IP networks do not need an autonomous system number, because they are controlled by a larger entity, such as an ISP. These companies use interior gateway protocols, such as RIP, EIGRP, OSPF, and IS-IS to route packets within their own networks. They are one of many independent and separate networks within the autonomous system of the ISP. The ISP is responsible for the routing of packets within its autonomous system and between other autonomous systems.

The autonomous system number used for EIGRP configuration is only significant to the EIGRP routing domain. It functions as a process ID to help routers keep track of multiple, running instances of EIGRP. This is required because it is possible to have more than one instance of EIGRP running on a network. Each instance of EIGRP can be configured to support and exchange routing updates for different networks.

Refer to
Online Course
for Illustration

7.2.1.3   The Router EIGRP Command

The Cisco IOS includes the processes to enable and configure several different types of dynamic routing protocols. The **router** global configuration mode command is used to begin the configuration of any dynamic routing protocol. The topology shown in Figure 1 is used to demonstrate this command.

As shown in Figure 2, when followed by a question mark (**?**), the **router** global configuration mode command lists of all the available routing protocols supported by this specific IOS release running on the router.

The following global configuration mode command is used to enter the router configuration mode for EIGRP and begin the configuration of the EIGRP process:

```
Router(config)# router eigrp autonomous-system
```

The autonomous-system argument can be assigned to any 16-bit value between the number 1 and 65,535. All routers within the EIGRP routing domain must use the same autonomous system number.

Figure 3 shows the configuration of the EIGRP process on routers R1, R2, and R3. Notice that the prompt changes from a global configuration mode prompt to router configuration mode.

In this example, **1** identifies this particular EIGRP process running on this router. To establish neighbor adjacencies, EIGRP requires all routers in the same routing domain to be configured with the same autonomous system number. In Figure 3, that same EIGRP is enabled on all three routers using the same autonomous system number of **1**.

Note   Both EIGRP and OSPF can support multiple instances of each routing protocol, although this type of multiple routing protocol implementation is not usually needed or recommended.

The `router eigrp` autonomous-system command does not start the EIGRP process itself. The router does not start sending updates. Rather, this command only provides access to configure the EIGRP settings.

To completely remove the EIGRP routing process from a device, use the `no router eigrp` autonomous-system global configuration mode command, which stops the EIGRP process and removes all existing EIGRP router configurations.

Refer to
Online Course
for Illustration

7.2.1.4 EIGRP Router ID

Determining the Router ID

The EIGRP router ID is used to uniquely identify each router in the EIGRP routing domain. The router ID is used in both EIGRP and OSPF routing protocols, although the role of the router ID is more significant in OSPF.

In EIGRP IPv4 implementations, the use of the router ID is not that apparent. EIGRP for IPv4 uses the 32-bit router ID to identify the originating router for redistribution of external routes. The need for a router ID becomes more evident in the discussion of EIGRP for IPv6. While the router ID is necessary for redistribution, the details of EIGRP redistribution are beyond the scope of this curriculum. For purposes of this curriculum, it is only necessary to understand what the router ID is and how it is derived.

Cisco routers derive the router ID based on three criteria, in the following precedence:

1. Use the IPv4 address configured with the `eigrp router-id` router configuration mode command.

2. If the router ID is not configured, the router chooses the highest IPv4 address of any of its loopback interfaces.

3. If no loopback interfaces are configured, the router chooses the highest active IPv4 address of any of its physical interfaces.

If the network administrator does not explicitly configure a router ID using the `eigrp router-id` command, EIGRP generates its own router ID using either a loopback or physical IPv4 address. A loopback address is a virtual interface and is automatically in the up state when configured. The interface does not need to be enabled for EIGRP, meaning that it does not need to be included in one of the EIGRP network commands. However, the interface must be in the up/up state.

Using the criteria described above, the figure shows the default EIGRP router IDs that are determined by the routers' highest active IPv4 address.

Note The `eigrp router-id` command is used to configure the router ID for EIGRP. Some versions of IOS will accept the command `router-id`, without first specifying `eigrp`. The running-config, however, will display `eigrp router-id` regardless of which command is used.

Refer to
Online Course
for Illustration

7.2.1.5   Configuring the EIGRP Router ID

`eigrp router-id` Command

The `eigrp router-id` command is used to configure the EIGRP router ID and takes precedence over any loopback or physical interface IPv4 addresses. The command syntax is:

```
Router(config)# router eigrp autonomous-system
Router(config-router)# eigrp router-id ipv4-address
```

Note   The IPv4 address used to indicate the router ID is actually any 32-bit number displayed in dotted-decimal notation.

The router ID can be configured with any IPv4 address with two exceptions: 0.0.0.0 and 255.255.255.255. The router ID should be a unique 32-bit number in the EIGRP routing domain; otherwise, routing inconsistencies can occur.

Figure 1 shows the configuration of the EIGRP router ID for routers R1 and R2 using the `router eigrp` autonomous-system command.

Loopback Address Used as the Router ID

Another option to specify the EIGRP router ID is to use an IPv4 loopback address. The advantage of using a loopback interface, instead of the IPv4 address of a physical interface, is that unlike physical interfaces, it cannot fail. There are no actual cables or adjacent devices on which the loopback interface depends for being in the up state. Therefore, using a loopback address for the router ID can provide a more consistent router ID than using an interface address.

If the `eigrp router-id` command is not used and loopback interfaces are configured, EIGRP chooses the highest IPv4 address of any of its loopback interfaces. The following commands are used to enable and configure a loopback interface:

```
Router(config)# interface loopback number
Router(config-if)#  ip address  ipv4-address subnet-mask
```

Note   The EIGRP router ID is not changed, unless the EIGRP process is removed with the `no router eigrp` command or if the router ID is manually configured with the `eigrp router-id` command.

Verifying the EIGRP Process

Figure 2 shows the `show ip protocols` output for R1, including its router ID. The `show ip protocols` command displays the parameters and current state of any active routing protocol processes, including both EIGRP and OSPF. The `show ip protocols` command displays different types of output specific to each routing protocol.

Use the Syntax Checker in Figure 3 to configure and verify the router ID for R3.

Refer to
Online Course
for Illustration

7.2.1.6   The Network Command

EIGRP router configuration mode allows for the configuration of the EIGRP routing protocol. Figure 1 shows that R1, R2, and R3 all have networks that should be included within a single EIGRP routing domain. To enable EIGRP routing on an interface, use the `network` router configuration mode command and enter the classful network address for each directly connected network.

The `network` command has the same function as in all IGP routing protocols. The `network` command in EIGRP:

■ Enables any interface on this router that matches the network address in the `network` router configuration mode command to send and receive EIGRP updates.

■ The network of the interfaces is included in EIGRP routing updates.

```
Router(config-router)# network ipv4-network-address
```

The ipv4-network-address argument is the classful IPv4 network address for this interface. Figure 2 shows the network commands configured for R1. In the figure, a single classful `network` statement, `network 172.16.0.0`, is used on R1 to include both interfaces in subnets 172.16.1.0/24 and 172.16.3.0/30. Notice that only the classful network address is used.

Figure 3 shows the `network` command used to enable EIGRP on R2's interfaces for subnets 172.16.1.0/24 and 172.16.2.0/24. When EIGRP is configured on R2's S0/0/0 interface, DUAL sends a notification message to the console stating that a neighbor adjacency with another EIGRP router on that interface has been established. This new adjacency happens automatically because both R1 and R2 use the same `eigrp 1` autonomous system number, and both routers now send updates on their interfaces in the 172.16.0.0 network.

By default, the `eigrp log-neighbor-changes` router configuration mode command is enabled. This command is used to:

■ Display any changes in EIGRP neighbor adjacencies.

■ Help verify neighbor adjacencies during configuration of EIGRP.

■ Advise the network administrator when any EIGRP adjacencies have been removed.

Refer to
Online Course
for Illustration

7.2.1.7   The Network Command and Wildcard Mask

By default, when using the `network` command and an IPv4 network address, such as 172.16.0.0, all interfaces on the router that belong to that classful network address are enabled for EIGRP. However, there may be times when the network administrator does not want to include all interfaces within a network when enabling EIGRP. For example, in Figure 1, assume that an administrator wants to enable EIGRP on R2, but only for the subnet 192.168.10.8 255.255.255.252, on the S0/0/1 interface.

To configure EIGRP to advertise specific subnets only, use the wildcard-mask option with the network command:

```
Router(config-router)#  network network-address [wildcard-mask]
```

Think of a wildcard mask as the inverse of a subnet mask. The inverse of subnet mask 255.255.255.252 is 0.0.0.3. To calculate the inverse of the subnet mask, subtract the subnet mask from 255.255.255.255 as follows:

```
  255.255.255.255
- 255.255.255.252
  ---------------
    0.  0.  0.  3   Wildcard mask
```

Figure 2 continues the EIGRP network configuration of R2. The `network 192.168.10.8 0.0.0.3` command specifically enables EIGRP on the S0/0/1 interface, a member of the 192.168.10.8 255.255.255.252 subnet.

Some IOS versions also let you enter the subnet mask instead of a wildcard mask. Figure 3 shows an example of configuring the same S0/0/1 interface on R2, but this time using a subnet mask in the `network` command. However, if the subnet mask is used, the IOS converts the command to the wildcard-mask format within the configuration. This is verified in the `show running-config` output in Figure 3.

Use the Syntax Checker in Figure 4 to configure the EIGRP `network` commands for router R3.

Refer to
Online Course
for Illustration

7.2.1.8   Passive Interface

As soon as a new interface is enabled within the EIGRP network, EIGRP attempts to form a neighbor adjacency with any neighboring routers to send and receive EIGRP updates.

At times it may be necessary, or advantageous, to include a directly connected network in the EIGRP routing update, but not allow any neighbor adjacencies off of that interface to form. The `passive-interface` command can be used to prevent the neighbor adjacencies. There are two primary reasons for enabling the `passive-interface` command:

- To suppress unnecessary update traffic, such as when an interface is a LAN interface, with no other routers connected

- To increase security controls, such as preventing unknown rogue routing devices from receiving EIGRP updates

Figure 1 shows R1, R2, and R3 do not have neighbors on their GigabitEthernet 0/0 interfaces.

The `passive-interface` router configuration mode command disables the transmission and receipt of EIGRP Hello packets on these interfaces.

```
Router(config)#   router eigrp as-number
Router(config-router)#   passive-interface interface-type interface-number
```

Figure 2 shows the `passive-interface` command configured to suppress Hello packets on the LANs for R1 and R3. R2 is configured using the Syntax Checker.

Without a neighbor adjacency, EIGRP cannot exchange routes with a neighbor. Therefore, the `passive-interface` command prevents the exchange of routes on the interface. Although EIGRP does not send or receive routing updates on an interface configured with the `passive-interface` command, it still includes the address of the interface in routing updates sent out of other non-passive interfaces.

Note   To configure all interfaces as passive, use the `passive-interface default` command. To disable an interface as passive, use the `no passive-interface` interface-type interface-number command.

An example of using the passive interface to increase security controls is when a network must connect to a third-party organization, for which the local administrator has no control, such as when connecting to an ISP network. In this case, the local network administrator would need to advertise the interface link through their own network, but would not want the third-party organization to receive or send routing updates to the local routing device, as this is a security risk.

Verifying the Passive Interface

To verify whether any interface on a router is configured as passive, use the `show ip protocols` privileged EXEC mode command, as shown in Figure 3. Notice that although R3's GigabitEthernet 0/0 interface is a passive interface, EIGRP still includes the interface's network address of 192.168.1.0 network in its routing updates.

Use the Syntax Checker in Figure 4 to configure R2 to suppress EIGRP Hello packets on its GigabitEthernet 0/0 interface.

Refer to
Online Course
for Illustration

7.2.2 Verifying EIGRP with IPv4

7.2.2.1 Verifying EIGRP: Examining Neighbors

Before EIGRP can send or receive any updates, routers must establish adjacencies with their neighbors. EIGRP routers establish adjacencies with neighbor routers by exchanging EIGRP Hello packets.

Use the `show ip eigrp neighbors` command to view the neighbor table and verify that EIGRP has established an adjacency with its neighbors. For each router, you should be able to see the IPv4 address of the adjacent router and the interface that this router uses to reach that EIGRP neighbor. Using this topology, each router has two neighbors listed in the neighbor table.

The `show ip eigrp neighbors` command output includes:

- **H column**- Lists the neighbors in the order that they were learned.

- **Address**- IPv4 address of the neighbor.

- **Interface**- Local interface on which this Hello packet was received.

- **Hold**- Current hold time. When a Hello packet is received, this value is reset to the maximum hold time for that interface, and then counts down to zero. If zero is reached, the neighbor is considered down.

- **Uptime**- Amount of time since this neighbor was added to the neighbor table.

- **Smooth Round Trip Timer (SRTT)** and **Retransmission Timeout (RTO)** - Used by RTP to manage reliable EIGRP packets.

- **Queue Count**- Should always be zero. If more than zero, then EIGRP packets wait to be sent.

- **Sequence Number**- Used to track updates, queries, and reply packets.

The `show ip eigrp neighbors` command is very useful for verifying and troubleshooting EIGRP. If a neighbor is not listed after adjacencies have been established with a router's neighbors, check the local interface to ensure it is activated with the `show ip interface brief` command. If the interface is active, try pinging the IPv4 address of the neighbor. If the ping fails, it means that the neighbor interface is down and must be activated. If the ping is successful and EIGRP still does not see the router as a neighbor, examine the following configurations:

- Are both routers configured with the same EIGRP autonomous system number?
- Is the directly connected network included in the EIGRP **network** statements?

Refer to
Online Course
for Illustration

7.2.2.2   Verifying EIGRP: show ip protocols Command

The **show ip protocols** command displays the parameters and other information about the current state of any active IPv4 routing protocol processes configured on the router. The **show ip protocols** command displays different types of output specific to each routing protocol.

The output in Figure 1 indicates several EIGRP parameters, including:

1. EIGRP is an active dynamic routing protocol on R1 configured with the autonomous system number 1.

2. The EIGRP router ID of R1 is 1.1.1.1.

3. The EIGRP administrative distances on R1 are internal AD of 90 and external of 170 (default values).

4. By default, EIGRP does not automatically summarize networks. Subnets are included in the routing updates.

5. The EIGRP neighbor adjacencies R1 has with other routers used to receive EIGRP routing updates.

Note   Prior to IOS 15, EIGRP automatic summarization was enabled by default.

The output from the **show ip protocols** command is useful in debugging routing operations. Information in the Routing Information Sources field can help identify a router suspected of delivering bad routing information. The Routing Information Sources field lists all the EIGRP routing sources the Cisco IOS software uses to build its IPv4 routing table. For each source, note the following:

- IPv4 address
- Administrative distance
- Time the last update was received from this source

As shown in Figure 2, EIGRP has a default AD of 90 for internal routes and 170 for routes imported from an external source, such as default routes. When compared to other IGPs, EIGRP is the most preferred by the Cisco IOS, because it has the lowest administrative distance. EIGRP has a third AD value of 5, for summary routes.

Refer to
Online Course
for Illustration

7.2.2.3   Verifying EIGRP: Examine the IPv4 routing table

Another way to verify that EIGRP and other functions of the router are configured properly is to examine the IPv4 routing tables with the **show ip route** command. As with any dynamic routing protocol, the network administrator must verify the information in the routing table to ensure that it is populated as expected, based on configurations entered.

For this reason, it is important to have a good understanding of the routing protocol configuration commands, as well as the routing protocol operations and the processes used by the routing protocol to build the IP routing table.

Notice that the outputs used throughout this course are from Cisco IOS 15. Prior to IOS 15, EIGRP automatic summarization was enabled by default. The state of automatic summarization can make a difference in the information displayed in the IPv4 routing table. If a previous version of the IOS is used, automatic summarization can be disabled using the `no auto-summary` router configuration mode command:

```
Router(config-router)#  no auto-summary
```

Figure 1 shows the topology for R1, R2, and R3.

In Figure 2, the IPv4 routing table is examined using the `show ip route` command. EIGRP routes are denoted in the routing table with a `D`. The letter D was used to represent EIGRP because the protocol is based upon the DUAL algorithm.

The `show ip route` command verifies that routes received by EIGRP neighbors are installed in the IPv4 routing table. The `show ip route` command displays the entire routing table, including remote networks learned dynamically, directly connected and static routes. For this reason, it is normally the first command used to check for convergence. After routing is correctly configured on all routers, the `show ip route` command reflects that each router has a full routing table, with a route to each network in the topology.

Notice that R1 has installed routes to three IPv4 remote networks in its IPv4 routing table:

■ 172.16.2.0/24 network, received from router R2 on the Serial0/0/0 interface

■ 192.168.1.0/24 network, received from router R2 on the Serial0/0/1 interface

■ 192.168.10.8/30 network, received from both R2 on the Serial0/0/0 interface, and from R3 on the Serial0/0/1 interface

R1 has two paths to the 192.168.10.8/30 network, because its cost or metric to reach that network is the same or equal using both routers. These are known as equal cost routes. R1 uses both paths to reach this network, which is known as load balancing. The EIGRP metric is discussed later in this chapter.

Figure 3 displays the routing table for R2. Notice similar results are displayed including an equal cost route for the 192.168.10.4/30 network.

Figure 4 displays the routing table for R3. Similar to the results for R1 and R2, remote networks are learned using EIGRP, including an equal cost route for the 172.16.3.0/30 network.

Refer to **Packet Tracer Activity** for this chapter

7.2.2.4   Packet Tracer - Configuring Basic EIGRP with IPv4

Background/Scenario

In this activity, you will implement basic EIGRP configurations including `network` commands, passive interfaces, and disabling automatic summarization. You will then verify your EIGRP configuration using a variety of `show` commands and testing end-to-end connectivity.

Refer to
Lab Activity
for this chapter

7.2.2.5   Lab - Configuring Basic EIGRP with IPv4

In this lab, you will complete the following objectives:

■ Part 1: Build the Network and Verify Connectivity

■ Part 2: Configure EIGRP Routing

■ Part 3: Verify EIGRP Routing

■ Part 4: Configure Bandwidth and Passive Interfaces

Refer to
Online Course
for Illustration

7.3   Operation of EIGRP

7.3.1   EIGRP Initial Route Discovery

7.3.1.1   EIGRP Neighbor Adjacency

The goal of any dynamic routing protocol is to learn about remote networks from other routers and to reach convergence in the routing domain. Before any EIGRP update packets can be exchanged between routers, EIGRP must first discover its neighbors. EIGRP neighbors are other routers running EIGRP on directly connected networks.

EIGRP uses Hello packets to establish and maintain neighbor adjacencies. For two EIGRP routers to become neighbors, several parameters between the two routers must match. For example, two EIGRP routers must use the same EIGRP metric parameters and both must be configured using the same autonomous system number.

Each EIGRP router maintains a neighbor table, which contains a list of routers on shared links that have an EIGRP adjacency with this router. The neighbor table is used to track the status of these EIGRP neighbors.

The figure shows two EIGRP routers exchanging initial EIGRP Hello packets. When an EIGRP enabled router receives a Hello packet on an interface, it adds that router to its neighbor table.

1. A new router (R1) comes up on the link and sends an EIGRP Hello packet through all of its EIGRP-configured interfaces.

2. Router R2 receives the Hello packet on an EIGRP-enabled interface. R2 replies with an EIGRP update packet that contains all the routes it has in its routing table, except those learned through that interface (split horizon). However, the neighbor adjacency is not established until R2 also sends an EIGRP Hello packet to R1.

3. After both routers have exchanged Hellos, the neighbor adjacency is established. R1 and R2 update their EIGRP neighbor tables adding the adjacent router as a neighbor.

Refer to
Online Course
for Illustration

7.3.1.2   EIGRP Topology Table

EIGRP updates contain networks that are reachable from the router sending the update. As EIGRP updates are exchanged between neighbors, the receiving router adds these entries to its EIGRP topology table.

Each EIGRP router maintains a topology table for each routed protocol configured, such as IPv4 and IPv6. The topology table includes route entries for every destination that the router learns from its directly connected EIGRP neighbors.

The figure shows the continuation of the initial route discovery process from the previous page. It now shows the update of the topology table.

When a router receives an EIGRP routing update, it adds the routing information to its EIGRP topology table and replies with an EIGRP acknowledgment.

1. R1 receives the EIGRP update from neighbor R2 and includes information about the routes that the neighbor is advertising, including the metric to each destination. R1 adds all update entries to its topology table. The topology table includes all destinations advertised by neighboring (adjacent) routers and the cost (metric) to reach each network.

2. EIGRP update packets use reliable delivery; therefore, R1 replies with an EIGRP acknowledgment packet informing R2 that it has received the update.

3. R1 sends an EIGRP update to R2 advertising the routes that it is aware of, except those learned from R2 (split horizon).

4. R2 receives the EIGRP update from neighbor R1 and adds this information to its own topology table.

5. R2 responds to the R1's EIGRP update packet with an EIGRP acknowledgment.

Refer to
Online Course
for Illustration

7.3.1.3   EIGRP Convergence

The figure illustrates the final steps of the initial route discovery process.

1. After receiving the EIGRP update packets from R2, using the information in the topology table, R1 updates its IP routing table with the best path to each destination, including the metric and the next-hop router.

2. Similar to R1, R2 updates its IP routing table with the best path routes to each network.

At this point, EIGRP on both routers is considered to be in the converged state.

Refer to
Interactive Graphic
in online course.

7.3.1.4   Activity - Identify the Steps in Establishing EIGRP Neighbor Adjacencies

Refer to
Online Course
for Illustration

7.3.2   Metrics

7.3.2.1   EIGRP Composite Metric

By default, EIGRP uses the following values in its composite metric to calculate the preferred path to a network:

- **Bandwidth**- The slowest bandwidth among all of the outgoing interfaces, along the path from source to destination.

- **Delay**- The cumulative (sum) of all interface delay along the path (in tens of microseconds).

The following values can be used, but are not recommended, because they typically result in frequent recalculation of the topology table:

- **Reliability**- Represents the worst reliability between the source and destination, which is based on keepalives.

- **Load**- Represents the worst load on a link between the source and destination, which is computed based on the packet rate and the configured bandwidth of the interface.

Note Although the MTU is included in the routing table updates, it is not a routing metric used by EIGRP.

The Composite Metric

Figure 1 shows the composite metric formula used by EIGRP. The formula consists of values K1 to K5, known as EIGRP metric weights. K1 and K3 represent bandwidth and delay, respectively. K2 represents load, and K4 and K5 represent reliability. By default, K1 and K3 are set to 1, and K2, K4, and K5 are set to 0. The result is that only the bandwidth and delay values are used in the computation of the default composite metric. EIGRP for IPv4 and EIGRP for IPv6 use the same formula for the composite metric.

The metric calculation method (k values) and the EIGRP autonomous system number must match between EIGRP neighbors. If they do not match, the routers do not form an adjacency.

The default k values can be changed with the `metric weights` router configuration mode command:

```
Router(config-router)#  metric weights tos k1 k2 k3 k4 k5
```

Note Modifying the `metric weights` value is generally not recommended and beyond the scope of this course. However, its relevance is important in establishing neighbor adjacencies. If one router has modified the metric weights and another router has not, an adjacency does not form.

Verifying the k Values

The `show ip protocols` command is used to verify the k values. The command output for R1 is shown in Figure 2. Notice that the k values on R1 are set to the default.

Refer to
Online Course
for Illustration

7.3.2.2   Examining Interface Values

Examining the Metric Values

The `show interfaces` command displays interface information, including the parameters used to compute the EIGRP metric. The figure shows the `show interfaces` command for the Serial 0/0/0 interface on R1.

- **BW**- Bandwidth of the interface (in kilobits per second).

- **DLY**- Delay of the interface (in microseconds).

- **Reliability**- Reliability of the interface as a fraction of 255 (255/255 is 100% reliability), calculated as an exponential average over five minutes. By default, EIGRP does not include its value in computing its metric.

- **Txload, Rxload**- Transmit and receive load on the interface as a fraction of 255 (255/255 is completely saturated), calculated as an exponential average over five minutes. By default, EIGRP does not include its value in computing its metric.

Note   Throughout this course, bandwidth is referenced as kb/s. However, router output displays bandwidth using the Kbit/sec abbreviation. Router output also displays delay as usec. In this course, delay is referenced as microseconds.

Refer to
Online Course
for Illustration

7.3.2.3   Bandwidth Metric

The bandwidth metric is a static value used by some routing protocols, such as EIGRP and OSPF, to calculate their routing metric. The bandwidth is displayed in kilobits per second (kb/s). Most serial interfaces use the default bandwidth value of 1544 kb/s or 1,544,000 b/s (1.544 Mb/s). This is the bandwidth of a T1 connection. However, some serial interfaces use a different default bandwidth value. Figure 1 shows the topology used throughout this section. The types of serial interfaces and their associated bandwidths may not necessarily reflect the more common types of connections found in networks today.

Always verify bandwidth with the **show interfaces** command.

The default value of the bandwidth may or may not reflect the actual physical bandwidth of the interface. If actual bandwidth of the link differs from the default bandwidth value, the bandwidth value should be modified.

Configuring the Bandwidth Parameter

On most serial links, the bandwidth metric defaults to 1544 kb/s. Because both EIGRP and OSPF use bandwidth in default metric calculations, a correct value for bandwidth is very important to the accuracy of routing information.

Use the following interface configuration mode command to modify the bandwidth metric:

```
Router(config-if)#  bandwidth  kilobits-bandwidth-value
```

Use the **no bandwidth** command to restore the default value.

In Figure 2, the link between R1 and R2 has a bandwidth of 64 kb/s, and the link between R2 and R3 has a bandwidth of 1,024 kb/s. The figure shows the configurations used on all three routers to modify the bandwidth on the appropriate serial interfaces.

Verifying the Bandwidth Parameter

Use the **show interfaces** command to verify the new bandwidth parameters, as shown in Figure 3. It is important to modify the bandwidth metric on both sides of the link to ensure proper routing in both directions.

Modifying the bandwidth value does not change the actual bandwidth of the link. The **bandwidth** command only modifies the bandwidth metric used by routing protocols, such as EIGRP and OSPF.

Refer to
Online Course
for Illustration

7.3.2.4   Delay Metric

Delay is the measure of the time it takes for a packet to traverse a route. The delay (DLY) metric is a static value based on the type of link to which the interface is connected and is expressed in microseconds. Delay is not measured dynamically. In other words, the router does not actually track how long packets take to reach the destination. The delay value, much like the bandwidth value, is a default value that can be changed by the network administrator.

When used to determine the EIGRP metric, delay is the cumulative (sum) of all interface delays along the path (measured in tens of microseconds).

The table in Figure 1 shows the default delay values for various interfaces. Notice that the default value is 20,000 microseconds for serial interfaces and 10 microseconds for GigabitEthernet interfaces.

Use the `show interfaces` command to verify the delay value on an interface, as shown in Figure 2. Although an interface with various bandwidths can have the same delay value, by default, Cisco recommends not modifying the delay parameter, unless the network administrator has a specific reason to do so.

Refer to
Online Course
for Illustration

7.3.2.5   How to Calculate the EIGRP Metric

Although EIGRP automatically calculates the routing table metric used to choose the best path, it is important that the network administrator understands how these metrics were determined.

The figure shows the composite metric used by EIGRP. Using the default values for K1 and K3, the calculation can be simplified to the slowest bandwidth (or minimum bandwidth), plus the sum of all of the delays.

In other words, by examining the bandwidth and delay values for all of the outgoing interfaces of the route, we can determine the EIGRP metric as follows:

Step 1.   Determine the link with the slowest bandwidth. Use that value to calculate bandwidth (10,000,000/bandwidth).

Step 2.   Determine the delay value for each outgoing interface on the way to the destination. Add the delay values and divide by 10 (sum of delay/10).

Step 3.   Add the computed values for bandwidth and delay, and multiply the sum by 256 to obtain the EIGRP metric.

The routing table output for R2 shows that the route to 192.168.1.0/24 has an EIGRP metric of 3,012,096.

Refer to
Online Course
for Illustration

7.3.2.6   Calculating the EIGRP Metric

Figure 1 displays the three router topology. This example illustrates how EIGRP determines the metric displayed in R2's routing table for the 192.168.1.0/24 network.

Bandwidth

EIGRP uses the slowest bandwidth in its metric calculation. The slowest bandwidth can be determined by examining each interface between R2 and the destination network 192.168.1.0. The Serial 0/0/1 interface on R2 has a bandwidth of 1,024 kb/s. The

GigabitEthernet 0/0 interface on R3 has a bandwidth of 1,000,000 kb/s. Therefore, the slowest bandwidth is 1,024 kb/s and is used in the calculation of the metric.

EIGRP divides a reference bandwidth value of 10,000,000 by the interface bandwidth value in kb/s. This results in higher bandwidth values receiving a lower metric and lower bandwidth values receiving a higher metric. 10,000,000 is divided by 1,024. If the result is not a whole number, then the value is rounded down. In this case, 10,000,000 divided by 1,024 equals 9,765.625. The .625 is dropped to yield 9,765 for the bandwidth portion of the composite metric, as shown in Figure 2.

Delay

The same outgoing interfaces are used to determine the delay value, as shown in Figure 3.

EIGRP uses the sum of all delays to the destination. The Serial 0/0/1 interface on R2 has a delay of 20,000 microseconds. The Gigabit 0/0 interface on R3 has a delay of 10 microseconds. The sum of these delays is divided by 10. In the example, (20,000+10)/10 results in a value of 2,001 for the delay portion of the composite metric.

Calculate Metric

Use the calculated values for bandwidth and delay in the metric formula. This results in a metric of 3,012,096, as shown in Figure 4. This value matches the value shown in the routing table for R2.

Refer to
Interactive Graphic
in online course.

7.3.2.7   Activity - Calculate the EIGRP Metric

7.3.3   DUAL and the Topology Table

Refer to
Online Course
for Illustration

7.3.3.1   DUAL Concepts

EIGRP uses the Diffusing Update Algorithm (DUAL) to provide the best loop-free path and loop-free backup paths.

DUAL uses several terms, which are discussed in more detail throughout this section:

- Successor
- Feasible Distance (FD)
- Feasible Successor (FS)
- Reported Distance (RD) or Advertised Distance (AD)
- Feasible Condition or Feasibility Condition (FC)

These terms and concepts are at the center of the loop avoidance mechanism of DUAL.

Refer to
Online Course
for Illustration

7.3.3.2   Introduction to DUAL

EIGRP uses convergence algorithm DUAL. Convergence is critical to a network to avoid routing loops.

Routing loops, even temporary ones, can be detrimental to network performance. Distance vector routing protocols, such as RIP, prevent routing loops with hold-down timers and split horizon. Although EIGRP uses both of these techniques, it uses them somewhat differently; the primary way that EIGRP prevents routing loops is with the DUAL algorithm.

Click Play in the figure to view the basic operation of DUAL.

The DUAL algorithm is used to obtain loop-freedom at every instance throughout a route computation. This allows all routers involved in a topology change to synchronize at the same time. Routers that are not affected by the topology changes are not involved in the recomputation. This method provides EIGRP with faster convergence times than other distance vector routing protocols.

The decision process for all route computations is done by the DUAL Finite State Machine (FSM). An FSM is a workflow model, similar to a flow chart that is composed of the following:

- A finite number of stages (states)

- Transitions between those stages

- Operations

The DUAL FSM tracks all routes, uses EIGRP metrics to select efficient, loop-free paths, and identify the routes with the least-cost path to be inserted into the routing table.

Recomputation of the DUAL algorithm can be processor-intensive. EIGRP avoids recomputation whenever possible by maintaining a list of backup routes that DUAL has already determined to be loop-free. If the primary route in the routing table fails, the best backup route is immediately added to the routing table.

7.3.3.3   Successor and Feasible Distance

Refer to **Online Course** for Illustration

Figure 1 shows the topology for this topic. A successor is a neighboring router that is used for packet forwarding and is the least-cost route to the destination network. The IP address of a successor is shown in a routing table entry right after the word via.

FD is the lowest calculated metric to reach the destination network. FD is the metric listed in the routing table entry as the second number inside the brackets. As with other routing protocols, this is also known as the metric for the route.

Examining the routing table for R2 in Figure 2, notice that EIGRP's best path for the 192.168.1.0/24 network is through router R3, and that the feasible distance is 3,012,096. This is the metric that was calculated in the previous topic.

7.3.3.4   Feasible Successors, Feasibility Condition, and Reported Distance

Refer to **Online Course** for Illustration

DUAL can converge quickly after a change in the topology because it can use backup paths to other networks without recomputing DUAL. These backup paths are known as Feasible Successors (FSs).

An FS is a neighbor that has a loop-free backup path to the same network as the successor, and it satisfies the Feasibility Condition (FC). R2's successor for the 192.168.1.0/24 network is R3, providing the best path or lowest metric to the destination network. Notice in Figure 1, that R1 provides an alternative path, but is it an FS? Before R1 can be an FS for R2, R1 must first meet the FC.

The FC is met when a neighbor's Reported Distance (RD) to a network is less than the local router's feasible distance to the same destination network. If the reported distance is less, it represents a loop-free path. The reported distance is simply an EIGRP neighbor's feasible distance to the same destination network. The reported distance is the metric that a router reports to a neighbor about its own cost to that network.

In Figure 2, R1's feasible distance to 192.168.1.0/24 is 2,170,112.

- R1 reports to R2 that its FD to 192.168.1.0/24 is 2,170,112.

- From R2's perspective, 2,170,112 is R1's RD.

R2 uses this information to determine if R1 meets the FC and, therefore, can be an FS.

As shown in Figure 3, because the RD of R1 (2,170,112) is less than R2's own FD (3,012,096), R1 meets the FC.

R1 is now an FS for R2 to the 192.168.1.0/24 network.

If there is a failure in R2's path to 192.168.1.0/24 via R3 (successor), then R2 immediately installs the path via R1 (FS) in its routing table. R1 becomes the new successor for R2's path to this network, as shown in Figure 4.

Refer to
Online Course
for Illustration

7.3.3.5   Topology Table: show ip eigrp topology Command

Figure 1 shows the topology.

The EIGRP topology table contains all of the routes that are known to each EIGRP neighbor. As an EIGRP router learns routes from its neighbors, those routes are installed in its EIGRP topology table.

As shown in Figure 2, use the `show ip eigrp topology` command to view the topology table. The topology table lists all successors and FSs that DUAL has calculated to destination networks. Only the successor is installed into the IP routing table.

Refer to
Online Course
for Illustration

7.3.3.6   Topology Table: show ip eigrp topology Command (Cont.)

As shown in Figure 1, the first line in the topology table displays:

- **P**- Route in the passive state. When DUAL is not performing its diffusing computations to determine a path for a network, the route is in a stable mode, known as the passive state. If DUAL recalculates or searches for a new path, the route is in an active state and displays an A. All routes in the topology table should be in the passive state for a stable routing domain.

- **192.168.1.0/24**- Destination network that is also found in the routing table.

- **1 successors**- Displays the number of successors for this network. If there are multiple equal cost paths to this network, there are multiple successors.

- **FD is 3012096**- FD, the EIGRP metric to reach the destination network. This is the metric displayed in the IP routing table.

As shown in Figure 2, the first subentry in the output shows the successor:

- **via 192.168.10.10**- Next-hop address of the successor, R3. This address is shown in the routing table.

- **3012096**- FD to 192.168.1.0/24. It is the metric shown in the IP routing table.

- **2816**- RD of the successor and is R3's cost to reach this network.

- **Serial 0/0/1**- Outbound interface used to reach this network, also shown in the routing table.

As shown in Figure 3, the second subentry shows the FS, R1 (if there is not a second entry, then there are no FSs):

- **via 172.16.3.1**- Next-hop address of the FS, R1.

- **41024256**- R2's new FD to 192.168.1.0/24, if R1 became the new successor and would be the new metric displayed in the IP routing table.

- **2170112**- RD of the FS, or R1's metric to reach this network. RD must be less than the current FD of 3,012,096 to meet the FC.

- **Serial 0/0/0**- This is the outbound interface used to reach FS, if this router becomes the successor.

Refer to
Online Course
for Illustration

7.3.3.7   Topology Table: No Feasible Successor

To see how DUAL uses successors and FSs, examine the routing table of R1, assuming the network is converged, as shown in Figure 1.

Figure 2 displays a partial output from the `show ip route` command on R1. The route to 192.168.1.0/24 shows that the successor is R3 via 192.168.10.6 with an FD of 2,170,112.

The IP routing table only includes the best path, the successor. To see if there are any FSs, we must examine the EIGRP topology table. The topology table in Figure 3 only shows the successor 192.168.10.6, which is R3. There are no FSs. By looking at the actual physical topology or network diagram, it is obvious that there is a backup route to 192.168.1.0/24 through R2. R2 is not an FS because it does not meet the FC. Although, looking at the topology, it is obvious that R2 is a backup route, EIGRP does not have a map of the network topology. EIGRP is a distance vector routing protocol and only knows about remote network information through its neighbors.

DUAL does not store the route through R2 in the topology table. All links can be displayed using the `show ip eigrp topology all-links` command. This command displays links whether they satisfy the FC or not.

As shown in Figure 4, the `show ip eigrp topology all-links` command shows all possible paths to a network, including successors, FSs, and even those routes that are not FSs. R1's FD to 192.168.1.0/24 is 2,170,112 via the successor R3. For R2 to be considered a FS, it must meet the FC. R2's RD to R1 to reach 192.168.1.0/24 must be less the R1's current FD. Per the figure, R2's RD is 3,012,096, which is higher than R1's current FD of 2,170,112.

Even though R2 looks like a viable backup path to 192.168.1.0/24, R1 has no idea that the path is not a potential loop back through itself. EIGRP is a distance vector routing protocol, without the ability to see a complete, loop-free topological map of the network. DUAL's method of guaranteeing that a neighbor has a loop-free path is that the neighbor's metric must satisfy the FC. By ensuring that the RD of the neighbor is less than its own FD, the router can assume that this neighboring router is not part of its own advertised route; thus, always avoiding the potential for a loop.

R2 can be used as a successor if R3 fails; however, there is a longer delay before adding it to the routing table. Before R2 can be used as a successor, DUAL must do further processing.

Refer to **Interactive Graphic** in online course.

7.3.3.8   Activity - Determine the Feasible Successor

Refer to **Online Course** for Illustration

7.3.4   DUAL and Convergence

7.3.4.1   DUAL Finite State Machine (FSM)

The centerpiece of EIGRP is DUAL and its EIGRP route-calculation engine. The actual name of this technology is DUAL Finite State Machine (FSM). This FSM contains all of the logic used to calculate and compare routes in an EIGRP network. The figure shows a simplified version of the DUAL FSM.

An FSM is an abstract machine, not a mechanical device with moving parts. FSMs define a set of possible states that something can go through, what events cause those states, and what events result from those states. Designers use FSMs to describe how a device, computer program, or routing algorithm reacts to a set of input events.

FSMs are beyond the scope of this course. However, the concept is used to examine some of the output from EIGRP's FSM using the `debug eigrp fsm` command. Use this command to examine what DUAL does when a route is removed from the routing table.

Refer to **Online Course** for Illustration

7.3.4.2   DUAL: Feasible Successor

R2 is currently using R3 as the successor to 192.168.1.0/24. In addition, R2 currently lists R1 as an FS, as shown in Figure 1.

The `show ip eigrp topology` output for R2 in Figure 2 verifies that R3 is the successor and R1 is the FS for the 192.168.1.0/24 network. To understand how DUAL can use a FS when the path using the successor is no longer available, a link failure is simulated between R2 and R3.

Before simulating the failure, DUAL debugging must be enabled using the `debug eigrp fsm` command on R2, as shown in Figure 3. A link failure is simulated using the `shutdown` command on the Serial 0/0/1 interface on R2.

The `debug` output displays the activity generated by DUAL when a link goes down. R2 must inform all EIGRP neighbors of the lost link, as well as update its own routing and topology tables. This example only shows selected `debug` output. In particular, notice that the DUAL FSM searches for and finds an FS for the route in the EIGRP topology table.

The FS R1 now becomes the successor and is installed in the routing table as the new best path to 192.168.1.0/24, as shown in Figure 4. With an FS, this change in the routing table happens almost immediately.

As shown in Figure 5, the topology table for R2 now shows R1 as the successor and there are no new FSs. If the link between R2 and R3 is made active again, then R3 returns as the successor and R1 once again becomes the FS.

Refer to
Online Course
for Illustration

7.3.4.3   DUAL: No Feasible Successor

Occasionally, the path to the successor fails and there are not any FSs. In this instance, DUAL does not have a guaranteed loop-free backup path to the network, so the path is not in the topology table as an FS. If there are not any FSs in the topology table, DUAL puts the network into the active state. DUAL actively queries its neighbors for a new successor.

R1 is currently using R3 as the successor to 192.168.1.0/24, as shown in Figure 1. However, R1 does not have R2 listed as an FS, because R2 does not satisfy the FC. To understand how DUAL searches for a new successor when there is no FS, a link failure is simulated between R1 and R3.

Before the link failure is simulated, DUAL debugging is enabled with the `debug eigrp fsm` command on R1, as shown in Figure 2. A link failure is simulated using the `shutdown` command on the Serial 0/0/1 interface on R1.

When the successor is no longer available and there is no feasible successor, DUAL puts the route into an active state. DUAL sends EIGRP queries asking other routers for a path to the network. Other routers return EIGRP replies, letting the sender of the EIGRP query know whether or not they have a path to the requested network. If none of the EIGRP replies have a path to this network, the sender of the query does not have a route to this network.

The selected debug output in Figure 2 shows the 192.168.1.0/24 network put into the active state and EIGRP queries sent to other neighbors. R2 replies with a path to this network, which becomes the new successor and is installed into the routing table.

If the sender of the EIGRP queries receives EIGRP replies that include a path to the requested network, the preferred path is added as the new successor and added to the routing table. This process takes longer than if DUAL had an FS in its topology table and was able to quickly add the new route to the routing table. In Figure 3, notice that R1 has a new route to the 192.168.1.0/24 network. The new EIGRP successor is router R2.

Figure 4 shows that the topology table for R1 now has R2 as the successor with no new FSs. If the link between R1 and R3 is made active again, R3 returns as the successor. However, R2 is still not the FS, because it does not meet the FC.

Refer to **Packet Tracer Activity** for this chapter

7.3.4.4   Packet Tracer - Investigating DUAL FSM

Background/Scenario

In this activity, you will modify the EIGRP metric formula to cause a change in the topology. This allows you to see how EIGRP reacts when a neighbor goes down due to unforeseen circumstances. You will then use the `debug` command to view topology changes and how the DUAL Finite State Machine determines successor and feasible successor paths to re-converge the network.

Refer to
Online Course
for Illustration

7.4   Configuring EIGRP for IPv6

7.4.1   EIGRP for IPv4 vs. IPv6

7.4.1.1   EIGRP for IPv6

Similar to its IPv4 counterpart, EIGRP for IPv6 exchanges routing information to populate the IPv6 routing table with remote prefixes. EIGRP for IPv6 was made available in Cisco IOS, Release 12.4(6)T.

Note   In IPv6, the network address is referred to as the prefix and the subnet mask is called the prefix length.

EIGRP for IPv4 runs over the IPv4 network layer, communicating with other EIGRP IPv4 peers, and advertising only IPv4 routes. EIGRP for IPv6 has the same functionality as EIGRP for IPv4, but uses IPv6 as the network layer transport, communicating with EIGRP for IPv6 peers and advertising IPv6 routes.

EIGRP for IPv6 also uses DUAL as the computation engine to guarantee loop-free paths and backup paths throughout the routing domain.

As with all IPv6 routing protocols, EIGRP for IPv6 has separate processes from its IPv4 counterpart. The processes and operations are basically the same as in the IPv4 routing protocol; however, they run independently. EIGRP for IPv4 and EIGRP for IPv6 each have separate EIGRP neighbor tables, EIGRP topology tables, and IP routing tables, as shown in the figure. EIGRP for IPv6 is a separate protocol-dependent module (PDM).

The EIGRP for IPv6 configuration and verification commands are very similar to those used in EIGRP for IPv4. These commands are described later in this section.

Refer to
Online Course
for Illustration

7.4.1.2   Comparing EIGRP for IPv4 and IPv6

The following is a comparison of the main features of EIGRP for IPv4 and EIGRP for IPv6:

- **Advertised routes**- EIGRP for IPv4 advertises IPv4 networks; whereas, EIGRP for IPv6 advertises IPv6 prefixes.

- **Distance vector**- Both EIGRP for IPv4 and IPv6 are advanced distance vector routing protocols. Both protocols use the same administrative distances.

- **Convergence technology**- EIGRP for IPv4 and IPv6 both use the DUAL algorithm. Both protocols use the same DUAL techniques and processes, including successor, FS, FD, and RD.

- **Metric**- Both EIGRP for IPv4 and IPv6 use bandwidth, delay, reliability, and load for their composite metric. Both routing protocols use the same composite metric and use only bandwidth and delay, by default.

- **Transport protocol**- The Reliable Transport Protocol (RTP) is responsible for guaranteed delivery of EIGRP packets to all neighbors for both protocols, EIGRP for IPv4 and IPv6.

- **Update messages**- Both EIGRP for IPv4 and IPv6 send incremental updates when the state of a destination changes. The terms, partial and bounded, are used when referring to updates for both protocols.

- **Neighbor discovery mechanism**- EIGRP for IPv4 and EIGRP for IPv6 use a simple Hello mechanism to learn about neighboring routers and form adjacencies.

- **Source and destination addresses**- EIGRP for IPv4 sends messages to the multicast address 224.0.0.10. These messages use the source IPv4 address of the outbound interface. EIGRP for IPv6 sends its messages to the multicast address FF02::A. EIGRP for IPv6 messages are sourced using the IPv6 link-local address of the exit interface.

- **Authentication**- EIGRP for IPv4 can use either plaintext authentication or Message Digest 5 (MD5) authentication. EIGRP for IPv6 uses MD5.

- **Router ID**- Both EIGRP for IPv4 and EIGRP for IPv6 use a 32-bit number for the EIGRP router ID. The 32-bit router ID is represented in dotted-decimal notation and is commonly referred to as an IPv4 address. If the EIGRP for IPv6 router has not been configured with an IPv4 address, the `eigrp router-id` command must be used to configure a 32-bit router ID. The process for determining the router ID is the same for both EIGRP for IPv4 and IPv6.

7.4.1.3   IPv6 Link-local Addresses

Refer to
Online Course
for Illustration

Routers running a dynamic routing protocol, such as EIGRP exchange messages between neighbors on the same subnet or link. Routers only need to send and receive routing protocol messages with their directly connected neighbors. These messages are always sent from the source IP address of the router that is doing the forwarding.

IPv6 link-local addresses are ideal for this purpose. An IPv6 link-local address enables a device to communicate with other IPv6-enabled devices on the same link and only on that link (subnet). Packets with a source or destination link-local address cannot be routed beyond the link from where the packet originated.

EIGRP for IPv6 messages are sent using:

- **Source IPv6 address**- This is the IPv6 link-local address of the exit interface.

- **Destination IPv6 address**- When the packet needs to be sent to a multicast address, it is sent to the IPv6 multicast address FF02::A, the all-EIGRP-routers with link-local scope. If the packet can be sent as a unicast address, it is sent to the link-local address of the neighboring router.

Note   IPv6 link-local addresses are in the FE80::/10 range. The /10 indicates that the first 10 bits are 1111 1110 10xx xxxx, which results in the first hextet having a range of 1111 1110 10**00 0000** (FE80) to 1111 1110 10**11 1111** (FEBF).

Refer to
Interactive Graphic
in online course.

7.4.1.4   Activity - Compare EIGRPv4 and EIGRPv6

7.4.2   Configuring EIGRP for IPv6

Refer to
Online Course
for Illustration

7.4.2.1   EIGRP for IPv6 Network Topology

Figure 1 shows the network topology that is used for configuring EIGRP for IPv6. If the network is running dual-stack, using both IPv4 and IPv6 on all devices, EIGRP for both IPv4 and IPv6 can be configured on all the routers. However, in this section, the focus is solely on EIGRP for IPv6.

Only the IPv6 global unicast addresses have been configured on each router.

Figures 2, 3, and 4 display the starting interface configurations on each router. Notice the interface bandwidth values from the previous EIGRP for IPv4 configuration. Because EIGRP for IPv4 and IPv6 use the same metrics, modifying the bandwidth parameters influences both routing protocols.

Refer to
Online Course
for Illustration

7.4.2.2   Configuring IPv6 Link-local Addresses

Link-local addresses are automatically created when an IPv6 global unicast address is assigned to the interface. Global unicast addresses are not required on an interface; however, IPv6 link-local addresses are.

Unless configured manually, Cisco routers create the link-local address using FE80::/10 prefix and the EUI-64 process, as shown in Figure 1. EUI-64 involves using the 48-bit Ethernet MAC address, inserting FFFE in the middle and flipping the seventh bit. For serial interfaces, Cisco uses the MAC address of an Ethernet interface. A router with several serial interfaces can assign the same link-local address to each IPv6 interface, because link-local addresses only need to be local on the link.

Link-local addresses created using the EUI-64 format, or in some cases random interface IDs, make it difficult to recognize and remember those addresses. Because IPv6 routing protocols use IPv6 link-local addresses for unicast addressing and next hop address information in the routing table, it is common practice to make it an easily recognizable address. Configuring the link-local address manually provides the ability to create an address that is recognizable and easier to remember.

Link-local addresses can be configured manually using the same interface configuration mode command used to create IPv6 global unicast addresses, but with different parameters:

```
Router(config-if)#   ipv6 address link-local-address link-local
```

A link-local address has a prefix within the range FE80 to FEBF. When an address begins with this hextet (16-bit segment), the `link-local` keyword must follow the address.

Figure 2 shows the configuration of a link-local address using the `ipv6 address` interface configuration mode command. The link-local address FE80::1 is used to make it easily recognizable as belonging to router R1. The same IPv6 link-local address is configured on all of R1's interfaces. FE80::1 can be configured on each link because it only has to be unique on that link.

Similar to R1, in Figure 3, router R2 is configured with FE80::2 as the IPv6 link-local address on all of its interfaces.

Use the Syntax Checker in Figure 4 to configure FE80::3 as the link-local address on all of R3's interfaces.

As shown in Figure 5, the `show ipv6 interface brief` command is used to verify the IPv6 link-local and global unicast addresses on all interfaces.

<table>
<tr><td>

Refer to
Online Course
for Illustration

</td><td>

7.4.2.3 Configuring the EIGRP for IPv6 Routing Process

</td></tr>
</table>

The `ipv6 unicast-routing` global configuration mode command enables IPv6 routing on the router. This command is required before any IPv6 routing protocol can be configured. This command is not required to configure IPv6 addresses on the interfaces, but is necessary for the router to be enabled as an IPv6 router.

EIGRP for IPv6

The following global configuration mode command is used to enter router configuration mode for EIGRP for IPv6:

```
Router(config)#  ipv6 router eigrp autonomous-system
```

Similar to EIGRP for IPv4, the autonomous-system value must be the same on all routers in the routing domain. In Figure 1, the EIGRP for IPv6 routing process could not be configured until IPv6 routing was enabled with the `ipv6 unicast-routing` global configuration mode command.

Router ID

As shown in Figure 2, the `eigrp router-id` command is used to configure the router ID. EIGRP for IPv6 uses a 32 bit value for the router ID. To obtain that value, EIGRP for IPv6 uses the same process as EIGRP for IPv4. The `eigrp router-id` command takes precedence over any loopback or physical interface IPv4 addresses. If an EIGRP for IPv6 router does not have any active interfaces with an IPv4 address, then the `eigrp router-id` command is required.

The router ID should be a unique 32-bit number in the EIGRP for IP routing domain; otherwise, routing inconsistencies can occur.

Note The `eigrp router-id` command is used to configure the router ID for EIGRP. Some versions of IOS will accept the command `router-id`, without first specifying `eigrp`. The running-config, however, will display `eigrp router-id` regardless of which command is used.

By default, the EIGRP for IPv6 process is in a shutdown state. The `no shutdown` command is required to activate the EIGRP for IPv6 process, as shown in Figure 3. This command is not required for EIGRP for IPv4. Although, EIGRP for IPv6 is enabled, neighbor adjacencies and routing updates cannot be sent and received until EIGRP is activated on the appropriate interfaces.

Both the `no shutdown` command and a router ID are required for the router to form neighbor adjacencies.

Figure 4 shows the complete EIGRP for IPv6 configuration for router R2.

Use the Syntax Checker in Figure 5 to configure the EIGRP for IPv6 process on router R3.

Refer to
Online Course
for Illustration

7.4.2.4   ipv6 eigrp Interface Command

EIGRP for IPv6 uses a different method to enable an interface for EIGRP. Instead of using the `network` router configuration mode command to specify matching interface addresses, EIGRP for IPv6 is configured directly on the interface.

Use the following interface configuration mode command to enable EIGRP for IPv6 on an interface:

```
Router(config-if)#  ipv6 eigrp  autonomous-system
```

The autonomous-system value must be the same as the autonomous system number used to enable the EIGRP routing process. Similar to the `network` command used in EIGRP for IPv4, the `ipv6 eigrp interface` command:

- Enables the interface to form adjacencies and send or receive EIGRP for IPv6 updates

- Includes the prefix (network) of this interface in EIGRP for IPv6 routing updates

Figure 1 shows the configuration to enable EIGRP for IPv6 on routers R1 and R2 interfaces. Notice the message following the serial 0/0/0 interface in R2:

```
%DUAL-5-NBRCHANGE: EIGRP-IPv6 2: Neighbor FE80::1 (Serial0/0/0) is up: new adjacency
```

This message indicates that R2 has now formed an EIGRP-IPv6 adjacency with the neighbor at link-local address FE80::1. Because static link-local addresses were configured on all three routers, it is easy to determine that this adjacency is with router R1 (FE80::1).

Use the Syntax Checker in Figure 2 to enable EIGRP for IPv6 on R3's interfaces.

Passive Interface with EIGRP for IPv6

The same `passive-interface` command used for IPv4 is used to configure an interface as passive with EIGRP for IPv6. As shown in Figure 3, the `show ipv6 protocols` command is used to verify the configuration.

Refer to
Online Course
for Illustration

7.4.3   Verifying EIGRP for IPv6

7.4.3.1   Verifying EIGRP for IPv6: Examining Neighbors

Similar to EIGRP for IPv4, before any EIGRP for IPv6 updates can be sent or received, routers must establish adjacencies with their neighbors, as shown in Figure 1.

Use the `show ipv6 eigrp neighbors` command to view the neighbor table and verify that EIGRP for IPv6 has established an adjacency with its neighbors. The output shown in

Figure 2 displays the IPv6 link-local address of the adjacent neighbor and the interface that this router uses to reach that EIGRP neighbor. Using meaningful link-local addresses makes it easy to recognize the neighbors R2 at FE80::2 and R3 at FE80::3.

The output from the `show ipv6 eigrp neighbors` command includes:

- **H column**- Lists the neighbors in the order they were learned.

- **Address**- IPv6 link-local address of the neighbor.

- **Interface**- Local interface on which this Hello packet was received.

- **Hold**- Current hold time. When a Hello packet is received, this value is reset to the maximum hold time for that interface and then counts down to zero. If zero is reached, the neighbor is considered down.

- **Uptime**- Amount of time since this neighbor was added to the neighbor table.

- **SRTT** and **RTO** - Used by RTP to manage reliable EIGRP packets.

- **Queue Count**- Should always be zero. If it is more than zero, then EIGRP packets are waiting to be sent.

- **Sequence Number**- Used to track updates, queries, and reply packets.

The `show ipv6 eigrp neighbors` command is useful for verifying and troubleshooting EIGRP for IPv6. If an expected neighbor is not listed, ensure that both ends of the link are up/up using the `show ipv6 interface brief` command. The same requirements exist for establishing neighbor adjacencies with EIGRP for IPv6 as it does for IPv4. If both sides of the link have active interfaces, check to see:

- Are both routers configured with the same EIGRP autonomous system number?

- Is the interface enabled for EIGRP for IPv6 with the correct autonomous system number?

Refer to
Online Course
for Illustration

7.4.3.2   Verifying EIGRP for IPv6: show ip protocols Command

The `show ipv6 protocols` command displays the parameters and other information about the state of any active IPv6 routing protocol processes currently configured on the router. The `show ipv6 protocols` command displays different types of output specific to each IPv6 routing protocol.

The output in the figure indicates several EIGRP for IPv6 parameters previously discussed, including:

1. EIGRP for IPv6 is an active dynamic routing protocol on R1 configured with the autonomous system number 2.

2. These are the *k* values used to calculate the EIGRP composite metric. K1 and K3 are 1, by default, and K2, K4, and K5 are 0, by default.

3. The EIGRP for IPv6 router ID of R1 is 1.0.0.0.

4. Same as EIGRP for IPv4, EIGRP for IPv6 administrative distances have internal AD of 90 and external of 170 (default values).

5. The interfaces enabled for EIGRP for IPv6.

The output from the `show ipv6 protocols` command is useful in debugging routing operations. The Interfaces section shows which interfaces EIGRP for IPv6 have been enabled. This is useful in verifying that EIGRP is enabled on all of the appropriate interfaces with the correct autonomous system number.

Refer to **Online Course** for Illustration

7.4.3.3 Verifying EIGRP for IPv6: Examine the IPv6 Routing Table

As with any routing protocol, the goal is to populate the IP routing table with routes to remote networks and the best paths to reaching those networks. As with IPv4, it is important to examine the IPv6 routing table and determine whether it is populated with the correct routes.

The IPv6 routing table is examined using the `show ipv6 route` command. EIGRP for IPv6 routes are denoted in the routing table with a D, similar to its counterpart for IPv4.

Figure 1 shows that R1 has installed three EIGRP routes to remote IPv6 networks in its IPv6 routing table:

■ 2001:DB8:CAFE:2::/64 via R3 (FE80::3) using its Serial 0/0/1 interface

■ 2001:DB8:CAFE:3::/64 via R3 (FE80::3) using its Serial 0/0/1 interface

■ 2001:DB8:CAFE:A002::/64 via R3 (FE80::3) using its Serial 0/0/1 interface

All three routes are using router R3 as the next-hop router (successor). Notice that the routing table uses the link-local address as the next-hop address. Because each router has had all its interfaces configured with a unique and distinguishable link-local address, it is easy to recognize that the next-hop router via FE80::3 is router R3.

Figure 2 displays the IPv6 routing table for R2.

Figure 3 displays the routing table for R3. Notice that R3 has two equal cost paths to the 2001:DB8:CAFE:A001::/64. One path is via R1 at FE80::1 and the other path is via R2 at FE80::2.

Refer to **Packet Tracer Activity** for this chapter

7.4.3.4 Packet Tracer - Configuring Basic EIGRP with IPv6

Background/Scenario

In this activity, you will configure the network with EIGRP routing for IPv6. You will also assign router IDs, configure passive interfaces, verify the network is fully converged, and display routing information using `show` commands.

■ EIGRP for IPv6 has the same overall operation and features as EIGRP for IPv4. There are a few major differences between them:

■ EIGRP for IPv6 is configured directly on the router interfaces.

■ With EIGRP for IPv6, a router-ID is required on each router or the routing process does not start.

■ The EIGRP for IPv6 routing process uses a shutdown feature.

Refer to
Lab Activity
for this chapter

7.4.3.5 Lab - Configuring Basic EIGRP for IPv6

In this lab, you will complete the following objectives:

■ Part 1: Build the Network and Verify Connectivity

■ Part 2: Configure EIGRP for IPv6 Routing

■ Part 3: Verify EIGRP for IPv6 Routing

■ Part 4: Configure and Verify Passive Interfaces

Refer to
Online Course
for Illustration

7.5 Summary

Refer to
Lab Activity
for this chapter

7.5.1.1 Class Activity - Portfolio RIP and EIGRP

Portfolio RIP and EIGRP

You are preparing a portfolio file for comparison of RIP and EIGRP routing protocols.

Think of a network with three interconnected routers with each router providing a LAN for PCs, printers, and other end devices. The graphic on this page depicts one example of a topology like this.

In this modeling activity scenario, you will be creating, addressing and configuring a topology, using verification commands, and comparing/contrasting RIP and EIGRP routing protocol outputs.

Complete the PDF reflection questions accompanying this activity. Save your work and be prepared to share your answers with the class. Also save a copy of your work for later use within this course or for portfolio reference.

Refer to
Online Course
for Illustration

7.5.1.2 Summary

EIGRP (Enhanced Interior Gateway Routing Protocol) is a classless, distance vector routing protocol. EIGRP is an enhancement of another Cisco routing protocol IGRP (Interior Gateway Routing Protocol) which is now obsolete. EIGRP was initially released in 1992 as a Cisco proprietary protocol available only on Cisco devices. In 2013, Cisco released a basic functionality of EIGRP as an open standard, to the IETF.

EIGRP uses the source code of "D" for DUAL in the routing table. EIGRP has a default administrative distance of 90 for internal routes and 170 for routes imported from an external source, such as default routes.

EIGRP is an advanced distance vector routing protocol that includes features not found in other distance vector routing protocols like RIP. These features include: Diffusing Update Algorithm (DUAL), establishing neighbor adjacencies, Reliable Transport Protocol (RTP), partial and bounded updates, and equal and unequal cost load balancing.

EIGRP uses PDMs (Protocol Dependent Modules) giving it the capability to support different Layer 3 protocols including IPv4 and IPv6. EIGRP uses RTP (Reliable Transport

Protocol) as the transport layer protocol for the delivery of EIGRP packets. EIGRP uses reliable delivery for EIGRP updates, queries and replies; and uses unreliable delivery for EIGRP Hellos and acknowledgments. Reliable RTP means an EIGRP acknowledgment must be returned.

Before any EIGRP updates are sent, a router must first discover their neighbors. This is done with EIGRP Hello packets. The Hello and hold-down values do not need to match for two routers to become neighbors. The `show ip eigrp neighbors` command is used to view the neighbor table and verify that EIGRP has established an adjacency with its neighbors.

EIGRP does not send periodic updates like RIP. EIGRP sends partial or bounded updates, which includes only the route changes and only to those routers that are affected by the change. EIGRP composite metric uses bandwidth, delay, reliability, and load to determine the best path. By default only bandwidth and delay are used.

At the center of EIGRP is DUAL (Diffusing Update Algorithm). The DUAL finite state machine is used to determine best path and potential backup paths to every destination network. The successor is a neighboring router that is used to forward the packet using the least-cost route to the destination network. Feasible distance (FD) is the lowest calculated metric to reach the destination network through the successor. A feasible successor (FS) is a neighbor who has a loop-free backup path to the same network as the successor, and also meets the feasibility condition. The feasibility condition (FC) is met when a neighbor's reported distance (RD) to a network is less than the local router's feasible distance to the same destination network. The reported distance is simply an EIGRP neighbor's feasible distance to the destination network.

EIGRP is configured with the `router eigrp` autonomous-system command. The autonomous-system value is actually a process-id and must be the same on all routers in the EIGRP routing domain. The `network` command is similar to that used with RIP. The network is the classful network address of the directly connected interfaces on the router. A wildcard mask is an optional parameter that can be used to include only specific interfaces.

Go to the online course to take the quiz and exam.

Chapter 7 Quiz

This quiz is designed to provide an additional opportunity to practice the skills and knowledge presented in the chapter and to prepare for the chapter exam. You will be allowed multiple attempts and the grade does not appear in the gradebook.

Chapter 7 Exam

The chapter exam assesses your knowledge of the chapter content.

Your Chapter Notes

EIGRP Advanced Configurations and Troubleshooting

8.0 EIGRP Advanced Configurations and Troubleshooting

8.0.1.1 Introduction

EIGRP is a versatile routing protocol that can be fine-tuned in many ways. Two of the most important tuning capabilities are the ability to summarize routes and the ability to implement load balancing. Other tuning capabilities include being able to propagate a default, fine-tune timers, and implement authentication between EIGRP neighbors to increase security.

This chapter discusses these additional tuning features and the configuration mode commands to implement these features for both IPv4 and IPv6.

> Refer to
> **Lab Activity**
> for this chapter

8.0.1.2 Class Activity - EIGRP - Back to the Future

Activity - EIGRP – Back to the Future

This chapter teaches you how to maintain your EIGRP networks and to influence them to do what you want them to do. EIGRP concepts from this chapter include:

- Auto-summarization
- Load balancing
- Default routes
- Hold-down timers
- Authentication

With a partner, write 10 EIGRP review questions based on the previous chapter's curriculum content. Three of the questions must focus on the bulleted items above. Ideally, Multiple Choice, True/False, or Fill in the Blank question types will be designed. As you design your questions, ensure that you record the curriculum section and page numbers of the supporting content in case you need to refer back for answer verification.

Save your work and then meet with another group, or the entire class, and quiz them using the questions you developed.

Refer to
Interactive Graphic
in online course.

8.1   Advanced EIGRP Configurations

8.1.1   Automatic summarization

8.1.1.1   Network Topology

Before fine tuning EIGRP features, start with a basic implementation of EIGRP.

Figure 1 shows the network topology used for this chapter.

Figures 2, 3, and 4 show the IPv4 interface configurations and the EIGRP implementations on R1, R2, and R3, respectively.

The types of serial interfaces and their associated bandwidths may not necessarily reflect the more common types of connections found in networks today. The bandwidths of the serial links used in this topology help explain the calculation of the routing protocol metrics and the process of best path selection.

Notice that the `bandwidth` commands on the serial interfaces were used to modify the default bandwidth of 1,544 kb/s.

In this chapter, the ISP router is used as the routing domain's gateway to the Internet. All three routers are running Cisco IOS, Release 15.2.

Refer to
Online Course
for Illustration

8.1.1.2   EIGRP Automatic summarization

One of the most common tuning methods of EIGRP is enabling and disabling automatic route summarization. Route summarization allows a router to group networks together and advertises them as one large group using a single, summarized route. The ability to summarize routes is necessary due to the rapid growth of networks.

A border router is a router that sits at the edge of a network. This router must be able to advertise all of the known networks within its route table to a connecting network router or ISP router. This convergence can potentially result in very large route tables. Imagine if a single router had 10 different networks and had to advertise all 10 route entries to a connecting router. What if that connecting router also had 10 networks, and had to advertise all 20 routes to an ISP router? If every enterprise router followed this pattern, the routing table of the ISP router would be huge.

Summarization decreases the number of entries in routing updates and lowers the number of entries in local routing tables. It also reduces bandwidth utilization for routing updates and results in faster routing table lookups.

To limit the number of routing advertisements and the size of routing tables, routing protocols such as EIGRP, use automatic summarization at classful boundaries. This means that EIGRP recognizes subnets as a single Class A, B, or C network, and creates only one entry in the routing table for the summary route. As a result, all traffic destined for the subnets travels across that one path.

The figure shows an example of how automatic summarization works. Routers R1 and R2 are both configured using EIGRP for IPv4 with automatic summarization. R1 has three subnets in its routing table: 172.16.1.0/24, 172.16.2.0/24, and 172.16.3.0/24. In the classful network addressing architecture, these subnets are all considered part of a larger class B network, 172.16.0.0/16. Because EIGRP on router R1 is configured for automatic summarization, when it sends its routing update to R2, it summarizes the three /24 subnets as a single network of 172.16.0.0/16, which reduces the number of routing updates sent and the number of entries in R2's IPv4 routing table.

All traffic destined for the three subnets travels across the one path. R2 does not maintain routes to individual subnets and no subnet information is learned. In an enterprise network, the path chosen to reach the summary route may not be the best choice for the traffic that is trying to reach each individual subnet. The only way that all routers can find the best routes for each individual subnet is for neighbors to send subnet information. In this situation, automatic summarization should be disabled. When automatic summarization is disabled, updates include subnet information.

Refer to
Online Course
for Illustration

8.1.1.3   Configuring EIGRP Automatic summarization

EIGRP for IPv4 automatic summarization is disabled by default beginning with Cisco IOS Release 15.0(1)M and 12.2(33). Prior to this, automatic summarization was enabled by default. This meant that EIGRP performed automatic summarization each time the EIGRP topology crossed a border between two different major class networks.

In Figure 1, the output from the `show ip protocols` command on R1 indicates that EIGRP automatic summarization is disabled. This router is running IOS 15.2; therefore, EIGRP automatic summarization is disabled by default. Figure 2 shows the current routing table for R3. Notice that the IPv4 routing table for R3 contains all of the networks and subnets within the EIGRP routing domain.

To enable automatic summarization for EIGRP, use the `auto-summary` command in router configuration mode, as shown in Figure 3:

```
R1(config)#  router eigrp as-number
R1(config-router)#  auto-summary
```

The `no` form of this command is used to disable automatic summarization.

Use the Syntax Checker in Figure 4 to enable automatic summarization for R3.

Refer to
Online Course
for Illustration

8.1.1.4   Verifying Auto-Summary: show ip protocols

In Figure 1, notice the EIGRP routing domain has three classful networks:

- 172.16.0.0/16 class B network consisting of 172.16.1.0/24, 172.16.2.0/24, and 172.16.3.0/30 subnets

- 192.168.10.0/24 class C network consisting of the 192.168.10.4/30 and 192.168.10.8/30 subnets

- 192.168.1.0/24 class C network, which is not subnetted

The output from R1's `show ip protocols` command in Figure 2 shows that automatic summarization is now enabled. The output also indicates the networks that are summarized and on which interfaces. Notice that R1 summarizes two networks in its EIGRP routing updates:

- 192.168.10.0/24 sent out the GigabitEthernet 0/0 and Serial 0/0/0 interfaces

- 172.16.0.0/16 sent out the Serial 0/0/1 interface

R1 has the subnets 192.168.10.4/30 and 192.168.10.8/30 in its IPv4 routing table.

As indicated in Figure 3, R1 summarizes the 192.168.10.4/30 and 192.168.10.8/30 subnet. It forwards the summarized address of 192.168.10.0/24 to its neighbors on its Serial 0/0/0 and GigabitEthernet 0/0 interfaces. Because R1 does not have any EIGRP neighbors on its GigabitEthernet 0/0 interface, the summarized routing update is only received by R2.

As indicated in Figure 4, R1 also has the 172.16.1.0/24, 172.16.2.0/24, and 172.16.3.0/30 subnets in its IPv4 routing table. R3 selects R1 as the successor to 172.16.0.0/16 because it has a lower feasible distance. The R3 S0/0/0 interface connecting to R1 uses a default bandwidth of 1,544 kb/s. The R3 link to R2 has a higher feasible distance because the R3 S0/0/1 interface has been configured with a lower bandwidth of 1,024 kb/s.

Notice that the 172.16.0.0/16 summarized update is not sent out R1's GigabitEthernet 0/0 and Serial 0/0/0 interfaces. This is because these two interfaces are members of the same 172.16.0.0/16 class B network. The 172.16.1.0/24 non-summarized routing update is sent by R1 to R2. Summarized updates are only sent out interfaces on different major classful networks.

Refer to
Online Course
for Illustration

8.1.1.5   Verifying Auto-Summary: Topology Table

In Figure 1, routers R1 and R2 will send R3 a summarized EIGRP routing update of 172.16.0.0/16. Routing tables for R1 and R2 contain subnets of the 172.16.0.0/16 network; therefore, both routers send the summary advertisement across a different major network to R3.

Figure 2 shows the output from the `show ip eigrp topology all-links` command used to view R3's complete EIGRP topology table. This verifies that R3 has received the 172.16.0.0/16 summary route from both R1 at 192.168.10.5 and R2 at 192.168.10.9. The first entry via 192.168.10.5 is the successor and the second entry via 192.168.10.9 is the feasible successor. R1 is the successor because its 1,544 kb/s link with R3 gives R3 a better EIGRP cost to 172.16.0.0/16 than R2, which is using a slower 1,024 kb/s link.

The `all-links` option shows all received updates, whether the route qualifies as a feasible successor (FS) or not. In this instance, R2 does qualify as an FS. R2 is considered an FS because its reported distance (RD) of 2,816 is less than the feasible distance (FD) of 2,170,112 via R1.

Refer to
Online Course
for Illustration

8.1.1.6   Verifying Auto-Summary: Routing Table

Examine the routing table to verify that the summarized route was received.

Figure 1 shows R3's routing table prior to automatic summarization, and then with automatic summarization enabled using the `auto-summary` command. Notice that with automatic summarization enabled, R3's routing table now only contains the single class B network address 172.16.0.0/16. The successor or next-hop router is R1 via 192.168.10.5.

Note   Automatic summarization is only an option with EIGRP for IPv4. Classful addressing does not exist in IPv6; therefore, there is no need for automatic summarization with EIGRP for IPv6.

When enabling automatic summarization, it is also necessary to understand the Null interface. Figure 2 shows the routing table for R1. Notice the two entries highlighted are using an exit interface of Null0. EIGRP has automatically included a summary route to Null0 for two classful networks 192.168.10.0/24 and 172.16.0.0/16.

The Null0 interface is a virtual IOS interface that is a route to nowhere, commonly known as "the bit bucket." Packets that match a route with a Null0 exit interface are discarded.

EIGRP for IPv4 automatically includes a Null0 summary route whenever the following conditions exist:

- There is at least one subnet that was learned via EIGRP.

- There are two or more **network** EIGRP router configuration mode commands.

- Automatic summarization is enabled.

The purpose of the Null0 summary route is to prevent routing loops for destinations that are included in the summary, but do not actually exist in the routing table.

Refer to
Online Course
for Illustration

8.1.1.7   Summary Route

The figure illustrates a scenario where a routing loop could occur:

1. R1 has a default route, 0.0.0.0/0 via the ISP router.

2. R1 sends a routing update to R2 containing the default route.

3. R2 installs the default route from R1 in its IPv4 routing table.

4. R2's routing table contains the 172.16.1.0/24, 172.16.2.0/24, and 172.16.3.0/24 subnets in its routing table.

5. R2 sends a summarized update to R1 for the 172.16.0.0/16 network.

6. R1 installs the summarized route for 172.16.0.0/16 via R2.

7. R1 receives a packet for 172.16.4.10. Because R1 has a route for 172.16.0.0/16 via R2, it forwards the packet to R2.

8. R2 receives the packet with the destination address 172.16.4.10 from R1. The packet does not match any specific route so using the default route in its routing table R2 forwards the packet back to R1.

9. The packet for 172.16.4.10 is looped between R1 and R2 until the TTL expires and the packet is dropped.

Refer to
Online Course
for Illustration

8.1.1.8   Summary Route (Cont.)

EIGRP uses the Null0 interface to prevent these types of routing loops. The figure illustrates a scenario where a Null0 route prevents the routing loop illustrated in the previous example:

1. R1 has a default route, 0.0.0.0/0 via the ISP router.

2. R1 sends a routing update to R2 containing the default route.

3. R2 installs the default route from R1 in its IPv4 routing table.

4. R2's routing table contains the 172.16.1.0/24, 172.16.2.0/24, and 172.16.3.0/24 subnets in its routing table.

5. R2 installs the 172.16.0.0/16 summary route to Null0 in its routing table.

6. R2 sends a summarized update to R1 for the 172.16.0.0/16 network.

7. R1 installs the summarized route for 172.16.0.0/16 via R2.

8. R1 receives a packet for 172.16.4.10. Because R1 has a route for 172.16.0.0/16 via R2, it forwards the packet to R2.

9. R2 receives the packet with the destination address 172.16.4.10 from R1. The packet does not match any specific subnet of 172.16.0.0 but does match the 172.16.0.0/16 summary route to Null0. Using the Null0 route, the packet is discarded.

A summary route on R2 for 172.16.0.0/16 to the Null0 interface, discards any packets that begin with 172.16.x.x, but do not have a longer match with any of the subnets: 172.16.1.0/24, 172.16.2.0/24, or 172.16.3.0/24.

Even if R2 has a default route of 0.0.0.0/0 in its routing table, the Null0 route is a longer match.

Note   The Null0 summary route is removed when autosummary is disabled using the **no auto-summary** router configuration mode command.

Refer to
Interactive Graphic
in online course.

8.1.1.9   Activity - Determine the Classful Summarization

Refer to
Interactive Graphic
in online course.

8.1.1.10   Activity - Determine the Exit Interface for a Given Packet

Refer to
Online Course
for Illustration

8.1.2   Manual Summarization

8.1.2.1   Manual Summary Routes

EIGRP can be configured to summarize routes, whether or not automatic summarization (**auto-summary**) is enabled. Because EIGRP is a classless routing protocol and includes the subnet mask in the routing updates, manual summarization can include supernet routes. Remember, a supernet is an aggregation of multiple major classful network addresses.

In Figure 1, two more networks are added to router R3 using loopback interfaces: 192.168.2.0/24 and 192.168.3.0/24. Although the loopback interfaces are virtual interfaces, they are used to represent physical networks for this example.

Figure 2 shows the commands on R3 to configure the two loopback interfaces and the configuration to enable both interfaces for EIGRP.

To verify that R3 sent EIGRP update packets to R1 and R2, the routing tables are examined on both routers.

In Figure 3, only the pertinent routes are shown. R1 and R2 routing tables show these additional networks in their routing tables: 192.168.2.0/24 and 192.168.3.0/24. Instead of sending three separate networks, R3 can summarize the 192.168.1.0/24, 192.168.2.0/24, and 192.168.3.0/24 networks as a single route.

Refer to
Online Course
for Illustration

8.1.2.2   Configuring EIGRP Manual Summary Routes

Determining the Summary EIGRP Route

Figure 1 shows the two manual summary routes that are configured on R3. These summary routes are sent out of the Serial 0/0/0 and Serial 0/0/1 interfaces to R3's EIGRP neighbors.

To determine the summary of these three networks, the same method is used to determine summary static routes, as shown in Figure 2:

Step 1.   Write out the networks to be summarized in binary.

Step 2.   To find the subnet mask for summarization, start with the far left bit.

Step 3.   Working from left to right, find all the bits that match consecutively.

Step 4.   When there is a column of bits that do not match, stop. This is the summary boundary.

Step 5.   Count the number of far left matching bits, which in this example is 22. This number is used to determine the subnet mask for the summarized route: /22 or 255.255.252.0.

Step 6.   To find the network address for summarization, copy the matching 22 bits and add all 0 bits to the end to make 32 bits.

The result is the summary network address and mask for 192.168.0.0/22.

Configure EIGRP Manual Summarization

To establish EIGRP manual summarization on a specific EIGRP interface, use the following interface configuration mode command:

```
Router(config-if)#  ip summary-address eigrp as-number network-address subnet-mask
```

Figure 2 shows the configuration to propagate a manual summary route on R3's Serial 0/0/0 interface. Because R3 has two EIGRP neighbors, the EIGRP manual summarization must be configured on both Serial 0/0/0 and Serial 0/0/1.

Use the Syntax Checker in Figure 3 to configure the same manual summary route on R3's Serial 0/0/1 interface.

Refer to
Online Course
for Illustration

8.1.2.3   Verifying Manual Summary Routes

The figure illustrates that, after the summary route is configured, the routing tables of R1 and R2 no longer include the individual 192.168.1.0/24, 192.168.2.0/24, and 192.168.3.0/24 networks. Instead, they show a single summary route of 192.168.0.0/22. Summary routes reduce the number of total routes in routing tables, which makes the routing table lookup process more efficient. Summary routes also require less bandwidth utilization for the routing updates, because a single route can be sent instead of multiple individual routes.

Refer to
Online Course
for Illustration

8.1.2.4   EIGRP for IPv6: Manual Summary Routes

While automatic summarization is not available for EIGRP IPv6 networks, it is possible to enable manual summarization for EIGRP IPv6.

Figure 1 shows an EIGRP IPv6 topology with four loopback addresses configured on R3. These virtual addresses are used to represent physical networks in R3's IPv6 routing table. These networks can be manually summarized in EIGRP for IPv6.

Figure 2 shows the configuration of the IPv6 loopback addresses on R3. Only four loopback addresses are shown in the topology and configured on R3; however, for this example it is assumed that all 2001:DB8:ACAD::/48 subnets can be reachable via R3.

To configure EIGRP for IPv6 manual summarization on a specific EIGRP interface, use the following interface configuration mode command:

```
Router(config-if)# ipv6 summary-address eigrp as-number prefix/prefix-length
```

Figure 3 shows the configuration to propagate an EIGRP for IPv6 manual summary route to R1 and R2 for the 2001:DB8:ACAD::/48 prefix. Similar to EIGRP for IPv4, R3 includes a summary route to null0 as a loop prevention mechanism.

The reception of the manual summary route can be verified by examining the routing table of the other routers in the routing domain. Figure 4 shows the 2001:DB8:ACAD::/48 route in the IPv6 routing table of R1.

Refer to **Packet Tracer Activity** for this chapter

8.1.2.5 Packet Tracer - Configuring EIGRP Manual Summary Routes for IPv4 and IPv6

Background/Scenario

In this activity, you will calculate and configure summary routes for the IPv4 and IPv6 networks. EIGRP is already configured; however, you are required to configure IPv4 and IPv6 summary routes on the specified interfaces. EIGRP will replace the current routes with a more specific summary route thereby reducing the size of the routing tables.

Refer to **Online Course** for Illustration

8.1.3 Default Route Propagation

8.1.3.1 Propagating a Default Static Route

Propagating a Default Static Route

Using a static route to 0.0.0.0/0 as a default route is not routing protocol-dependent. The "quad zero" static default route can be used with any currently supported routing protocols. The static default route is usually configured on the router that has a connection to a network outside the EIGRP routing domain; for example, to an ISP.

In Figure 1, R2 is the gateway router connecting the EIGRP routing domain with the Internet. When the static default route is configured, it is necessary to propagate that route throughout the EIGRP domain, as shown in Figure 2.

One method of propagating a static default route within the EIGRP routing domain is by using the **redistribute static** command. The **redistribute static** command tells EIGRP to include static routes in its EIGRP updates to other routers. Figure 3 shows the configuration of the static default route and the **redistribute static** command on router R2.

Figure 4 verifies that the default route has been received by router R2 and installed in its IPv4 routing table.

In Figure 5, the `show ip protocols` command verifies that R2 is redistributing static routes within the EIGRP routing domain.

Refer to
Online Course
for Illustration

8.1.3.2   Verifying the Propagated Default Route

The figure displays a portion of the IPv4 routing tables for R1 and R3.

In the routing tables for R1 and R3, notice the routing source and administrative distance for the new default route learned using EIGRP. The entry for the EIGRP learned default route is identified by the following:

- **D**- This route was learned from an EIGRP routing update.

- *****- The route is a candidate for a default route.

- **EX**- The route is an external EIGRP route, in this case a static route outside of the EIGRP routing domain.

- **170**- This is the administrative distance of an external EIGRP route.

Notice that R1 selects R3 as the successor to the default route because it has a lower feasible distance. Default routes provide a default path to outside the routing domain and, like summary routes, minimize the number of entries in the routing table.

Refer to
Online Course
for Illustration

8.1.3.3   EIGRP for IPv6: Default Route

Recall that EIGRP maintains separate tables for IPv4 and IPv6; therefore, an IPv6 default route must be propagated separately, as shown in Figure 1. Similar to EIGRP for IPv4, a default static route is configured on the gateway router (R2), as shown in Figure 2:

```
R2(config)#  ipv6 route ::/0 serial 0/1/0
```

The ::/0 prefix and prefix-length is equivalent to the 0.0.0.0 0.0.0.0 address and subnet mask used in IPv4. Both are all-zero addresses with a /0 prefix-length.

The IPv6 default static route is redistributed into the EIGRP for IPv6 domain using the same `redistribute static` command used in EIGRP for IPv4.

Note   Some IOSs may require that the `redistribute static` command include the EIGRP metric parameters before the static route can be redistributed.

Verifying Propagation of Default Route

The propagation of the IPv6 static default route can be verified by examining R1's IPv6 routing table using the `show ipv6 route` command, as shown in Figure 3. Notice that the successor or next-hop address is not R2, but R3. This is because R3 provides a better path to R2, at a lower cost metric than R1.

Refer to **Packet
Tracer Activity**
for this chapter

8.1.3.4   Packet Tracer - Propagating a Default Route in EIGRP for IPv4 and IPv6

Background/Scenario

In this activity, you will configure and propagate a default route in EIGRP for IPv4 and IPv6 networks. EIGRP is already configured. However, you are required to configure an

IPv4 and an IPv6 default route. Then, you will configure the EIGRP routing process to propagate the default route to downstream EIGRP neighbors. Finally, you will verify the default routes by pinging hosts outside the EIGRP routing domain.

Refer to
Online Course
for Illustration

8.1.4   Fine-tuning EIGRP Interfaces

8.1.4.1   EIGRP Bandwidth Utilization

EIGRP Bandwidth for IPv4

By default, EIGRP uses only up to 50 percent of an interface's bandwidth for EIGRP information. This prevents the EIGRP process from over-utilizing a link and not allowing enough bandwidth for the routing of normal traffic.

Use the `ip bandwidth-percent eigrp` command to configure the percentage of bandwidth that can be used by EIGRP on an interface.

```
Router(config-if)#  ip bandwidth-percent eigrp as-number percent
```

In Figure 1, R1 and R2 share a very slow 64 kb/s link. The configuration to limit how much bandwidth EIGRP uses is shown in Figure 2. The `ip bandwidth-percent eigrp` command uses the amount of configured bandwidth (or the default bandwidth) when calculating the percent that EIGRP can use. In this example, EIGRP is limited to no more than 40 percent of the link's bandwidth. Therefore, EIGRP never uses more the 32 kb/s of the link's bandwidth for EIGRP packet traffic.

To restore the default value, use the `no` form of this command.

Use the Syntax Checker in Figure 3 to limit the bandwidth used by EIGRP between R2 and R3, to 75 percent of the link's bandwidth.

EIGRP Bandwidth for IPv6

To configure the percentage of bandwidth that can be used by EIGRP for IPv6 on an interface, use the `ipv6 bandwidth-percent eigrp` command in interface configuration mode. To restore the default value, use the `no` form of this command.

```
Router(config-if)#  ipv6 bandwidth-percent eigrp as-number percent
```

Figure 4 shows the configuration of the interfaces between R1 and R2 to limit the bandwidth used by EIGRP for IPv6.

Refer to
Online Course
for Illustration

8.1.4.2   Hello and Hold Timers

Hello Intervals and Hold Times with EIGRP for IPv4

EIGRP uses a lightweight Hello protocol to establish and monitor the connection status of its neighbor. The Hold time tells the router the maximum time that the router should wait to receive the next Hello before declaring that neighbor as unreachable.

Hello intervals and Hold times are configurable on a per-interface basis and do not have to match with other EIGRP routers to establish or maintain adjacencies. The command to configure a different Hello interval is:

```
Router(config-if)#  ip hello-interval eigrp as-number seconds
```

If the Hello interval is changed, ensure that the Hold time value is equal to, or greater than, the Hello interval. Otherwise, neighbor adjacency goes down after the Hold time expires and before the next Hello interval. Use the following command to configure a different Hold time:

```
Router(config-if)#  ip hold-time eigrp as-number seconds
```

The seconds value for both Hello and Hold time intervals can range from 1 to 65,535.

Figure 1 shows the configuration of R1 to use a 50-second Hello interval and 150-second Hold time. The **no** form can be used on both of these commands to restore the default values.

The Hello interval time and Hold time do not need to match for two routers to form an EIGRP adjacency.

Use the Syntax Checker in Figure 2 to configure the adjacent interface on R2 with the same values as R1.

Hello Intervals and Hold Times with EIGRP for IPv6

EIGRP for IPv6 uses the same Hello interval and Hold times as EIGRP for IPv4. The interface configuration mode commands are similar to those for IPv4:

```
Router(config-if)#  ipv6 hello-interval eigrp as-number seconds
Router(config-if)#  ipv6 hold-time eigrp as-number seconds
```

Figure 3 shows the Hello interval and Hold times configurations for R1 and R2 with EIGRP for IPv6.

Refer to
Online Course
for Illustration

8.1.4.3   Load Balancing IPv4

Equal-cost load balancing is the ability of a router to distribute outbound traffic using all interfaces that have the same metric from the destination address. Load balancing uses network segments and bandwidth more efficiently. For IP, Cisco IOS Software applies load balancing using up to four equal-cost paths by default.

Figure 1 shows the EIGRP for IPv4 network topology. In this topology, R3 has two EIGRP equal-cost routes for the network between R1 and R2, 172.16.3.0/30. One route is via R1 at 192.168.10.4/30 and the other route is via R2 at 192.168.10.8/30.

The **show ip protocols** command can be used to verify the number of equal-cost paths currently configured on the router. The output in Figure 2 shows that R3 is using the default of four equal-cost paths.

The routing table maintains both routes. Figure 3 shows that R3 has two EIGRP equal-cost routes for the 172.16.3.0/30 network. One route is via R1 at 192.168.10.5 and the other route is via R2 at 192.168.10.9. Looking at the topology in Figure 1, it may seem as if the path via R1 is the better route because there is a 1544 kb/s link between R3 and R1, whereas the link to R2 is only a 1024 kb/s link. However, EIGRP only uses the slowest bandwidth in its composite metric which is the 64 kb/s link between R1 and R2. Both paths have the same 64 kb/s link as the slowest bandwidth, this results in both paths being equal.

When a packet is process-switched, load balancing over equal-cost paths occurs on a per-packet basis. When packets are fast-switched, load balancing over equal-cost paths occurs on a per-destination basis. Cisco Express Forwarding (CEF) can perform both per packet and per-destination load balancing.

Cisco IOS, by default, allows load balancing using up to four equal-cost paths; however, this can be modified. Using the `maximum-paths` router configuration mode command, up to 32 equal-cost routes can be kept in the routing table.

```
Router(config-router)#  maximum-paths value
```

The value argument refers to the number of paths that should be maintained for load balancing. If the value is set to **1**, load balancing is disabled.

Refer to
Online Course
for Illustration

8.1.4.4   Load Balancing IPv6

Figure 1 shows the EIGRP for IPv6 network topology. The serial links in the topology have the same bandwidth that is used in the EIGRP for IPv4 topology.

Similar to the previous scenario for IPv4, R3 has two EIGRP equal-cost routes for the network between R1 and R2, 2001:DB8:CAFE:A001::/64. One route is via R1 at FE80::1 and the other route is via R2 at FE80::2.

Figure 2 shows that the EIGRP metrics are the same in the IPv6 routing table and in the IPv4 routing table for the 2001:DB8:CAFE:A001::/64 and 172.16.3.0/30 networks. This is because the EIGRP composite metric is the same for both EIGRP for IPv6 and for IPv4.

Unequal-Cost Load Balancing

EIGRP for IPv4 and IPv6 can also balance traffic across multiple routes that have different metrics. This type of balancing is called unequal-cost load balancing. Setting a value using the `variance` command in router configuration mode enables EIGRP to install multiple loop-free routes with unequal cost in a local routing table.

A route learned through EIGRP must meet two criteria to be installed in the local routing table:

- The route must be loop-free, being either a feasible successor or having a reported distance that is less than the total distance.

- The metric of the route must be lower than the metric of the best route (the successor) multiplied by the variance configured on the router.

For example, if the variance is set to 1, only routes with the same metric as the successor are installed in the local routing table. If the variance is set to 2, any EIGRP-learned route with a metric less than 2 times the successor metric will be installed in the local routing table.

To control how traffic is distributed among routes when there are multiple routes for the same destination network that have different costs, use the `traffic-share balanced` command. Traffic is then distributed proportionately to the ratio of the costs.

Refer to
Interactive Graphic
in online course.

8.1.4.5   Activity - Determine the EIGRP Fine Tuning Commands

8.1.5   Secure EIGRP

Refer to
Online Course
for Illustration

8.1.5.1   Routing Protocol Authentication Overview

Routing Protocol Authentication

Network administrators must be aware that routers are at risk from attack just as much as end-user devices. Anyone with a packet sniffer, such as Wireshark, can read information propagating between routers. In general, routing systems can be attacked through the disruption of peer devices or the falsification of routing information.

Disruption of peers is the less critical of the two attacks because routing protocols heal themselves, making the disruption last only slightly longer than the attack itself.

The falsification of routing information is a more subtle class of attack that targets the information carried within the routing protocol. The consequences of falsifying routing information are as follows:

- Redirect traffic to create routing loops

- Redirect traffic to monitor on an insecure line

- Redirect traffic to discard it

A method to protect routing information on the network is to authenticate routing protocol packets using the Message Digest 5 (MD5) algorithm. MD5 allows the routers to compare signatures that should all be the same, confirming that it is from a credible source.

The three components of such a system include:

- Encryption algorithm, which is generally public knowledge

- Key used in the encryption algorithm, which is a secret shared by the routers authenticating their packets

- Contents of the packet itself

In the figure, click the Play button to view an animation of how each router authenticates the routing information. Generally, the originator of the routing information produces a signature using the key and routing data it is about to send as inputs to the encryption algorithm. The router receiving the routing data can then repeat the process using the same key and the same routing data it has received. If the signature the receiver computes is the same as the signature, the sender computes the update is authenticated and considered reliable.

Routing protocols such as RIPv2, EIGRP, OSPF, IS-IS, and BGP all support various forms of MD5 authentication.

8.1.5.2   Configuring EIGRP with MD5 Authentication

Refer to
Online Course
for Illustration

EIGRP message authentication ensures that routers only accept routing messages from other routers that know the same pre-shared key. Without authentication configured, if an unauthorized person introduces another router with different or conflicting route information on the network, the routing tables on the legitimate routers can become corrupt and a DoS attack may ensue. Thus, when authentication is added to the EIGRP messages sent between routers, it prevents someone from purposely, or accidentally, adding another router to the network and causing a problem.

EIGRP supports routing protocol authentication using MD5. The configuration of EIGRP message authentication consists of two steps: the creation of a keychain and key, and the configuration of EIGRP authentication to use that keychain and key.

Step 1. **Create a Keychain and Key**Routing authentication requires a key on a keychain to function. Before authentication can be enabled, create a keychain and at least one key.

    a. In global configuration mode, create the keychain. Although multiple keys can be configured, this section focuses on the use of a single key.

```
Router(config)# key chain name-of-chain
```

    b. Specify the key ID. The key ID is the number used to identify an authentication key within a keychain. The range of keys is from 0 to 2,147,483,647. It is recommended that the key number be the same on all routers in the configuration.

```
Router(config-keychain)# key key-id
```

    c. Specify the key string for the key. The key string is similar to a password. Routers exchanging authentication keys must be configured using the same key string.

```
Router(config-keychain-key )# key-string key-string-text
```

Step 2. **Configure EIGRP Authentication Using Keychain and Key**Configure EIGRP to perform message authentication with the previously defined key. Complete this configuration on all interfaces enabled for EIGRP.

    a. In global configuration mode, specify the interface on which to configure EIGRP message authentication.

```
Router(config)# interface type number
```

    b. Enable EIGRP message authentication. The **md5** keyword indicates that the MD5 hash is to be used for authentication.

```
Router(config-if)# ip authentication mode eigrp as-number md5
```

    c. Specify the keychain that should be used for authentication. The name-of-chain argument specifies the keychain that was created in Step 1.

```
Router(config-if)# ip authentication key-chain eigrp as-number name-of-chain
```

Each key has its own key ID, which is stored locally. The combination of the key ID and the interface associated with the message uniquely identifies the authentication algorithm and MD5 authentication key in use. The keychain and the routing update are processed using the MD5 algorithm to produce a unique signature.

8.1.5.3 EIGRP Authentication Example

Refer to **Online Course** for Illustration

To authenticate routing updates, all EIGRP-enabled interfaces must be configured to support authentication. Figure 1 shows the IPv4 topology and which interfaces are configured with authentication.

Figure 2 shows the configuration for router R1 using the **EIGRP_KEY** keychain and the **cisco123** key string. After R1 is configured, the other routers receive authenticated routing updates. Adjacencies are lost until the neighbors are configured with routing protocol authentication.

Figure 3 shows a similar configuration for router R2. Notice that the same key string, **cisco123**, is used to authenticate information with R1 and ultimately R3.

Use the Syntax Checker in Figure 4 to configure EIGRP authentication for R3.

Configuring EIGRP for IPv6 Authentication

The algorithms and the configuration to authenticate EIGRP for IPv6 messages are the same as EIGRP for IPv4. The only difference is the interface configuration mode commands use **ipv6**, instead of **ip**.

```
Router(config-if)#  ipv6 authentication mode eigrp as-number md5
Router(config-if)#  ipv6 authentication key-chain eigrp as-number name-of-chain
```

Figure 5 shows the commands to configure EIGRP for IPv6 authentication on router R1 using the **EIGRP_IPV6_KEY** keychain and the **cisco123** key string. Similar configurations would be entered on R2 and R3.

Refer to
Online Course
for Illustration

8.1.5.4   Verify Authentication

After EIGRP message authentication is configured on one router, any adjacent neighbors that have not yet been configured for authentication are no longer EIGRP neighbors. For example, when R1's Serial 0/0/0 interface was configured for MD5 authentication, but R2 had not yet been configured, the following IOS message appeared on R1:

```
%DUAL-5-NBRCHANGE: EIGRP-IPv4 1: Neighbor 172.16.3.2 (Serial0/0/0) is down: au-
thentication mode changed
```

When the adjacent Serial 0/0/0 interface on R2 is configured, the adjacency is re-established and the following IOS message is displayed on R1:

```
%DUAL-5-NBRCHANGE: EIGRP-IPv4 1: Neighbor 172.16.3.2 (Serial0/0/0) is up: new ad-
jacency
```

Similar messages are also displayed on R2.

Adjacencies are only formed when both connecting devices have authentication configured, as shown in Figure 1. To verify that the correct EIGRP adjacencies were formed after being configured for authentication, use the **show ip eigrp neighbors** command on each router. Figure 2 shows that all three routers have re-established neighbor adjacencies after being configured for EIGRP authentication.

To verify the neighbor adjacencies EIGRP for IPv6, use the **show ipv6 eigrp neighbors** command.

Refer to
Lab Activity
for this chapter

8.1.5.5   Lab - Configuring Advanced EIGRP for IPv4 Features

In this lab, you will complete the following objectives:

- Part 1: Build the Network and Configure Basic Device Settings
- Part 2: Configure EIGRP and Verify Connectivity
- Part 3: Configure Summarization for EIGRP
- Part 4: Configure and Propagate a Default Static Route
- Part 5: Fine-Tune EIGRP
- Part 6: Configure EIGRP Authentication

Refer to
Online Course
for Illustration

8.2   Troubleshoot EIGRP

8.2.1   Components of Troubleshooting EIGRP

8.2.1.1   Basic EIGRP Troubleshooting Commands

EIGRP is commonly used in large enterprise networks. Troubleshooting problems related to the exchange of routing information is an essential skill for a network administrator. This is particularly true for administrators who are involved in the implementation and maintenance of large, routed enterprise networks that use EIGRP as the interior gateway protocol (IGP). There are several commands that are useful when troubleshooting an EIGRP network.

The **show ip eigrp neighbors** command verifies that the router recognizes its neighbors. The output in Figure 1 indicates two successful EIGRP neighbor adjacencies on R1.

In Figure 2, the **show ip route** command verifies that the router learned the route to a remote network through EIGRP. The output shows that R1 has learned about four remote networks through EIGRP.

Figure 3 shows the output from the **show ip protocols** command. This command verifies that the EIGRP displays the currently configured values for various properties of any enabled routing protocols.

EIGRP for IPv6

Similar commands and troubleshooting criteria also apply to EIGRP for IPv6.

The following are the equivalent commands used with EIGRP for IPv6:

- Router# **show ipv6 eigrp neighbors**

- Router# **show ipv6 route**

- Router# **show ipv6 protocols**

Refer to
Online Course
for Illustration

8.2.1.2   Components

The figure shows a flowchart for diagnosing EIGRP connectivity issues.

After configuring EIGRP, the first step is to test connectivity to the remote network. If the ping fails, confirm the EIGRP neighbor adjacencies. Neighbor adjacency might not be formed for a number of reasons, including the following:

- The interface between the devices is down.

- The two routers have mismatching EIGRP autonomous system numbers (process IDs).

- Proper interfaces are not enabled for the EIGRP process.

- An interface is configured as passive.

Aside from these issues, there are a number of other, more advanced issues that can cause neighbor adjacencies to not be formed. Two examples are misconfigured EIGRP authentication or mismatched K values, which EIGRP uses to calculate its metric.

If the EIGRP neighbor adjacency is formed between the two routers, but there is still a connection issue, there may be a routing problem. Some issues that may cause a connectivity problem for EIGRP include:

- Proper networks are not being advertised on remote routers.

- An incorrectly-configured passive interface, or an ACL, is blocking advertisements of remote networks.

- Automatic summarization is causing inconsistent routing in a discontiguous network.

If all of the required routes are in the routing table, but the path that traffic takes is not correct, verify the interface bandwidth values.

Refer to **Interactive Graphic** in online course.

8.2.1.3   Activity - Identify the Troubleshooting Command

Refer to **Online Course** for Illustration

8.2.2   Troubleshoot EIGRP Neighbor Issues

8.2.2.1   Layer 3 Connectivity

A prerequisite for a neighbor adjacency to form between two directly connected routers is Layer 3 connectivity. By examining the output of the `show ip interface brief` command, a network administrator can verify that the status and protocol of connecting interfaces are up. A ping from one router to another, directly connected router, should confirm IPv4 connectivity between the devices. The figure displays the `show ip interface brief` command output for R1. R1 shows connectivity to R2, and pings are successful.

If the ping is unsuccessful, check the cabling and verify that the interfaces on connected devices are on a common subnet. A log message that states that EIGRP neighbors are `not on common subnet` indicates that there is an incorrect IPv4 address on one of the two EIGRP neighbor interfaces.

EIGRP for IPv6

Similar commands and troubleshooting criteria also apply to EIGRP for IPv6.

The equivalent command used with EIGRP for IPv6 is `show ipv6 interface brief`.

Refer to **Online Course** for Illustration

8.2.2.2   EIGRP Parameters

When troubleshooting an EIGRP network, one of the first things to verify is that all routers that are participating in the EIGRP network are configured with the same autonomous system number. The `router eigrp` as-number command starts the EIGRP process and is followed by a number that is the autonomous system number. The value of the as-number argument must be the same in all routers that are in the EIGRP routing domain.

Figure 1 shows that all routers should be participating in autonomous system number 1. In Figure 2, the `show ip protocols` command verifies that R1, R2, and R3 all use the same autonomous system number.

EIGRP for IPv6

Similar commands and troubleshooting criteria also apply to EIGRP for IPv6.

The following are the equivalent commands used with EIGRP for IPv6:

- Router(config)# **ipv6 router eigrp** as-number
- Router# **show ipv6 protocols**

Note At the top of the output, "IP Routing is NSF aware" refers to Nonstop Forwarding (NSF). This capability allows the EIGRP peers of a failing router to retain the routing information that it has advertised, and to continue using this information until the failed router resumes normal operation and is able to exchange routing information. For more information refer to: http://www.cisco.com/en/US/docs/ios-xml/ios/iproute_eigrp/configuration/15-mt/eigrp-nsf-awa.html

Refer to **Online Course** for Illustration

8.2.2.3 EIGRP Interfaces

In addition to verifying the autonomous system number, it is necessary to verify that all interfaces are participating in the EIGRP network. The **network** command that is configured under the EIGRP routing process indicates which router interfaces participates in EIGRP. This command is applied to the classful network address of the interface or to a subnet when the wildcard mask is included.

In Figure 1, the **show ip eigrp interfaces** command displays which interfaces are enabled for EIGRP on R1. If connected interfaces are not enabled for EIGRP, then neighbors do not form an adjacency.

In Figure 2, the "Routing for Networks" section of the **show ip protocols** command indicates which networks have been configured; any interfaces in those networks participate in EIGRP.

If the network is not present in this section, use **show running-config** to ensure that the proper **network** command was configured.

In Figure 3, the output from the **show running-config** command confirms that any interfaces with these addresses, or a subnet of these addresses, are enabled for EIGRP.

EIGRP for IPv6

Similar commands and troubleshooting criteria also apply to EIGRP for IPv6.

The following are the equivalent commands used with EIGRP for IPv6:

- Router# **show ipv6 protocols**
- Router# **show ipv6 eigrp interfaces**

Refer to
Interactive Graphic
in online course.

8.2.2.4 Activity - Troubleshoot EIGRP Neighbor Issues

Refer to
Online Course
for Illustration

8.2.3 Troubleshoot EIGRP Routing Table Issues

8.2.3.1 Passive Interface

One reason that route tables may not reflect the correct routes is due to the **passive-interface** command. With EIGRP running on a network, the **passive-interface** command stops both outgoing and incoming routing updates. For this reason, routers do not become neighbors.

To verify whether any interface on a router is configured as passive, use the **show ip protocols** command in privileged EXEC mode. Figure 1 shows that R2's GigabitEthernet 0/0 interface is configured as a passive interface, because there are no neighbors on that link.

In addition to being configured on interfaces that have no neighbors, a passive interface can be enabled on interfaces for security purposes. In Figure 2, notice that the shading for the EIGRP routing domain is different from previous topologies. The 209.165.200.224/27 network is now included in the R2's EIGRP updates. However, for security reasons, the network administrator does not want R2 to form an EIGRP neighbor adjacency with the ISP router.

Figure 3 shows the addition of the 209.165.200.224/27 **network** command on R2. R2 now advertises this network to the other routers in the EIGRP routing domain.

The **passive-interface** router configuration mode command is configured on Serial 0/1/0 to prevent R2's EIGRP updates from being sent to the ISP router. The **show ip eigrp neighbors** command on R2 verifies that R2 has not established a neighbor adjacency with ISP.

Figure 4 shows that R1 has an EIGRP route to the 209.165.200.224/27 network in its IPv4 routing table (R3 will also have an EIGRP route to that network in its IPv4 routing table). However, R2 does not have a neighbor adjacency with the ISP router.

EIGRP for IPv6

Similar commands and troubleshooting criteria also apply to EIGRP for IPv6.

The following are the equivalent commands used with EIGRP for IPv6:

- Router# **show ipv6 protocols**

- Router(config-rtr)# **passive-interface** type number

Refer to
Online Course
for Illustration

8.2.3.2 Missing Network Statement

Figure 1 shows that R1's GigabitEthernet 0/1 interface has now been configured with the 10.10.10.1/24 address and is active.

R1 and R3 still have their neighbor adjacency, but a ping test from the R3 router to a R1's G0/1 interface of 10.10.10.1 is unsuccessful. Figure 2 shows a failed connectivity test from R3 to the destination network of 10.10.10.0/24.

In Figure 3, using the `show ip protocols` on the R1 router shows that the network 10.10.10.0/24 is not advertised to EIGRP neighbors.

As shown in Figure 4, R1's EIGRP process is configured to include the advertisement of the 10.10.10.0/24 network.

Figure 5 shows that there is now a route in R3's routing table for the 10.10.10.0/24 network and reachability is verified by pinging R1's GigabitEthernet 0/1 interface.

EIGRP for IPv6

Similar commands and troubleshooting criteria also apply to EIGRP for IPv6.

The following are the equivalent commands used with EIGRP for IPv6:

- Router# **show ipv6 protocols**

- Router# **show ipv6 route**

- Router(config-rtr)# **network** ipv6-prefix/prefix-length

Note   Another form of missing route may result from the router filtering inbound or outbound routing updates. ACLs provide filtering for different protocols, and these ACLs may affect the exchange of the routing protocol messages that cause routes to be absent from the routing table. The `show ip protocols` command shows whether there are any ACLs that are applied to EIGRP.

Refer to
Online Course
for Illustration

8.2.3.3   Automatic summarization

Another issue that may create problems for the network administrator is EIGRP automatic summarization.

Figure 1 shows a different network topology than what has been used throughout this chapter. There is no connection between R1 and R3. R1's LAN has the network address 10.10.10.0/24, while R3's LAN is 10.20.20.0/24. The serial connections between both routers and R2 have the same bandwidth of 1024 kb/s.

R1 and R3 have their LAN and serial interfaces enabled for EIGRP, as shown in Figure 2. Both routers perform EIGRP automatic summarization.

EIGRP for IPv4 can be configured to automatically summarize routes at classful boundaries. If there are discontiguous networks, automatic summarization causes inconsistent routing.

In Figure 3, R2's routing table shows that it does not receive individual routes for the 10.10.10.0/24 and 10.20.20.0/24 subnets. Both R1 and R3 automatically summarized those subnets to the 10.0.0.0/8 classful boundary when sending EIGRP update packets to R2. The result is that R2 has two equal-cost routes to 10.0.0.0/8 in the routing table, which can result in inaccurate routing and packet loss. Depending upon whether per-packet, per-destination, or CEF load balancing is being used, packets may or may not be forwarded out the proper interface.

In Figure 4, the `show ip protocols` command verifies that automatic summarization is performed on both R1 and R3. Notice that both routers summarize the 10.0.0.0/8 network using the same metric.

The `auto-summary` command is disabled by default on Cisco IOS Software versions of 15 and newer versions of 12.2(33). By default, older software has automatic summarization enabled. To disable automatic summarization, enter the `no auto-summary` command in `router EIGRP` configuration mode.

To correct this problem, R1 and R3 have automatic summarization disabled:

```
R1(config)#  router eigrp 1
R1(config-router)#  no auto-summary
R3(config)#  router eigrp 1
R3(config-router)#  no auto-summary
```

After automatic summarization has been disabled on R1 and R3, R2's routing table now indicates that it receives the individual 10.10.10.0/24 and 10.20.20.0/24 subnets from R1 and R3, respectively, as shown in Figure 5. Accurate routing and connectivity to both subnets is now restored.

EIGRP for IPv6

Classful networks do not exist in IPv6; therefore EIGRP for IPv6 does not support automatic summarization. All summarization must be accomplished using EIGRP manual summary routes.

Refer to
Interactive Graphic
in online course.

8.2.3.4   Activity - Troubleshoot EIGRP Routing Table Issues

Refer to **Packet Tracer Activity**
for this chapter

8.2.3.5   Packet Tracer - Troubleshooting EIGRP for IPv4

Background/Scenario

In this activity, you will troubleshoot EIGRP neighbor issues. Use `show` commands to identify errors in the network configuration. Then, you will document the errors you discover and implement an appropriate solution. Finally, you will verify full end-to-end connectivity is restored.

Refer to
Lab Activity
for this chapter

8.2.3.6   Lab - Troubleshooting Basic EIGRP for IPv4 and IPv6

In this lab, you will complete the following objectives:

- Part 1: Build the Network and Load Device Configurations
- Part 2: Troubleshoot Layer 3 Connectivity
- Part 3: Troubleshoot EIGRP for IPv4
- Part 4: Troubleshoot EIGRP for IPv6

Refer to
Lab Activity
for this chapter

8.2.3.7   Lab - Troubleshooting Advanced EIGRP

In this lab, you will complete the following objectives:

- Part 1: Build the Network and Load Device Configurations
- Part 2: Troubleshoot EIGRP

Refer to
Online Course
for Illustration

Refer to
Lab Activity
for this chapter

8.3 Summary

8.3.1.1 Class Activity - Tweaking EIGRP

Tweaking EIGRP

The purpose of this activity is to review EIGRP routing protocol fine-tuning concepts.

You will work with a partner to design one EIGRP topology. This topology is the basis for two parts of the activity. The first uses default settings for all configurations and the second incorporates, at least, three of the following fine-tuning EIGRP options:

- Manual summary route

- Default routes

- Default routes propagation

- Hello interval timer settings

Refer to the labs, Packet Tracer activities, and interactive activities to help you as you progress through this modeling activity.

Directions are listed on the PDF file for this activity. Share your completed work with another group. You may want to save a copy of this activity to a portfolio.

Refer to **Packet Tracer Activity**
for this chapter

8.3.1.2 Packet Tracer - Skills Integration Challenge

Background/Scenario

In this activity, you are tasked with implementing EIGRP for IPv4 and IPv6 on two separate networks. Your task includes enabling EIGRP, assigning router-IDs, changing the Hello timers, configuring EIGRP summary routes, and limiting EIGRP advertisements.

Refer to
Online Course
for Illustration

8.3.1.3 Summary

EIGRP is one of the routing protocols commonly used in large enterprise networks. Modifying EIGRP features and troubleshooting problems is one of the most essential skills for a network engineer involved in the implementation and maintenance of large routed enterprise networks that use EIGRP.

Summarization decreases the number of entries in routing updates and lowers the number of entries in local routing tables. It also reduces bandwidth utilization for routing updates and results in faster routing table lookups. EIGRP for IPv4 automatic summarization is disabled by default beginning with Cisco IOS Release 15.0(1)M and 12.2(33). Prior to this, automatic summarization was enabled by default. To enable automatic summarization for EIGRP use the `auto-summary` command in router configuration mode. Use the `show ip protocols` command to verify the status of automatic summarization. Examine the routing table to verify that automatic summarization is working.

EIGRP automatically includes summary routes to Null0 to prevent routing loops that are included in the summary but do not actually exist in the routing table. The Null0 interface is a virtual IOS interface that is a route to nowhere, commonly known as "the bit bucket". Packets that match a route with a Null0 exit interface are discarded.

To establish EIGRP manual summarization on a specific EIGRP interface, use the following interface configuration mode command:

```
Router(config-if)# ip summary-address eigrp  as-number network-address subnet-mask
```

To configure EIGRP for IPv6 manual summarization on a specific EIGRP interface, use the following interface configuration mode command:

```
Router(config-if)# ipv6 summary-address eigrp as-number prefix/prefix-length
```

One method of propagating a default route within the EIGRP routing domain is to use the **redistribute static** command. This command tells EIGRP to include this static route in its EIGRP updates to other routers. The **show ip protocols** command verifies that static routes within the EIGRP routing domain are being redistributed.

Use the **ip bandwidth-percent eigrp** as-number percent interface configuration mode command to configure the percentage of bandwidth that can be used by EIGRP on an interface.

To configure the percentage of bandwidth that can be used by EIGRP for IPv6 on an interface, use the **ipv6 bandwidth-percent eigrp** command in interface configuration mode. To restore the default value, use the **no** form of this command.

Hello intervals and Hold times are configurable on a per-interface basis in EIGRP and do not have to match with other EIGRP routers to establish or maintain adjacencies.

For IP in EIGRP, Cisco IOS software applies load balancing using up to four equal-cost paths by default. With the **maximum-paths** router configuration mode command, up to 32 equal-cost routes can be kept in the routing table.

EIGRP supports routing protocol authentication using MD5. The algorithms and the configuration to authenticate EIGRP for IPv4 messages are the same as EIGRP for IPv6. The only difference is that the interface configuration mode commands use **ip**, instead of **ipv6**.

```
Router(config-if)# ipv6 authentication mode eigrp  as-number  md5
Router(config-if)# ipv6 authentication key-chain eigrp as-number name-of-chain
```

To verify that the correct EIGRP adjacencies were formed after being configured for authentication, use the **show ip eigrp neighbors** command on each router.

The **show ip route** command verifies that the router learned EIGRP routes. The **show ip protocols** command is used to verify that EIGRP displays the currently configured values.

Go to the online course to take the quiz and exam.

Chapter 8 Quiz

This quiz is designed to provide an additional opportunity to practice the skills and knowledge presented in the chapter and to prepare for the chapter exam. You will be allowed multiple attempts and the grade does not appear in the gradebook.

Chapter 8 Exam

The chapter exam assesses your knowledge of the chapter content.

Your Chapter Notes

IOS Images and Licensing

9.0 IOS Images and Licensing

9.0.1.1 Introduction

Cisco IOS (originally Internetwork Operating System) is software used on most Cisco routers and switches. IOS is a package of routing, switching, security, and other internetworking technologies integrated into a single multitasking operating system.

The Cisco IOS portfolio supports a broad range of technologies and features. Customers choose an IOS based on a set of protocols and features supported by a particular image. Understanding the Cisco portfolio of feature sets is helpful in selecting the proper IOS to meet the needs of an organization.

Cisco made significant changes in the packaging and licensing of its IOS when transitioning from IOS 12.4 to 15.0. This chapter explains the naming conventions and packaging of IOS 12.4 and 15. Beginning with IOS 15, Cisco also implemented a new packaging format and licensing process for IOS. This chapter discusses the process of obtaining, installing, and managing Cisco IOS 15 software licenses.

Note   The release of IOS after 12.4 is 15.0. There is no IOS software release 13 or 14.

Refer to **Lab Activity** for this chapter

9.0.1.2 Class Activity - IOS Detection

IOS Detection

Your school or university has just received a donation of Cisco routers and switches. You transport them from your shipping and receiving department to your Cisco networking lab and start sorting them into switch and router groups.

Refer to the accompanying PDF for directions on how to proceed with this modeling activity. Save your work and share the data you found with another group or the entire class.

Refer to **Interactive Graphic** in online course.

9.1 Managing IOS System Files

9.1.1 Naming Conventions

9.1.1.1 Cisco IOS Software Release Families and Trains

Cisco IOS Software has evolved from a single platform operating system for routing, to a sophisticated operating system that supports a large array of features and technologies such as VoIP, NetFlow, and IPsec. To better meet the requirements of the different market segments, the software is organized into software release families and software trains.

A software release family is comprised of multiple IOS software release versions that:

- Share a code base

- Apply to related hardware platforms

- Overlap in support coverage (as one OS comes to end-of-life, another OS is introduced and supported)

Examples of IOS software releases, within a software release family, include 12.3, 12.4, 15.0, and 15.1.

Along with each software release, there are new versions of the software created to implement bug fixes and new features. IOS refers to these versions as trains.

A Cisco IOS train is used to deliver releases with a common code base to a specific set of platforms and features. A train may contain several releases, each release being a snapshot of the code base of the train at the moment of the release. Because different software release families can apply to different platforms or market segments, several trains can be current at any point in time.

This chapter examines the trains of both IOS 12.4 and 15.

Refer to
Online Course
for Illustration

9.1.1.2   Cisco IOS 12.4 Mainline and T Trains

12.4 Trains

The figure shows the migration from software release 12.3 to 12.4. Within a software release family there may be two or more closely related and active trains. For example, the Cisco IOS Software 12.4 release family has two trains, the 12.4 mainline and the 12.4T trains.

The Cisco IOS Software 12.4 train is considered the mainline train. The mainline train receives mostly software (bug) fixes with the goal of increasing software quality. The mainline train releases are also designated as Maintenance Deployment releases (MD).

A mainline train is always associated with a technology train (T train). A T train, such as 12.4T, receives the same software bug fixes as the mainline train. The T train also receives new software and hardware support features. Releases in the Cisco IOS Software 12.4T train are considered Early Deployment (ED) releases.

There may be other trains, depending on the software release family. For example, another train available is the service provider train (S train). An S train will contain specific features designed to meet service provider requirements.

All child trains of the mainline train (T, S, etc.) typically contain an uppercase letter designating the train type.

Mainline train = 12.4

T train = 12.4T (12.4 + new software and hardware support features)

Up to and including the Cisco IOS Software 12.4 release family, the mainline and T trains were separated. In other words, from the mainline train, a T train would branch out and become a separate code base that received new features and hardware support. Eventually, a new mainline train would evolve from an established T train and the cycle would start again. This use of multiple trains was changed with the software release, Cisco IOS 15.

The figure illustrates the relationships between the release of the Cisco IOS Software 12.4 mainline train and the 12.4T train.

Refer to
Online Course
for Illustration

9.1.1.3   Cisco IOS 12.4 Mainline and T Numbering

The IOS release numbering convention is used to identify the release of the IOS software, including any bug fixes and new software features. An example of the numbering scheme is shown in the figure for both the mainline and T trains:

- The software release numbering scheme for a mainline train is composed of a train number, a maintenance identifier, and a rebuild identifier. For example, the Cisco IOS Software Release 12.4(21a) is a mainline train. The release for a T train is composed of a train number, a maintenance identifier, a train identifier, and a rebuild identifier. For example, Cisco IOS Software Release 12.4(20)T1 belongs to the Cisco IOS Software 12.4T train.

- Each maintenance identifier of Cisco IOS Software 12.4 mainline, such as 12.4(7), includes additional software and maintenance fixes. This change is indicated with the number within the parentheses. Each maintenance release of Cisco IOS Software 12.4T, such as 12.4(20)T, includes these same software fixes, along with additional software features, and hardware support.

- Cisco uses rebuilds of an individual release to integrate fixes for significant issues. This reduces the possible impact on customers who have already deployed and certified an individual release. A rebuild typically includes fixes to a limited number of software defects, which are known as caveats. It is indicated by a lowercase letter inside the parenthesis of mainline trains, or by a final number in other trains. For example, Cisco IOS Software Release 12.4(21) received a few caveat fixes and the resulting rebuild was named 12.4(21a). Similarly, 12.4(15)T8 is the eighth rebuild of 12.4(15)T. Each new rebuild increments the rebuild identifier and delivers additional software fixes on an accelerated schedule, prior to the next planned individual release. The criteria for making changes in a rebuild are strict.

A single set of individual release numbers are used for all Cisco IOS Software 12.4 trains. Cisco IOS Software Maintenance Release 12.4 and Cisco IOS Software Release 12.4T use a pool of individual release numbers that are shared across the entire Cisco IOS Software 12.4 release family. Cisco IOS Software Release 12.4(6)T was followed by 12.4(7)T and 12.4(8)T. This permits the administrator to track changes introduced in the code.

Note   Any caveat that is fixed in a T train release should be implemented in the next mainline release.

Refer to
Online Course
for Illustration

9.1.1.4   Cisco IOS 12.4 System Image Packaging

Prior to Cisco IOS Software Release 15.0, Cisco IOS Software Packaging consisted of eight packages for Cisco routers, as shown in the figure. This packaging scheme was introduced with the Cisco IOS Software 12.3 mainline train and was later used in other trains. The image packaging consists of eight IOS images, three of which are considered premium packages.

The five non-premium packages are:

- **IP Base**- IP Base is the entry level Cisco IOS Software Image
- **IP Voice**- Converged voice and data, VoIP, VoFR, and IP Telephony
- **Advanced Security**- Security and VPN features including Cisco IOS Firewall, IDS/ IPS, IPsec, 3DES, and VPN
- **SP (Service Provider) Services**- Adds SSH/SSL, ATM, VoATM, and MPLS to IP Voice
- **Enterprise Base**- Enterprise protocols: Appletalk, IPX, and IBM Support

Note Starting with the Cisco IOS Software 12.4 release family SSH is available in all images.

Three other premium packages offer additional IOS software feature combinations that address more complex network requirements. All features merge in the Advanced Enterprise Services package. This package integrates support for all routing protocols with Voice, Security, and VPN capabilities:

- **Advanced Enterprise Services**- Full Cisco IOS Software features
- **Enterprise Services**- Enterprise Base and Service Provider Services
- **Advanced IP Services**- Advanced Security, Service Provider Services, and support for IPv6

Note The Cisco Feature Navigator is a tool used to find the right Cisco operating system depending on the features and technologies needed.

Refer to
Online Course
for Illustration

9.1.1.5 Cisco IOS 15.0 M and T Trains

Following the Cisco IOS 12.4(24)T release, the next release of Cisco IOS Software was 15.0.

IOS 15.0 provides several enhancements to the operating system including:

- New feature and hardware support
- Broadened feature consistency with other major IOS releases
- More predictable new feature release and rebuild schedules
- Proactive individual release support policies
- Simplified release numbering
- Clearer software deployment and migration guidelines

As shown in the figure, Cisco IOS 15.0 uses a different release model from the traditional separate mainline and T trains of 12.4. Instead of diverging into separate trains, Cisco IOS Software 15 mainline and T will have extended maintenance release (EM release) and standard maintenance release (T release). With the new IOS release model, Cisco IOS 15 mainline releases are referred to as M trains.

Beginning with 15.0, new releases in the form of a T train are available approximately two to three times per year. EM releases are available approximately every 16 to 20 months. T releases enable faster Cisco feature delivery before the next EM release becomes available.

An EM release incorporates the features and hardware support of all the previous T releases. This makes newer EM releases available that contain the full functionality of the train at the time of release.

In summary, the benefits of the new Cisco IOS release model include:

- Feature inheritance from Cisco IOS Software Releases 12.4T and 12.4 mainline

- New feature releases approximately two to three times a year delivered sequentially from a single train

- EM releases approximately every 16 to 20 months and includes new features

- T releases for the very latest features and hardware support before next EM release becomes available on Cisco.com

- Maintenance rebuilds of M and T releases contain bug fixes only

Refer to
Online Course
for Illustration

9.1.1.6   Cisco IOS 15 Train Numbering

The release numbering convention for IOS 15 identifies the specific IOS release, including bug fixes and new software features, similar to previous IOS release families. The figure shows examples of this convention for both the EM release and T release.

Extended Maintenance Release

The EM release is ideal for long-term maintenance, enabling customers to qualify, deploy, and remain on the release for an extended period. The mainline train incorporates features delivered in previous releases plus incremental new feature enhancements and hardware support.

The first maintenance rebuild (for bug fixes only, not new features or new hardware support) of Release 15.0(1)M is numbered 15.0(1)M1. Subsequent maintenance releases are defined by an increment of the maintenance rebuild number (i.e., M2, M3, etc.).

Standard Maintenance Release

The T release is used for short deployment releases ideal for the latest new features and hardware support before the next EM release becomes available. The T release provides regular bug fix maintenance rebuilds, plus critical fix support for network affecting bugs such as Product Security Incident Report Team (PSIRT) issues.

The first planned 15 T new feature release is numbered Release 15.1(1)T. The first maintenance rebuild (for bug fixes only, not new features or new hardware support) of Release 15.1(1)T will be numbered 15.1(1)T1. Subsequent releases are defined by an increment of the maintenance rebuild number (i.e., T2, T3, etc.).

Refer to
Online Course
for Illustration

9.1.1.7   IOS 15 System Image Packaging

Cisco Integrated Services Routers Generation Two (ISR G2) 1900, 2900, and 3900 Series support services on demand through the use of software licensing. The Services on Demand process enables customers to realize operational savings through ease of software ordering and management. When an order is placed for a new ISR G2 platform, the router is shipped with a single universal Cisco IOS Software image and a license is used to enable the specific feature set packages, as shown in Figure 1.

There are two types of universal images supported in ISR G2:

- **Universal images with the "universalk9" designation in the image name**- This universal image offers all of the Cisco IOS Software features, including strong payload cryptography features, such as IPsec VPN, SSL VPN, and Secure Unified Communications.

- **Universal images with the "universalk9_npe" designation in the image name**- The strong enforcement of encryption capabilities provided by Cisco Software Activation satisfies requirements for the export of encryption capabilities. However, some countries have import requirements that require that the platform does not support any strong cryptography functionality, such as payload cryptography. To satisfy the import requirements of those countries, the npe universal image does not support any strong payload encryption.

With the ISR G2 devices, IOS image selection has been made easier because all features are included within the universal image. Features are activated through licensing. Each device ships with Universal image. The technology packages IP Base, Data, UC (Unified Communications), and SEC (Security), are enabled in the universal image using Cisco Software Activation licensing keys. Each licensing key is unique to a particular device and is obtained from Cisco by providing the product ID and serial number of the router and a Product Activation Key (PAK). The PAK is provided by Cisco at the time of software purchase. The IP Base is installed by default.

Figure 2 shows the suggested migration for the next generation ISRs from the IOS 12 (IOS Reformation Packaging) to IOS 15 (Simplified Packaging).

Refer to
Online Course
for Illustration

9.1.1.8 IOS Image Filenames

When selecting or upgrading a Cisco IOS router, it is important to choose the proper IOS image with the correct feature set and version. The Cisco IOS image file is based on a special naming convention. The name for the Cisco IOS image file contains multiple parts, each with a specific meaning. It is important to understand this naming convention when upgrading and selecting a Cisco IOS Software.

As shown in Figure 1, the `show flash` command displays the files stored in flash memory, including the system image files.

An example of an IOS 12.4 software image name is shown in Figure 2.

- **Image Name (c2800nm)**- Identifies the platform on which the image runs. In this example, the platform is a Cisco 2800 router with a network module.

- **advipservicesk9**- Specifies the feature set. In this example, advipservicesk9 refers to the advanced IP services feature set which includes both the advanced security and service provider packages, along with IPv6.

- **mz**- Indicates where the image runs and if the file is compressed. In this example, mz indicates that the file runs from RAM and is compressed.

- **124-6.T**- The filename format for image 12.4(6)T. This is the train number, maintenance release number, and the train identifier.

- **bin**- The file extension. This extension indicates that this file is a binary executable file.

Figure 3 illustrates the different parts of an IOS 15 system image file on an ISR G2 device:

- **Image Name (c1900)**- Identifies the platform on which the image runs. In this example, the platform is a Cisco 1900 router.

- **universalk9**- Specifies the image designation. The two designations for an ISR G2 are universalk9 and universalk9_npe. Universalk9_npe does not contain strong encryption and is meant for countries with encryption restrictions. Features are controlled by licensing and can be divided into four technology packages. These are IP Base, Security, Unified Communications, and Data.

- **mz**- Indicates where the image runs and if the file is compressed. In this example, mz indicates that the file runs from RAM and is compressed.

- **SPA**- Designates that file is digitally signed by Cisco.

- **152-4.M3**- Specifies the filename format for the image 15.2(4)M3. This is the version of IOS, which includes the major release, minor release, maintenance release, and maintenance rebuild numbers. The M indicates this is an extended maintenance release.

- **bin**- The file extension. This extension indicates that this file is a binary executable file.

The most common designation for memory location and compression format is mz. The first letter indicates the location where the image is executed on the router. The locations can include:

- **f** - flash

- **m**- RAM

- **r**- ROM

- **l** - relocatable

The compression format can be either z for zip or x for mzip. Zipping is a method Cisco uses to compress some run-from-RAM images that is effective in reducing the size of the image. It is self-unzipping, so when the image is loaded into RAM for execution, the first action is to unzip.

Note   The Cisco IOS Software naming conventions, field meaning, image content, and other details are subject to change.

Memory Requirements

On most Cisco routers including the integrated services routers, the IOS is stored in compact flash as a compressed image and loaded into DRAM during boot-up. The Cisco IOS Software Release 15.0 images available for the Cisco 1900 and 2900 ISR require 256MB of flash and 512MB of RAM. The 3900 ISR requires 256MB of flash and 1GB of RAM. This does not include additional management tools such as Cisco Configuration Professional (Cisco CP). For complete details, refer to the product data sheet for the specific router.

Refer to **Packet Tracer Activity** for this chapter

9.1.1.9   Packet Tracer - Decode IOS Image Names

Background/Scenario

As a network technician, it is important that you are familiar with the IOS image naming convention so that you can, at a glance, determine important information about operating systems currently running on a device. In this scenario, Company A has merged with Company B. Company A has inherited network equipment from Company B. You have been assigned to document the features for the IOS images on these devices.

Refer to **Online Course** for Illustration

9.1.2   Managing Cisco IOS Images

9.1.2.1   TFTP Servers as a Backup Location

As a network grows, Cisco IOS Software images and configuration files can be stored on a central TFTP server. This helps to control the number of IOS images and the revisions to those IOS images, as well as the configuration files that must be maintained.

Production internetworks usually span wide areas and contain multiple routers. For any network, it is good practice to keep a backup copy of the Cisco IOS Software image in case the system image in the router becomes corrupted or accidentally erased.

Widely distributed routers need a source or backup location for Cisco IOS Software images. Using a network TFTP server allows image and configuration uploads and downloads over the network. The network TFTP server can be another router, a workstation, or a host system.

Refer to **Online Course** for Illustration

9.1.2.2   Creating Cisco IOS Image Backup

To maintain network operations with minimum down time, it is necessary to have procedures in place for backing up Cisco IOS images. This allows the network administrator to quickly copy an image back to a router in case of a corrupted or erased image.

In Figure 1, the network administrator wants to create a backup of the current image file on the router (c1900-universalk9-mz.SPA.152-4.M3.bin) to the TFTP server at 172.16.1.100.

To create a backup of the Cisco IOS image to a TFTP server, perform the following three steps:

Step 1.   Ensure that there is access to the network TFTP server. Ping the TFTP server to test connectivity, as shown in Figure 2.

Step 2.   Verify that the TFTP server has sufficient disk space to accommodate the Cisco IOS Software image. Use the `show flash0:` command on the router to determine the size of the Cisco IOS image file. The file in the example is 68831808 bytes long.

Step 3.   Copy the image to the TFTP server using the `copy` source-url destination-url command, as shown in Figure 3.

After issuing the command using the specified source and destination URLs, the user is prompted for the source file name, IP address of the remote host, and destination file name. The transfer will then begin.

Use the Syntax Checker in Figure 4 on R2 to copy the IOS to a TFTP server.

Refer to
Online Course
for Illustration

9.1.2.3   Copying a Cisco IOS Image

Cisco consistently releases new Cisco IOS software versions to resolve caveats and provide new features. This example uses IPv6 for the transfer to show that TFTP can also be used across IPv6 networks.

Figure 1 illustrates copying a Cisco IOS software image from a TFTP server. A new image file (c1900-universalk9-mz.SPA.152-4.M3.bin) will be copied from the TFTP server at 2001:DB8:CAFE:100::99 to the router.

Follow these steps to upgrade the software on the Cisco router:

Step 1.   Select a Cisco IOS image file that meets the requirements in terms of platform, features, and software. Download the file from cisco.com and transfer it to the TFTP server.

Step 2.   Verify connectivity to the TFTP server. Ping the TFTP server from the router. The output in Figure 2 shows the TFTP server is accessible from the router.

Step 3.   Ensure that there is sufficient flash space on the router that is being upgraded. The amount of free flash can be verified using the `show flash0:` command. Compare the free flash space with the new image file size. The `show flash0:` command in Figure 3 is used to verify free flash size. Free flash space in the example is 182,394,880 bytes.

Step 4.   Copy the IOS image file from the TFTP server to the router using the `copy` command shown in Figure 4. After issuing this command with specified source and destination URLs, the user will be prompted for IP address of the remote host, source file name, and destination file name. The transfer of the file will begin.

Refer to
Online Course
for Illustration

9.1.2.4   Boot System

To upgrade to the copied IOS image after that image is saved on the router's flash memory, configure the router to load the new image during bootup using the `boot system` command. Save the configuration. Reload the router to boot the router with new image. After the router has booted, to verify the new image has loaded, use the `show version` command.

During startup, the bootstrap code parses the startup configuration file in NVRAM for the `boot system` commands that specify the name and location of the Cisco IOS Software image to load. Several `boot system` commands can be entered in sequence to provide a fault-tolerant boot plan.

Shown in Figure 1, the `boot system` command is a global configuration command that allows the user to specify the source for the Cisco IOS Software image to load. Some of the syntax options available include:

- Specify the flash device as the source of the Cisco IOS image.

```
Router(config)#  boot system flash0://c1900-universalk9-mz.SPA.152-4.M3.bin
```

- Specify the TFTP server as a source of Cisco IOS image, with ROMmon as backup.

```
Router(config)#  boot system tftp://c1900-universalk9-mz.SPA.152-4.M3.bin
Router(config)#  boot system rom
```

If there are no **boot system** commands in the configuration, the router defaults to loading the first valid Cisco IOS image in flash memory and running it.

As shown in Figure 2, the **show version** command can be used to verify the software image file.

Refer to **Packet Tracer Activity** for this chapter

9.1.2.5   Packet Tracer - Using a TFTP Server to Upgrade a Cisco IOS Image

Background/Scenario

A TFTP server can help manage the storage of IOS images and revisions to IOS images. For any network, it is good practice to keep a backup copy of the Cisco IOS Software image in case the system image in the router becomes corrupted or accidentally erased. A TFTP server can also be used to store new upgrades to the IOS and then deployed throughout the network where it is needed. In this activity, you will upgrade the IOS images on Cisco devices by using a TFTP server. You will also backup an IOS image with the use of a TFTP server.

Refer to **Interactive Graphic** in online course.

9.1.2.6   Video Demonstration - Managing Cisco IOS Images

Refer to **Online Course** for Illustration

9.2   IOS Licensing

9.2.1   Software Licensing

9.2.1.1   Licensing Overview

Beginning with Cisco IOS Software release 15.0, Cisco modified the process to enable new technologies within the IOS feature sets. Cisco IOS Software release 15.0 incorporates cross-platform feature sets to simplify the image selection process. It does this by providing similar functions across platform boundaries. Each device ships with the same universal image. Technology packages are enabled in the universal image via Cisco Software Activation licensing keys. The Cisco IOS Software Activation feature allows the user to enable licensed features and register licenses. The Cisco IOS Software Activation feature is a collection of processes and components used to activate Cisco IOS software feature sets by obtaining and validating Cisco software licenses.

Figure 1 shows the technology packages that are available:

- IP Base
- Data
- Unified Communications (UC)
- Security (SEC)

Click the buttons in Figure 2 to learn more about technology packages.

Note   The IP Base license is a prerequisite for installing the Data, Security, and Unified Communications licenses. For earlier router platforms that can support Cisco IOS Software release 15.0, a universal image is not available. It is necessary to download a separate image that contains the desired features.

Technology Package Licenses

Technology package licenses are supported on Cisco ISR G2 platforms (Cisco 1900, 2900, and 3900 Series routers). The Cisco IOS universal image contains all packages and features in one image. Each package is a grouping of technology-specific features. Multiple technology package licenses can be activated on the Cisco 1900, 2900, and 3900 series ISR platforms.

Note   Use the `show license feature` command to view the technology package licenses and feature licenses supported on the router.

Refer to **Online Course** for Illustration

9.2.1.2   Licensing Process

When a new router is shipped, it comes preinstalled with the software image and the corresponding permanent licenses for the customer-specified packages and features.

The router also comes with the evaluation license, known as a temporary license, for most packages and features supported on the specified router. This allows customers to try a new software package or feature by activating a specific evaluation license. If customers want to permanently activate a software package or feature on the router, they must get a new software license.

The figure shows the three steps to permanently activate a new software package or feature on the router.

Refer to **Online Course** for Illustration

9.2.1.3   Step 1. Purchase the Software Package or Feature to Install

Step 1.   Purchase the software package or feature to install.

The first step is to purchase the software package or feature needed. This may be the IP Base license for a specific software release or adding a package to IP Base, such as Security.

Software Claim Certificates are used for licenses that require software activation. The claim certificate provides the Product Activation Key (PAK) for the license and important information regarding the Cisco End User License Agreement (EULA). In most instances, Cisco or the Cisco channel partner will have already activated the licenses ordered at the time of purchase and no Software Claim Certificate is provided.

In either instance, customers receive a PAK with their purchase. The PAK serves as a receipt and is used to obtain a license. A PAK is an 11 digit alpha numeric key created by Cisco manufacturing. It defines the Feature Set associated with the PAK. A PAK is not tied to a specific device until the license is created. A PAK can be purchased that generates any specified number of licenses. As shown in the figure, a separate license is required for each package, IP Base, Data, UC, and SEC.

Refer to
Online Course
for Illustration

9.2.1.4 Step 2. Obtain a License

Step 2. Obtain a license.

The next step is to obtain the license, which is actually a license file. A license file, also known as a Software Activation License, is obtained using one of the following options:

- **Cisco License Manager (CLM)**- This is a free software application available at http://www.cisco.com/go/clm. Cisco License Manager is a standalone application from Cisco that helps network administrators rapidly deploy multiple Cisco software licenses across their networks. Cisco License Manager can discover network devices, view their license information, and acquire and deploy licenses from Cisco. The application provides a GUI that simplifies installation and helps automate license acquisition, as well as perform multiple licensing tasks from a central location. CLM is free of charge and can be downloaded from CCO.

- **Cisco License Registration Portal**- This is the web-based portal for getting and registering individual software licenses, available at http://www.cisco.com/go/license.

Both of these processes require a PAK number and a Unique Device Identifier (UDI).

The PAK is received during purchase.

The UDI is a combination of the Product ID (PID), the Serial Number (SN), and the hardware version. The SN is an 11 digit number which uniquely identifies a device. The PID identifies the type of device. Only the PID and SN are used for license creation. This UDI can be displayed using the `show license udi` command shown in Figure 1. This information is also available on a pull-out label tray found on the device. Figure 2 shows an example of the pull-out label on a Cisco 1941 router.

After entering the appropriate information, the customer receives an email containing the license information to install the license file. The license file is an XML text file with a .lic extension.

Use the Syntax Checker in Figure 3 to determine the UDI on router R2.

Refer to
Online Course
for Illustration

9.2.1.5 Step 3. Install the License

Step 3. Install the License

After the license has been purchased, the customer receives a license file, which is an XML text file with a .lic extension. Installing a permanent license requires two steps:

Step 1. Use the `license install` stored-location-url privileged exec mode command to install a license file.

Step 2. Reload the router using the privileged exec command `reload`. A reload is not required if an evaluation license is active.

Figure 1 shows the configuration for installing the permanent license for the Security package on the router.

Note   Unified Communications is not supported on 1941 routers.

A permanent license is a license that never expires. After a permanent license is installed on a router, it is good for that particular feature set for the life of the router, even across IOS versions. For example, when a UC, SEC, or Data license is installed on a router, the subsequent features for that license are activated even if the router is upgraded to a new IOS release. A permanent license is the most common license type used when a feature set is purchased for a device.

Note   Cisco manufacturing preinstalls the appropriate permanent license on the ordered device for the purchased feature set. No customer interaction with the Cisco IOS Software Activation processes is required to enable that license on new hardware.

Use the Syntax Checker in Figure 2 to install a permanent license file on router R2.

> Refer to
> **Online Course**
> for Illustration

9.2.2   License Verification and Management

9.2.2.1   License Verification

After a new license has been installed the router must be rebooted using the `reload` command. As shown in Figure 1, the `show version` command is used after the router is reloaded to verify that license has been installed.

The `show license` command in Figure 2 is used to display additional information about Cisco IOS software licenses. This command displays license information used to help with troubleshooting issues related to Cisco IOS software licenses. This command displays all the licenses installed in the system. In this example, both the IP Base and Security licenses have been installed. This command also displays the features that are available, but not licensed to execute, such as the Data feature set. Output is grouped according to how the features are stored in license storage.

The following is a brief description of the output:

- **Feature**- Name of the feature
- **License Type**- Type of license; such as Permanent or Evaluation
- **License State**- Status of the license; such as Active or In Use
- **License Count**- Number of licenses available and in use, if counted. If non-counted is indicated, the license is unrestricted.
- **License Priority**- Priority of the license; such as high or low

Note   Refer to the Cisco IOS 15 command reference guide for complete details on the information displayed in the `show license` command.

Refer to
Online Course
for Illustration

9.2.2.2   Activate an Evaluation Right-To-Use License

The Evaluation license process has gone through three revisions on the ISR G2 devices. The latest revision, starting with Cisco IOS Releases 15.0(1)M6, 15.1(1)T4, 15.1(2)T4, 15.1(3) T2, and 15.1(4)M Evaluation licenses are replaced with Evaluation Right-To-Use licenses (RTU) after 60 days. An Evaluation license is good for a 60 day evaluation period. After the 60 days, this license automatically transitions into an RTU license. These licenses are available on the honor system and require the customer's acceptance of the EULA. The EULA is automatically applied to all Cisco IOS software licenses.

The **license accept end user agreement** global configuration mode command is used to configure a one-time acceptance of the EULA for all Cisco IOS software packages and features. After the command is issued and the EULA accepted, the EULA is automatically applied to all Cisco IOS software licenses and the user is not prompted to accept the EULA during license installation.

Figure 1 shows how to configure a one-time acceptance of the EULA:

```
Router(config)#  license accept end user agreement
```

In addition, Figure 1 shows the command to activate an Evaluation RTU license:

```
Router#  license boot module  module-name  technology-package  package-name
```

Use the **?** in place of the arguments to determine which module names and supported software packages are available on the router. Technology package names for Cisco ISR G2 platforms are:

- **ipbasek9** - IP Base technology package
- **securityk9** - Security technology package
- **datak9** - Data technology package
- **uck9** - Unified Communications package (not available on 1900 series)

Note   A reload using the **reload** command is required to activate the software package.

Evaluation licenses are temporary, and are used to evaluate a feature set on new hardware. Temporary licenses are limited to a specific usage period (for example, 60 days).

Reload the router after a license is successfully installed using the **reload** command. The **show license** command in Figure 2 verifies that the license has been installed.

Use the Syntax Checker in Figure 3 to accept the EULA and activate an Evaluation RTU data package license on the 1900 router.

Refer to
Online Course
for Illustration

9.2.2.3   Back up the License

The **license save** command is used to copy all licenses in a device and store them in a format required by the specified storage location. Saved licenses are restored by using the **license install** command.

The command to back up a copy of the licenses on a device is:

```
Router#  license save  file-sys://lic-location
```

Use the **show flash0:** command to verify that the licenses have been saved (Figure 1).

The license storage location can be a directory or a URL that points to a file system. Use the ? command to see the storage locations supported by a device.

Use the Syntax Checker in Figure 2 to save all license files on router R2.

Refer to
Online Course
for Illustration

9.2.2.4 Uninstall the License

To clear an active permanent license from the Cisco 1900 series, 2900 series, and 3900 series routers, perform the following steps:

Step 1. Disable the technology package.

- Disable the active license with the command:

```
Router(config)#  license boot module module-name technology-package
package-name  disable
```

- Reload the router using the **reload** command. A reload is required to make the software package inactive.

Step 2. Clear the license.

- Clear the technology package license from license storage.

```
Router#  license clear feature-name
```

- Clear the **license boot module** module-name **technology-package** package-name **disable** command used for disabling the active license:

```
Router(config)#  no license boot module  module-name  technology-pack-
age  package-name  disable
```

Note Some licenses, such as built-in licenses, cannot be cleared. Only licenses that have been added by using the **license install** command are removed. Evaluation licenses are not removed.

Figure 1 shows an example of clearing an active license.

Use the Syntax Checker in Figure 2 to uninstall the security license on router R2.

Refer to
Interactive Graphic
in online course.

9.2.2.5 Video Demonstration - Working with IOS 15 Image Licenses

Refer to
Online Course
for Illustration

Refer to
Lab Activity
for this chapter

9.3 Summary

9.3.1.1 Class Activity - Powerful Protocols

Powerful Protocols

At the end of this course, you are asked to complete two Capstone Projects where you will create, configure, and verify two network topologies using the two main routing protocols taught in this course, EIGRP and OSPF.

To make things easier, you decide to create a chart of configuration and verification commands to use for these two design projects. To help devise the protocol charts, ask another student in the class to help you.

Refer to the PDF for this chapter for directions on how to create a design for this modeling project. When complete, share your work with another group or with the class. You may also want to save the files created for this project in a network portfolio for future reference.

Refer to
Lab Activity
for this chapter

9.3.1.2   EIGRP Capstone Project

In this Capstone Project activity, you will demonstrate your ability to:

- Design, configure, verify, and secure EIGRP, IPv4, or IPv6 on a network

- Design a VLSM addressing scheme for the devices connected to the LANs

- Present your design using network documentation from your Capstone Project network

Refer to
Lab Activity
for this chapter

9.3.1.3   OSPF Capstone Project

In this Capstone Project activity, you will demonstrate your ability to:

- Configure basic OSPFv2 to enable internetwork communications in a small- to medium-sized IPv4 business network.

- Implement advanced OSPF features to enhance operation in a small- to medium-sized business network.

- Implement multiarea OSPF for IPv4 to enable internetwork communications in a small- to medium-sized business network.

- Configure basic OSPFv3 to enable internetwork communications in a small- to medium-sized IPv6 business network.

Refer to **Packet
Tracer Activity**
for this chapter

9.3.1.4   Packet Tracer - Skills Integration Challenge

Background/Scenario

As network technician familiar with IPv4 addressing, routing, and network security, you are now ready to apply your knowledge and skills to a network infrastructure. Your task is to finish designing the VLSM IPv4 addressing scheme, implement multiarea OSPF, and secure access to the VTY lines using access control lists.

Refer to
Online Course
for Illustration

9.3.1.5   Summary

Examples of Cisco IOS software releases include 12.3, 12.4, 15.0, and 15.1. Along with each software release there are new versions of the software used to implement bug fixes and new features.

Cisco IOS software 12.4 incorporates new software features and hardware support that was introduced in the Cisco IOS Software 12.3T train and additional software fixes. Mainline releases (also called maintenance releases) contain no uppercase letter in their release designation and inherit new Cisco IOS Software functionality and hardware from lower numbered T releases. Prior to and including 12.4, the mainline "M" train received bug fixes only. The technology "T" train includes fixes as well as new feature and platforms. The 12.4T train provides Cisco IOS software functionality and hardware adoption that introduces new technology, functionality, and hardware advances that are not available in the Cisco IOS Software 12.4 mainline train.

In the Cisco IOS Software 15.0 release family a new strategy is in place. Cisco IOS 15.0 release family does not diverge into separate M and T trains but into M and T releases in the same train. For example, the first release in the Cisco IOS Software 15.0 release family is 15.0(1)M, where M indicates it is an extended maintenance release. An extended maintenance release is ideal for long-term maintenance. Not all releases in the Cisco IOS Software 15.0 release family will be extended maintenance releases; there will also be standard maintenance releases that receive the latest features and hardware support. The standard maintenance releases will have an uppercase T in their designation.

When selecting or upgrading a Cisco IOS router, it is important to choose the proper IOS image with the correct feature set and version. The Cisco IOS image file is based on a special naming convention. The name for the Cisco IOS image file contains multiple parts, each with a specific meaning. Example: c1900-universalk9-mz.SPA.152-4.M3.bin

Commands are available for upgrading and verification of flash. The `show flash` command displays the files store in flash memory including the system image files. This command can also be used to verify free flash size. The `boot system` command is a global configuration command which allows the user to specify the source for the Cisco IOS.

Using a network TFTP server allows image and configuration uploads and downloads over the network. The network TFTP server can be another router, a workstation, or a host system.

Beginning with Cisco IOS Software release 15.0, Cisco modified the process to enable new technologies within the IOS feature sets. Each device ships with the same universal image. Technology packages such as IP Base, Data, UC, and SEC are enabled in the universal image via Cisco software activation licensing keys. Each licensing key is unique to a particular device and is obtained from Cisco by providing the product ID and serial number of the router and a Product Activation Key (PAK).

License activation is not necessary for factory ordered preconfigured licenses prior to use. IP Base comes shipped as a permanent license on all ISR-G2 devices. The other three technology packages: Data, Security, and Unified Communications come with an Evaluation license as the default, but a permanent license may be purchased.

A Permanent License is a license that never expires. For example, once a UC (Unified Communications), Security or Data license is installed on a router, the subsequent features for that license will be activated even if the router is upgraded to a new IOS release.

Installing a License

Prerequisites:

- Obtain the necessary PAK, which is an 11 digit ID that can be delivered by mail or electronically

- Need to have a valid Cisco username/password

- Retrieve serial number and PID with the `show license udi` command or from the router label tray

The `show version` command is used after the router is reloaded to verify that license has been installed.

The `show license` command is used to display additional information about Cisco IOS software licenses.

The `license accept end user agreement` global configuration command is used to configure a one-time acceptance of the EULA for all Cisco IOS software packages and features.

Use the cisco.com web site to research other benefits and information on IOS 15.

Go to the online course to take the quiz and exam.

Chapter 9 Quiz

This quiz is designed to provide an additional opportunity to practice the skills and knowledge presented in the chapter and to prepare for the chapter exam. You will be allowed multiple attempts and the grade does not appear in the gradebook.

Chapter 9 Exam

The chapter exam assesses your knowledge of the chapter content.

Your Chapter Notes

Notes

Notes

Notes

Notes

Notes

Notes

Notes

Notes

Notes

Notes

Notes

Notes

Notes

Notes

Notes

Notes

Notes

Notes

Notes

Notes

Notes